Errol Flynn

Errol Flynn

Michael Freedland

ARTHUR BARKER LIMITED   LONDON
A subsidiary of Weidenfeld (Publishers) Limited

For Doreen and Yisrolic, Marilyn
and Geoffrey in the spirit
of brotherly love

ISBN 0 213 16652 6

Printed in Great Britain by
Butler & Tanner Ltd
Frome and London

Contents

Illustrations

Acknowledgments

Errol Flynn, known throughout the western world more as a playboy than an actor, a man's man whose principal hobby was women, became a legend within months of his first Hollywood starring vehicle. With the help of people who knew, loved – and sometimes detested – Flynn, this is aimed at breaking down the legend and establishing the facts. A series of detailed interviews formed a pattern that gradually developed into a picture that was different from the one that people thought they knew; a picture that was never black and white, nor quite as technicolored as some of his own writings about his life (it is also clear that at times Flynn himself tinted his tales in hues that were altogether too subdued).

To the people who shared with me their memories – mostly never revealed publicly before, some of them extremely intimate – I offer my thanks.

At the top of the list must be Mrs Nora Flynn Black and that veteran wizard of a director, Raoul Walsh. But I thank sincerely all those to whom I spoke – sometimes at very great length, taking time they could ill afford – including Larry Adler, Martin Benson, Sammy Cahn, Joan Blondell, Jack Cummings, Bette Davis (at the time of an extensive interview originally for *The Times*, London), Deirdre Flynn, Trevor Howard, the late James Wong Howe, the late Allen Jenkins, Christopher Lee, Ida Lupino, Lewis Milestone, Fred MacMurray, Walter Pidgeon, Vincent Price, Irving Rapper, Anthony Quinn, Randolph Scott, Alexis Smith, Melville Shavelson and the late Herbert Wilcox. Also to the staff of Alan McAfee, London.

Special thanks go to Paul Welsh for his invaluable assistance in dotting numerous "i"s and crossing various "t"s and also to a veritable walking encyclopaedia of the cinema, Dennis Sykes – whose idea this book originally was.

I cannot sufficiently thank all the librarians of the Motion Picture Academy, Los Angeles, and of the British Library and British Film Institute, London. Nor could I leave out my wife, Sara, who put up with so much and helped by pretending that she didn't. To Beryl Whiteman for typing the manuscript, my gratitude.

1

Uncertain Glory

He was a very lucky boy. He had the whole
world in the palm of his hand and threw
it all away.
Irving Rapper

The scene at Forest Lawn, the Valhalla to which film idols have
gone since the days of Valentino, is a familiar one: black-veiled
women and somber-suited men standing silently watching a coffin
being lowered into an unmarked grave. Heads are bowed while the
Episcopalian clergyman intones the burial rites, so it is possible that
few notice the statue at the head of the newly-opened dark, damp
pit – the figure of a nude woman picking flowers.

But if the whole thing had been dreamed up at a Warner Brothers
story conference, no more appropriate setting could have been
devised for the final resting place of Errol Flynn. Certainly he would
have asked no more of death than he had of life, the promise of
a beautiful, undraped woman giving him her undivided attention
night and day.

The man who had once said "I like the whisky old and the women
young" had listed his own priorities and had had them to the full.
When he died in October 1959, few shed tears. His had been a
roistering, rip-roaring life, ten times as colourful as any role he had
played on the screen; yet to people who knew him only as a
swashbuckler who seemed to win every battle single-handed, he was
a romantic who had helped colour a drab world.

On the surface there was little to like about him. He seemed
to live for himself and always for today, because he knew that
expecting a tomorrow was asking too much. A judge with a
gift for prose decided eight years after that funeral that Flynn

had been very different from most people's ideas of an upright
citizen.

In the High Court in London, Mr Justice McGarry, asked to
rule on the fate of Flynn's property, declared:

"As a sexual athlete, Errol may in truth have attained Olympic
standards.... In his career, in his three marriages, in his
friendships, in his quarrels and in bed with the many women he
took there, he lived with zest and irregularity. The lives of film
stars are not cast in the ordinary mould; and in some respects
Errol Flynn's was more stellar than most.... Hollywood has
never been deficient in what was then, as always, one of Errol's
great interests in life – namely a generous pool of available
pulchritude."

There was never any doubt that his activities far away from the
studio were the most important in his life. He never considered
himself an actor, even though other people in his business admired
his capabilities, both in front of a camera and away from it. He was
a ladykiller in the tradition of Casanova and Bluebeard – young girls
who found him devastatingly attractive would give away more than
their virtue to spend a night with him. Probably never before or
since has there been a bedside manner to beat his.

Everything about him was outrageous. *Newsweek* magazine
described him once as "a rebel without a cause, but seldom without
a case". He seemed to find himself before courts of law almost as
often as he appeared in a different sort of court to play tennis –
and in tennis he was as successful as he was at sexual athletics.

He once said: "Dammit, the main difference between me and
thousands of other men is that they are careful, cautious and
discreet. Me, I am not. I never have been. I felt that whatever I
did was not unpleasant enough to affect anyone's opinion or
interest."

The son of a professor, he had an intellect that could have made
him an outstanding academic; after all he wrote with a fluency as
keen as the ease with which he handled a sword in a scene from
Robin Hood or *Captain Blood*. But life to him was not intended to
be taken that seriously.

To his father he was always "impetuous and irresponsible". To his women fans, always a Greek god born into the wrong age which fortunately for them happened to be their own. To his friends, he was the good-company guy with whom they could be swapping blows as frequently as risqué stories, trading drinks as often as women. His wit, his charm, his prejudices inspired a phrase that lived after him: "In like Flynn". In truth it would be difficult to imagine anyone or anything else ever being "like Flynn".

Unique, too, was the effect that these features had on people who knew and worked with Errol Flynn. Those who punched with him in bars, challenged him in the courts and jumped with him from carpet to bed, from bed to boat and back to bed again often had reason to despise him. Now they tend to smile at his idiosyncrasies, and remember more than anything else his charm.

This is his story.

2
The Sun Also Rises

He was like a child. He liked to have several
things going at the same time.
Joan Blondell

It took the charm and the beauty of a girl to make Theodore Thomson Flynn even momentarily forsake his laboratory bench and the collection of test tubes and preserved specimens that had always seemed to represent his idea of the perfect life.

Theodore was tall and good-looking, but, until Lily Marelle Young had come his way, he rarely allowed his thoughts to stray in the direction of girls. The ones he had known had been too flighty, too bored with his work to merit his attention. But Marelle – one of the first things she did was to tell him to ignore her first name, which she hated – was different. She had an intoxicatingly beautiful face, an enticing curving body and a smile that showed she really cared whenever – as he always would – he steered the conversation in the direction of his latest experiments.

Flynn with his red, bushy eyebrows, may not have thought himself much of a romantic figure, but Marelle did. As the daughter of a sailor, she had a spirit about her that craved the unexpected and the unusual and she was convinced the young scientist had the promise of excitement about him. But he courted her slowly, respectfully, and when he finally found the courage to propose, it was as though she had willed him to do it.

From their wedding day, she began to encourage and push him. When, almost a year later, the opportunity arose for an ocean voyage, she persuaded him it could be the cruise of a lifetime. He was just twenty-five and she three years his junior.

The ss *Aurora* was not really most people's idea of a cruise liner. There was no saloon, no luxurious restaurant and the captain's table was the one that the cabin boy used, too. But Theodore and Marelle asked for nothing more.

For a girl who might have thought her red and white blood corpuscles swam in a solution of sea water, the journey around the coast of Australia was an ambition fulfilled. It offered the promise of experiences about which many of the most intrepid explorers had only read.

Together, they were joining an expedition to the South Pole and Theodore was going to be the team's biologist. Marelle's father might not have approved. To men like Captain Young, skipper of the *William S. Bowden*, women on board ship spelled trouble, but his strong-willed daughter would have it no other way. Certainly, her husband raised no objections – once, somewhat to his surprise, he found that nobody else on board seemed to mind. Of course, news of Marelle's pedigree had gone before her.

The Youngs had been seafarers for as long as anyone could remember and Marelle was the proud owner of a sword once belonging to Captain Bligh of the *Bounty* – brought home by her ancestor Midshipman Richmond Young. The young officer had been one of Fletcher Christian's aides but was acquitted of any part in the famous mutiny. As if it were a symbol of loyalty to Marelle's past, the sword went wherever she and Theodore did – including their voyage on the *Aurora*.

It was not the sort of ship that her father liked very much. The *Aurora* was a "smokepot", one of those new-fangled steam-powered monsters that he despised as could only a man who had spent most of his days listening to the sound of sails snapping in the wind.

Not that the captain's ancestry had been so perfect. A few generations after the *Bounty* adventure, other Youngs went marauding around the South Seas, picking up natives to go to work on the sugar plantations of Queensland. "Blackbirding" they called it. Other people had another word for the practice: slave trading.

Marelle's family had settled in Australia more than a hundred years before. Not so the Flynns. Any elementary knowledge of European family names would indicate that their stock was Irish, and Irish they had stayed until Theodore's parents emigrated to Australia just before his birth. Even now the Irish influence was still strong and Theodore usually added a touch of brogue to his antipodean accent.

He was not a particularly religious man, although he considered himself a member, if an agnostic one, of the Church of Ireland, the Ulster version of Anglicanism. The Flynn family had been converted to the faith after his grandfather had had a row with a Catholic priest. But his real religion now was his love for his work – and for his wife.

The voyage southwards seemed idyllic. The fact that Marelle was sick a lot – a symptom which even the daughter of an old salt couldn't always fight – she put down to the rolling of the ship.

But by the time the *Aurora* reached Hobart, capital of Tasmania, she knew there was another reason – and one which was confirmed by the ship's doctor. She was pregnant.

The Flynns pondered on this totally unexpected development. They were stolid, unemotional people at moments that called for serious decisions, and this, they decided, was no time for sentimentality. Theodore had his work to think of and there was no question he had to continue his journey. Pregnant or not, Marelle would set up home in Tasmania on her own.

At Hobart they kissed goodbye and Theodore continued on to the Pole, knowing that he would probably not hear from his wife again until after their child had been born.

And it was to the bitterly cold wastes of Antarctica that a supply ship brought the news: on 20 June 1909, Marelle had given birth to their son. It was not until Theodore joined her several months later that they chose his names: Errol Leslie Thomson Flynn.

Tasmania, they decided, would be their permanent home. It was a cold island, much more provincial than Sydney where they had lived before, but that was not something that bothered them. How could it when there was such a marvellous beach? It was the beach that had become baby Errol's natural playground and he probably began to think of it more as his home than the actual bricks and mortar of the house where they lived. He was certainly a lot happier there than he ever was indoors.

He loved everything about it – the feel of the sand on his feet, the fresh cool water so close by and the mysterious shells washed up all around him as he sat and played.

By the age of three, he was a strong swimmer. He was also developing an equally strong will. Errol was the apple of his father's eye and the affection was returned twofold. There was no better reward for the child than a cheery nod from his father when he was being good. But even then, that was not very often. Errol, still so young, was constantly getting into trouble.

If he and his father were kindred spirits, the boy's relationship with his mother was more tense. It would always be so. There was a strong will about the child that Marelle could recognize, if not admit to it as being perhaps a little too much like her own. His good looks which had the local matrons muttering "ooh" and "ah" every time they saw him peering round at them from his baby carriage confirmed that in this respect he was like her, too. But she found it difficult to show him affection. It was as if even at this stage, she saw him competing with her for the love of her husband.

Errol also shared with her a thirst for adventure, but instead of indulgently smiling at his antics, Marelle made the child feel the perpetrator of some dreadful crime every time he misbehaved. Theodore could laugh when Errol climbed out of his cot, smeared his face with boot polish and excitedly told his father: "I'm a black man." Marelle could not.

Instead of changing or growing inhibited by her attitude, Errol simply became more daring than ever. And it was not only his mother who showed concern. The neighbours didn't take too kindly either to Master Flynn's influence on their own children.

Errol was no more than five when he attended a tea party at the local deanery, a party that was to be the talk of Hobart for weeks and remembered by the small guests – with good cause – for years.

It had been going on for little more than an hour when the flustered hostess, wife of a rather staid clergyman, plucked up the courage to use the new-fangled telephone, an instrument with which she had not yet fully come to terms. She nervously cranked the handle, asked the operator for the number of the Flynn's house and began a call to Marelle which plainly was not entirely social.

"Errol," she screeched, "he is a mischievous boy, isn't he?" Mrs Flynn waited for the inevitable sting in the tail of the woman's conversation. It came like a volley of shots from a machine gun. "We're very sorry," she snapped, "but we've had to send him home. You see ... he's tipped all the other little boys and girls into the fountain – one by one."

Errol arrived home and was beaten. Not even that cooled his ardour for the unconventional. A year after the party episode, he found more excitement on the beach. His parents thought they had detected an artistic trait in the boy when he developed a love for watercolours. But he was not satisfied, just painting pictures. Instead he took his colours to the beach, found a rowing boat which he managed to prize from its moorings – and sitting astride its seat covered his body in a dozen hues that would have looked better on a sheet of paper. But not to Errol. At that moment, he was a pirate. The Flynns searched for him for a whole day, not knowing that for that day Errol Flynn, aged six, was Long John Silver or, perhaps more aptly, Captain Blood. He had sailed for miles in his boat and then found his own way home. It was his first swashbuckling role.

Mrs Flynn ought to have appreciated her luck that Errol was simply demonstrating a healthy urge to see the world into which he had been born. But she considered the child was becoming a degenerate, a state of affairs hardly helped by a further conversation with another young mother. This one regaled Marelle with news of a discovery Errol had made through the courtesy of her own daughter, a moppet called Nerida.

It was Nerida who had just schooled Errol in the differences between boys and girls, an event that surely must be enshrined as of historic importance, since up to then he had fondly believed there was nothing more to it than that females wore dresses and males wore trousers and, for a reason he couldn't begin to understand, girls had longer hair than boys. Nerida changed all that.

When Errol returned home, he knew he was in for the thrashing of his life. His mother was looking at him with a gaze of disgust in her eyes, the like of which even he had never seen before. She then began to shout. "Go on," she screamed, while pulling the unwilling child into her husband's study. "Go on – tell him what you did, you nasty little boy. Go on. Don't stand there. Tell your father what you were doing."

It was the last thing in the world that Errol intended to tell his father and he fled in tears to his bedroom. He had had enough, he decided, of what George Bernard Shaw had called middle-class morality. He would prove that disenchantment again – many times.

He was so disturbed by the parental reaction to this honest enough bit of scientific fact-finding, that at that precise moment he decided he had lost all faith in the goodness of human nature. There was nothing for it but to take his talents where they would be better appreciated.

For three days, Errol disappeared from home. His parents were frantic. The police were called. Neighbours joined a search party and the area around the Flynns' home was combed. The beaches were minutely gone over once and then again. No one knew that all the time Errol was just a few hundred yards away from home, sitting in the top branch of a tree, contemplating his station in life.

When he finally decided he had had enough, he resigned himself to more chastising, more beatings. But this time, he was wrong. He arrived home to find his mother in bed – not because it was late, but convinced she was about to die from either a broken heart or a nervous breakdown. When she saw the dirty face and tattered jersey of Errol, she dissolved in a flood of tears and hugged her boy until he felt squashed by her embrace. Did that mean then that, after all, she really loved him? In his autobiography, he says he could never be sure.

Other questions were more easily settled – and usually at the expense of someone, or something. He was about eight when he chose a group of unsuspecting ducks as his victims. He had been watching a duck playing with a piece of fatty pork when the idea for a novel kind of sport first hit him. The duck, he saw, ate the meat and then almost immediately passed it out through its rectum. How long, he wondered, would it take three or perhaps six ducks to pass the same piece of meat? There was but one way to find out. He tied a piece of string to the end of the pork and watched it being transmitted from one bird to the next, going in one way and coming out the other, and doing what damage to their digestive systems he neither knew nor cared.

His father, however, did both know and care, and beat Errol so hard that his umbrella snapped in two.

Some forty years later, Theodore Flynn was to say: "Errol was always a naughty boy. He was always high spirited, just like Huckleberry Finn, and he was always good-looking. He was quite a handful. No, he was not a manageable child."

The beating with the umbrella was a rare occurrence, but Errol now worried constantly about the risks of displeasing his father. His mother was a completely lost cause.

It was obvious Errol had a good mind. The affair over the ducks proved that and so did the occasions at the school when a sea story or a tale of adventure on desert islands read to the class by their teacher transported his imagination over continents. But he did not want to bother with more formal lessons and was notoriously lazy.

In this respect, he was very different from his father, who was now professor of biology at Hobart University. He was also the recognized authority on sea creatures and marsupials like Australia's emblem, the kangaroo.

The professor knew a great deal too, about the Tasmanian tiger which, until recently, had been considered a prehistoric animal but which through a freak of nature was found to be still living on the island. He hunted the creature and even kept one caged near his laboratory.

Errol thought the tiger the most majestic thing on four legs. He showed so much interest in it that his father agreed to let him accompany him on expeditions to retrieve specimens. Errol regarded every caged tiger as a friend and when he heard that one of them was being put down, he felt as though he had personally been bereaved.

But these were rare moments of tenderness on Errol's part. More frequently, he was making a nuisance of himself in some way or another, although his parents did not entirely lose faith in their son. When he was about ten and his sister Rosemary was born, they even began to trust him – which was a mistake. She was two years old when they, nevertheless, felt sufficiently secure to leave the two children at home together while they themselves went out. They saw little reason to worry. After all, Carrie the maid was there, too.

Now, Carrie was not particularly beautiful but even to the immature twelve year old, it was obvious that she had been provided with the usual equipment in the right places. It was also obvious that Errol and Carrie were of a similar mind, perhaps borne of a mutual distrust of Mrs Flynn. Errol liked her so much that he actually raided his money box when she was in need and lent her the princely sum of 1s 9d.

On this evening, with Rosemary asleep in her cot and Carrie sitting in her chair, Master Flynn decided that the time had come for another experiment. He began it courageously by touching Carrie's leg – near where the calf seemed to swell so invitingly. At that stage, he did not know whether she would shout, blush or merely push away his hand. In any event, he figured it was worth trying. And it was. As his hand moved higher, she adjusted herself on the chair to accommodate him more comfortably. It was when he reached the part of her thigh where the smoothness of her skirt was interrupted by the raised bump of a suspender that she uttered her first sound. She quivered and asked Errol how much money she owed. When he told her, Carrie suggested a means of repayment.

They rushed into her bedroom and the debt was settled very quickly.

He was never quite the same after that. Carrie represented his first awakening, the first serious brush with the mores of society. If he could get away with that, he thought, there was so much more that he could do. But for the moment he was concentrating on playing truant from school and on running away from home as frequently as his personal finances allowed.

This waywardness, of course, led to even more conflict with parental authority. His mother reacted predictably. His father was more unsure. He did not enjoy whacking him although he knew Errol deserved it. He tried to leave that sort of thing to Marelle, but every time she beat Errol and shouted at him, Theodore squirmed.

In truth the professor was captivated by his son. Even by his disrespect for conformity, which somehow he saw as a distortion but nevertheless a direct inheritance of his own sense of adventure. The academic in the professor also admired his son for being so articulate. Errol had started using words of more than one syllable almost from the time that he could speak. The professor also liked watching him dress up. In that way, he thought the child was surely following his mother's love of amateur dramatics. Certainly, Errol loved the occasional visits he was allowed to make to the theater and when he was taken to see Anna Pavlova dancing, he was enchanted.

Despite his laziness at school, Errol was always willing to learn; just as long as there was a germ of excitement in his lessons. The professor knew that too, and tried to find ways of helping the boy himself – and particularly through his own work. An invitation he received from the University of London, he thought, provided just such an opportunity. It offered the greatest excitement of all – travel. Theodore was not going to London merely to lecture. He was also to deliver a consignment of duck-billed platypi, which would be the first ever seen alive in the British capital. Not really a difficult task – in the normal course of events, that is, but as the elder Flynn should have realized, things were never normal with Errol around.

The only problem the professor really considered was the food that the animals from "down under" had to consume – a special kind of worm. Errol, naturally enough, knew that and watched very carefully as the worms were loaded aboard after the platypi. He spent much of the journey studying the habits of the creatures – somehow living things attracted him a lot more than did the engine room or other parts of the ship which normally dominated the attentions of small boys. But even Errol got fed up with duck-billed platypi and by the time the ship docked at Durban, one of the first ports of call, he was downright bored.

The family spent a day ashore and Errol found his way to a park. There, in a pond he saw a mass of swimming tadpoles. What, he wondered, if instead of the worms, he gave those to the platypi? There was but one way to find out. Errol bought himself a small bucket which he hid under his jacket and then took it aboard the ship without anyone knowing.

He soon discovered the precise difference between a tadpole and a worm, and so did two of the very rare creatures being transported from one end of the world to the other – they died. Even Errol worried about that little mishap and decided that he had to own up and explain the animals' sudden demise to his father. The professor was distinctly unamused. From that moment on, the remaining specimens were closely guarded and so was Errol.

It was going to be a longish stay in Britain for the Flynns – long enough for Errol's education to be considered. A private school, the impressively named South London College at Barnes in south-west London, was chosen for the boy. It turned out to be an establishment that would do even less for the young Flynn's schooling than had the places from which he absconded in Tasmania. Considerably less – apart from one thing. He learned there what one of the masters intended whenever he put his hand on a boy's knee. He also got to hear what the man did in what should have been the privacy of his own bedroom, and didn't like it. Before long the master was fired and Errol was expelled. He was fourteen and dismissed for a combination of truancy and fighting.

Despite its shortcomings, the school produced its share of middle-class gentlemen. Among these was one L. G. Pine, who was to become managing editor of that mirror of the British aristocracy, *Burke's Peerage*. In later years, he remembered the young Errol Flynn as a stockily-built boy who by the time he was expelled had both shot up and acquired good looks and height.

Before the additional shock of the expulsion to her system, Errol's mother had moved to Paris. Not because she and the professor were in the midst of a matrimonial crisis, simply that she wanted to see something of *la vie Parisienne* while Theodore was more concerned with some fossilized find. It was another example of Marelle's own restless spirit. Stories that Errol attended the Lycée Louis Le Grand in Paris at this time are as farfetched as others that he was educated at St Paul's School in London. St Paul's denies the oft told story which is regaled as much by its own boys – and with a wide variety of detail as to the reasons for his expulsion from this school too – as anyone else. It is certain he never went there.

The professor and his wife had to face the fact that their son was likely to remain something of a handful, which for Theodore Flynn was not an easy state of affairs to contemplate. As he said years later: "I don't think *I* ever did any swashbuckling. Never had much leisure for that sort of thing."

He desperately wanted Errol to follow him, if not into permanent academic life then at least into a university as a student. But a new school at which, through influence, he had managed to get Errol a place could hold on to his son even less efficiently than could the South London College. Once again, he was expelled.

A period of doing nothing in London came to an end when the Flynn family moved back to Australia. This time, Errol was installed – and again none too happily for anyone concerned – in a Sydney grammar school, the Northshore. Here the most important part of the curriculum centered around his exploits chasing the maid, Elsie, who was at least twice Errol's age and who tried none too successfully to educate him in the arts of seduction.

Errol now decided that the time had come to lay more formal romantic roots. While still at school he borrowed enough money to buy an engagement ring which he presented to a pretty but unsophisticated lady called Naomi Dibbs. He tired of her when it became obvious that neither of them seemed to know what went where and how.

Errol was becoming proficient at more conventional athletics. He was a good boxer – good enough to persuade other boys at the school not to engage him in too many playing-field bouts – and his tennis was outstanding. Matches on the school courts led to area heats and from these he went on to national competitions. He entered the Davis Cup and before long was Australian Junior Champion. But he was still under par in the sport he considered the most important. He tried hard to improve his form with Elsie but could never really summon up the courage to do all that was required of him, although he did now get increasingly more daring.

Every night he would meet her in the bushes below his dormitory, an easy enough move since he merely had to escape through the window above his bed. Not only had he found a way of achieving this without hurting himself, but he could do it silently.

It was a fifteen-foot drop, yet the soft grass and the nearby hedge all managed to soften the fall. Until, that is, the night when a rattling of corrugated iron replaced the usual gentle thud of boy meeting lawn. The metal had been placed there by a jealous rival for Elsie's affections. Everyone, including the headmaster, now discovered Flynn's nocturnal liaison and Errol was expelled from Northshore, too.

If he couldn't have Elsie, Errol decided he didn't want Naomi either – nor for that matter the prospect of married life. He persuaded the young lady to return his ring, which he promptly sold for about £9, half of what he had paid for it.

All this happened without the doubtful benefit of having his parents' shoulders to cry upon, and his chastising mother's voice to listen to. The professor was in England once more – he had taken a fossilized whale for display at the British Museum – and Marelle was again in France. Now that he was quite alone, Errol decided he was ready to take a stab at the world of commerce.

He joined a wool firm belonging to a close friend of his father, but it was hardly a challenging experience. Seventeen-year-old Errol Flynn spent most of the time sticking stamps on to envelopes and eyeing the cash box – an occupation he shared with a chap in his twenties called Thomson. Before long, the temptation was too great for them both and between them they emptied the box. They were lucky to be no more than fired. Friends in adversity, they decided to stay together.

Thomson was ambitious for the big time and was not too fussy about how he got there. He also was prepared to share his knowledge with his young friend. "Ever heard of the Razor Gang?" he asked Errol. "Of course," replied Flynn, who didn't want to be thought unworldly.

Thomson sketched out the gang's general policy – robbing greedy, rich people of their wealth – without bothering to go into precise details. But he did mention that occasionally, members of the gang had been known to complete a deal by smartly moving a razor over their victim's face. All Errol knew was that he was being offered a bit of excitement and a chance to share in the profits. Thomson's share was too generous, as it turned out. He ended up with his own throat cut. Errol decided the time had come to end his association.

He had other plans for his immediate future – in the territory of New Guinea which was administered by Australia, and where an interesting discovery had been made: gold.

3

In the Wake of the Bounty

Work was like eating and drinking to him.
He was a primitive like Van Gogh.
Herbert Wilcox

Whether he knew it or not, New Guinea was to offer Errol all he would ever ask of life – adventure, danger, money and a great deal of sex, a commodity with which he had still not really come to terms. He knew that he enjoyed it, but he was all too conscious that he had still to reach the pinnacle of his achievements.

At seventeen, he had begun to mature into early manhood. He was tall, muscular and was shaving regularly. It had been no secret that the girls near Northshore did not exactly flee from his presence and he knew it well, but he still needed some other kind of stimulation. The gold rush seemed to offer just that.

His fare to the island cost him £18, twice the amount he had received from the proceeds of Naomi's engagement ring, but with a considerable amount of guile he had managed to prize the missing sum from an assortment of friends, and he set sail for New Guinea knowing only that it sounded like good sport.

The dirty craft on which he sailed smelled of a combination of human bodies and sea water.

It was not at all the sort of pampered sea voyage he had been used to on those trips to England with his parents. But as this relic of a bygone age of marine navigation chugged its way on to the coast of New Britain, the part of the island first colonized by white settlers, Errol thought only of the fortune he was to make and the fun he would have getting it.

Once on the island and when he had safely checked into a sleazy lodging house, Errol had to think of his priorities. Rightly, he came to the conclusion that before he could embark on an enterprise like gold prospecting, he had to have some sort of financial base on which to operate. He had to look for a job. From conversations with other young men starting new lives in New Guinea, it became clear that the local administration was in dire need of people who by their natural air of good breeding and self-confidence would leave the islanders in no doubt as to who was boss. There was a desperate shortage of officers and gentlemen. Now, of course, Errol was neither. But he was also a natural actor and a man of resource – his activities with Elsie showed that. When he met the District Commissioner, a figure in a crisp white uniform who looked as though he had just stepped from the pages of a story by Rudyard Kipling, Errol put his guile to the test.

"Know anything about sanitation?" asked the man. "Certainly do," said Errol. "My father's a professor of biology and that's the first thing he told me. . . ." The colonial administrator seemed more impressed than young Flynn could have imagined possible. "OK," he said, "you will earn £4 a week." Errol needed to hear no more. He bought himself a uniform like the commissioner's, complete with pith helmet, and was so thorough in his apparent enthusiasm, that he almost convinced himself he wanted nothing more out of life than to serve the king.

Exactly what he did thereafter will never be known for certain. The only available evidence is confused. Flynn himself spent the rest of his life talking about New Guinea and his exploits there, but the trouble is that he told a different story each time.

In his own book, he says that he did, indeed, become a sanitation expert until he was caught bathing in a pool with a pretty girl. That was not a good idea – since his boss happened to have a similar notion at the same time and asked whether he really considered this method of sampling the waters could be regarded as a true test of sanitary facilities. The girl appears in a number of versions of the story, but the detail changes.

Australian and American troops serving in New Guinea during World War Two came back with a stack of legends about Flynn's exploits there, none of which seem entirely consistent with any

other. In one of these he was a cook. In another he worked as an
oyster pirate.

In the early 1940s, Errol talked about those days to Mark Hellinger, the respected Broadway columnist who had become a Hollywood producer. "For heaven's sake, Errol," Hellinger told him as
Flynn rhapsodized about his adventures in New Guinea, "you're
not talking to a fan magazine writer or to the publicity department.
You're talking to *me*."

Hellinger did, however, allow Errol to continue and smiled indulgently at what he considered to be merely part of the evening's
entertainment. But in 1944 the producer went to New Guinea himself as a war correspondent. The stories he heard in the bars there
left him with the distinct impression that Mr Flynn had simply been
a modest raconteur unwilling to make too much out of incidents
from his past. Errol's parting words on the occasion they met had
been: "It's all true, sport." After what he heard in the bars he began
to believe it possibly was.

The girl in the pool, it turned out, had been the wife of another
colonial officer, a man who when he heard of the meeting decided
to teach a lesson to this young bounder Flynn. The wife's name
was Maura – with a face as pretty to Errol as her voice, and, he
decided, well worth fighting over. The husband thought so too and
was anything but impressed with Flynn's apparent courage. He was
older but not wiser than the young Australian. By the time the two
had settled their differences, Errol felt as though he had been beaten
to a pulp. He managed to make the husband both feel and look in
a similar state. In later years, that fight would serve as a useful experience for Errol Flynn. It surely would not be his last bout in
those circumstances.

Plainly unsuited as he was to the disciplines of the colonial service, he decided it was an appropriate moment for a change of job.
Errol found one – in charge of a group of native policemen. But
since he never respected other people's conventions he was
hardly suited to the role of a law enforcement officer. That job
lasted only a couple of months. In the meantime, the girl all the
trouble had been about met an untimely death, killed when the
ancient German Junkers aircraft in which she was taking a joy

ride smashed into a cliff. It took quite a time for Errol to forget her.

Without His Majesty – in the form of the Commonwealth of Australia's administrative force – to pay for his growing taste for women and alcohol, Errol went looking for more rewarding employment. He still had his heart set on the really big money – a gold strike – but even at this tender age he realized that it would take time. Somehow he had to find a way of getting to the gold fields, staking a claim and, before too long an interval, striking it rich. When you are seventeen nothing seems impossible. So why not aim for the top?

The surprising thing is that Errol did actually find time to muse about his role in life. He began keeping a diary into which he confided his determination to be bogged down neither by a quest for adventure for adventure's sake nor by the unreal world of reading about other people's search for excitement.

"Whenever you waste your time over printed words that neither enlighten nor amuse you," he wrote in an extremely illuminating entry, "you are, in a sense, committing suicide. The value, the intrinsic value of our actions, emotions, thoughts, possessions, occupations, the manner in which we are living – this is the first thing to be determined."

He was thinking on paper but sometimes his thoughts were more mature than his actions.

"Unless we are satisfied that any of these things has a true value, even if only relative," he wrote, "our lives are futile and there is no more hopeless realization than this."

But the young Errol Flynn's real values still centered around his abiding quest for gold – and the means he would adopt to get it.

In a bar he met a man who offered him a job running a copra business. He did not even know what copra was, but just the same assured his drinking companion that he had had the stuff in his mother's milk. For £40 a month, he agreed to operate the coconut plantation producing the copra. The naïvety with which he accepted the assignment matched the immaturity of his years.

All he had to do, he had been assured, was to seek out the foreman of the gang – known as the "boss boy" – and tell him, like a company commander giving instructions to a dependable old sergeant-major, to "Carry on, boss boy."

Of course, it turned out to be neither quite as pleasant nor as simple as he had imagined it would be. This was cannibal country and not far from his plantation a particularly vicious tribe had gone on the rampage. Pregnant women had been impaled on large spikes. Children had been decapitated and their brains removed – a much sought-after delicacy in those parts, he discovered.

The massacre sharpened both his sense of adventure and what he claimed to be the love of justice he had learned during his brief time in the police. He and his "boys" brought back a dozen of the cannibals and entertained something like two thousand of the local populace to the spectacle of a public hanging. Like locusts ravaging a harvest they swarmed from the surrounding hills into the field that had become the execution ground. By all accounts they left well satisfied.

Errol was not unduly disturbed by this particular piece of rough justice, but he did decide that the time had come to move to new adventures, and particularly to more palatable ones. His trouble was that he was not really sure in which direction he wanted to go. The only thing he did know for certain was that he intended to keep out of the way of his mother. He was confident that she would monopolize any reunion they might have with the shrill delivery of a sermon attacking his wayward morals. And that, he considered, would be terribly unfair since he hadn't had half the opportunities that she believed he had to justify such treatment.

The journey back to his wooden hut, however, changed all that. As he waded through the long jungle grass, he found himself facing the slim, quaking figure of a young girl. It was quite clear she thought the white stranger was about to kill her. But as she stood there, rooted to the spot, her anguish subsided. She could see that if anyone was nervous, it was the white stranger.

Errol was better educated in the physical side of life than most young men of his age, but before him now was a vision that could never have been conjured by any of those books hungrily devoured by schoolboys. The girl wore nothing more than a grass skirt and a shy smile on a bronze face. But he was just eighteen and not even that smile could keep his eyes away from the rest of her body. She had the most enchanting figure he had ever seen. Long, beautifully shaped legs, a waist ... he didn't really allow her waist to register. He gazed instead, as though mesmerized, at her breasts. He had never seen anything like this in his life. As he stared, the girl's innate sense of modesty made her turn her head away, but when she sneaked a look in his direction she could tell that it was now he who was avoiding her gaze. It seemed that he was more concerned for his own safety than she was for hers.

He stumbled for words, although there was really little point in trying to get them to make sense; she would never have understood his English. The girl, however, had no problem at all in communicating. When she held out her hand, her intentions were clear. Together they went into her family's hut, not a hundred yards away from their meeting place.

Errol says in his book *My Wicked, Wicked Ways* that his father had anticipated such an event. He had written him a note, warning: "My boy, always remember that a man who has anything to do with a native woman stinks in the nostrils of a decent white man." The son wrote back to the father: "Dad, I stink."

If Errol did not accept his father's European code of morals, he was doing no more than entering fully into the traditional way of life of most of the local settlers. Men who would never have dreamed of having a black man to their table considered it their right to take a black girl to their bed.

Flynn found no difficulty at all in adopting most of their prejudices, few of which he would ever lose. When a much older Chinese dared to address him as "Flynn", he punched the man for his insolence. Officially, that was a crime and such an action was punishable by a jail sentence. Errol was indeed hauled before the local magistrate and given a week's imprisonment, but the jail turned out to be the comfortable home of a sympathetic Englishman and for that week the two men whiled away the time playing poker.

Once he was "freed", Errol reluctantly thought again about earning a living. This time, the search resulted in an introduction to a lifestyle. He joined a team of fishermen and discovered at that precise moment that for him a boat was like an extra limb, something without which he would never again feel completely alive.

Soon, Errol was in business for himself. He hired an assortment of canoes, together with a few native workmen casually "thrown in" as part of the deal. But it was fishing without line or net. Instead, Errol and his "boys" used dynamite, picking up the proceeds whenever the fish rose to the surface in the wake of the explosion. It would, of course, ruin the fishing in the waters for ever and cause hideous pollution of the sea, but he cared as little about this as he did about deflowering a native maiden – and by now he had no inhibitions in that direction either. He had become as hungry for sex as was a drug addict for a "shot" of heroin. He was as indiscriminate in his sources of supply, too. Before very long he contracted a particularly nasty form of gonorrhoea. He found a local quack to administer a healing potion, took a double dose and very nearly died from the experience, but he was young, otherwise virile and determined not to change his ways.

It didn't cure him of his need for women any more than an experience with one of his boats – he nearly blew himself as well as his quarry out of the water – made him think twice about heaven being a place that moved on water.

He extended his activities to include a schooner called the *Maskai* – a Polynesian word which he was convinced meant "screw you", but which others said was the local name for the jungle.

For a time he used the boat to take copra from one place to another. Later he saw the opportunities it offered for ferrying passengers. His first trip should have lasted two days but took as many weeks. Yet somehow at that stage Flynn was like one of those toy soldiers that were weighted at the bottom: every time he was knocked over, he rose up again. Sometimes his activities had unforeseen consequences that were to prove as important to him as was his education at the hands of the beautiful-breasted native girl.

He arranged to take a film crew through uncharted waters. The men said they were working on a Hollywood movie and the glamorous image which that presented excited Errol. He didn't know that they were really employed by the Australian Government, who anticipated trouble from the local inhabitants and needed a record of the territory.

Neither did Errol know that he was acting as more than just the skipper of the *Maskai*. He was featuring in the cameramen's lenses, too. He was young, rugged, and with his bare chest catching the rays of the sun, a superb foreground figure for the film. As far as he was concerned, however, these were merely a bunch of interesting clients.

At the end of the expedition, Errol and the *Maskai* journeyed around the coast of New Guinea and finally put in at Port Moresby. None of the crew had either money or food, but there was just about enough fuel to reach a nearby Portuguese-administered island. They decided to move on.

Ashore again, one of the sailors joined in a poker game and came away with $50. "I often wonder what would have happened to me but for that poker game," Flynn said some fifteen years later. "None of those taking part knew that the guy who won had got into the game without a cent. He was playing strictly on bluff."

But there was no bluff about Errol's oft-stated ambitions. He was still searching for gold. When he realized that the only way he might get near it was by selling his precious *Maskai*, he reluctantly did so. With the proceeds of the sale, he could buy the services of eight young natives who would help in his quest.

One thing became apparent before very long: it was easier to blow yourself up looking for fish than it was to pan for gold. He had gone to the territory with one thing in mind and once the difficulties of terrain were clear, that mind was wandering, mostly back to dusky maidens.

Years later he was to say that he wished he had more often remembered a saying of Marx – Groucho Marx that is: "Lookee, no touchee." But with girls like the ones constantly before him, there was no competition, if sometimes he did think about the consequences.

He realized that the best chance of avoiding infection was to keep out of the way of women who had had their initial experiences elsewhere. A nubile virgin had distinct advantages. It was to be a thought he would always remember.

For the moment, his principal concern had to be with making a living. As first mate on a boat called the *Matupi* he led a party of natives almost to the frontiers of Dutch New Guinea. There he had more plans – this time, to hunt another priceless product, feathers.

As any milliner will confirm, the bird of paradise has the most beautiful feathers in the world. They are also the rarest. Hunting its plumage can be like searching for oil – and considerably more dangerous. Yet in the heart of nearby Dutch New Guinea there were birds of paradise flying freely, a situation that was just too tempting for Errol who saw in them the prospects of another fortune. The Dutch were a lot less kindly disposed to the idea of shooting the birds than he was. When Flynn's party were spotted by a colonial police task force, they gave chase – killing one of the boys in the process and, as Errol was to say years later, leaving him shaking with fright.

He did manage to get back to the boat. Once ashore and with the dust washed off his body, he again went looking for yet another new job. He found one dealing in human flesh, as a slave trader. For a sound New Guinea native he soon discovered he could get between £30 and £40. Always ready to learn his trade properly, Flynn became adept at feeling a black man's muscles, looking into his teeth and weighing up how much he could be worth.

As with everything else, however, he grew tired of this business venture. Not that he had any sudden pangs of conscience, simply that he found the whole thing dreadfully dull. So what was it all for? In his diary, he wrote: "The best part of life is spent earning money in order to enjoy a questionable liberty during the least valuable part of it. To hell with money! Pursuit of it is not going to mould my life for me!"

And he went on: "I'm going to live sturdily and spartan-like – to drive life into a corner and reduce it to its lowest terms and if I find it sublime, I shall know by experience – and not make wistful conjectures about it, conjured up by illustrated magazines." If ever words were made to be swallowed!

He had always read voraciously but now he had doubts about adventures that were never more than second-hand. He was equally determined to question other people's ideas about living, most

notably the ones that had been fostered during his painful years at
school.

"I refuse to accept", he wrote, "the ideology of a business world
which believes that man at hard work is the noblest work of God."

Yet he had become sharp in his business practices, particularly
in his ability to recognize a going concern, or a potentially going
one, when he saw it.

He didn't abandon his slave operation straight away. He went
on to "buy" a band of blacks from a sea captain who ought to have
known better. It took the mariner more than a week to realize what
had gone wrong and by that time Errol had sailed away into the
wide blue yonder. From that moment on, the captain swore there
was a loaded revolver waiting for Mr Flynn. He was one of the
people whom Mark Hellinger came across. Flynn, he told him, still
bristling with anger, had bought his slaves not with coins but with
St Louis World's Fair tokens. "Wrong," maintained an affronted
Errol when he heard the outrageous suggestion. "They were from
the San Francisco Exposition."

Once again, accounts vary of what happened after this particular
period in Flynn's life. But there seems general agreement that he
then became a jungle guide – until a vicious native tribe decided
that Flynn and party were a useful quarry and succeeded in killing
one of Errol's men with a single neat thrust of a spear that would
have done credit to a javelin thrower in the Olympics.

Errol had been hired to pilot a new group of photographers
through the *maskai*. When things got sticky, he suggested that they
might, perhaps, like to go back. "Hell no," said the leader of the
party. "We came here for pictures and we're not leaving till we get
them." According to a magazine article published in 1935, Errol
replied: "Right you are. We'll go on!" It was just the image that
Flynn fancied for himself, both as an adult and as a teenager. Life
was an adventure, danger its most fascinating ingredient. To know
that he would be able to talk about it when he got home was perhaps
the best part of all. Numerous veterans of the New Guinea campaign
have confirmed the rest of the episode. The party was surrounded
by a circle of fire. Three more of the bearers let out eerie screams
and fell to the ground in pools of blood and as more headhunters

charged from the bushes, Flynn himself caught one with a shot from his revolver. The native died instantly. Errol's relief at what seemed to be beating the attacker at his own game was to be short-lived. During the retreat back to base, Errol, too, was hit. An arrow pierced his heel. It was not a severe wound and only slightly slowed his progress through the *maskai*, but he bore the scar till his dying day.

Flynn limped on to the town of Salamaua. There, he added another detail to a curriculum vitae that had already included the occupations of slave trader, explorer, gold prospector and sailor. But this new one he didn't relish in the least.

He blinked his hazel eyes in disbelief as a pair of handcuffs was fastened around his wrists. Two men in the uniform of the New Guinea police were frogmarching him into a bamboo cage. "The charge," one of them told him gruffly, "is murder."

"Murder?" He had done many things in a ridiculously short space of time. Been found out on most of them, too. But he was now being charged with something that he protested he had not only not done, but from which he had no idea how he was going to escape.

His alleged victim was the native he had killed in the *maskai*. As far as the police were concerned, Flynn was a tearaway young prospector with no more respect for human life than he had had for local custom. He had failed to recognize the rule of the jungle that declared that the place belonged to the natives and the white man went there at his peril.

There was, however, just one weakness to the police case. No one was able to produce a body. So, as in many a later film, Errol was rescued at the eleventh hour, released with a warning to be much more careful in future.

Now even Errol knew it was time to get back to civilization. He was miserable, unsettled, with no responsibilites. There was no one person in his life who really mattered and, apart from the father he had not seen for so long, no one who seemed to care about him either. Errol Leslie Thomson Flynn felt a much chastened man, but not a careful one. When he sailed for Sydney, he was nursing another attack of gonorrhoea and was virtually broke.

He tried hard to pick up where he had left off before sailing for

New Guinea. But that was easier said than done. He even once more courted Naomi and gave her another engagement ring. But to him she was unexciting and colourless. Naomi had none of the mystery offered by the maidens of the island and he always thought that half the fun of taking a girl came from the surprises she offered. There were none from Naomi. The engagement ended speedily.

Jobs were so hard to come by that when he took one on a sheep farm, he didn't even bother to ask about his responsibilities. It turned out he was needed as a sort of veterinary surgeon who only had one task: to castrate the lambs. He was not provided with any particular instruments. "What da ya need them for, cobber?" asked the farmer. "You've got a good set of teeth, ain't you?" Errol contemplated the reasoning and agreed. "Right enough, sport," he said, and went about his duties, alternately biting and spitting out the hopes for what were to be a lost generation of sheep.

As far as can be gathered, the main worry this engendered for Errol concerned its possible effect on his love life. He bolstered his flagging nerves and suspect smell with the knowledge that in the one department now so lacking in his sheep he himself was perfectly intact.

At that stage, money represented not the beginning of a trail to riches but simply a means of obtaining the necessities of life. For a short period he was even able to ensure a luxury meal for himself for no more than sixpence – the price of a packet of cigarettes at a Sydney hotel.

He nonchalantly bought the cigarettes at the hotel kiosk and then with the packet protruding from his hand, casually walked into the restaurant. Errol, the natural actor, succeeded where anyone else would surely have been kicked into the road. He ordered his meal, ate his fill, and just as casually walked out again. Without paying, of course. He had earlier taken the precaution of using his ever-present charm to win over a group of street peddlers outside. Like them, he said, he was a small man bucking a system that kept him poor while it made others rich. He got so friendly with one of the men that the peddler readily agreed to buy back the cigarettes for no less than the sixpence Flynn had paid in the first place.

He had not forgotten about the higher stakes he had sought in New

Guinea. When he happened to mention to a drinking companion that he still had a registered gold claim, he sold it to the man for the unbelievable price of £2000. These were riches beyond which Errol had never dreamed. But they did not last.

The money somehow now seemed to be no more than a means of getting drunk and for buying more women. The Sydney prostitutes vied with each other to satisfy the boy's needs. He was not only an easy catch, but was so much better looking than the fat businessmen and uncouth sailors with whom they usually had to be content. But he still wasn't happy. For the first time in his life he was seriously depressed. Somehow, he had to get away.

The opportunity came in the midst of a drunken stupor. He signed away most of what remained of his £2000 fortune and bought a 44-foot rigged cutter called the *Sirocco*, a name that would recur in the Errol Flynn story. The *Sirocco* was his means of getting back to New Guinea. It was also a floating brothel. As he wrote to his father – in a letter addressed "Dear Pater" – there were "maidens from stem to stern".

Once the *Sirocco* had docked in New Guinea, Errol decided to spend his last remaining pounds on a tiny plot of land with a couple of weather-beaten tobacco plants. It made him a plantation owner, although not a happy one. He began to think that he wanted more out of life than was offered by the primitive, humid wastes of the jungle.

His father had sent him a constant supply of books to read and he devoured them. "They're the best education I've had," he wrote his "pater". But if the books taught him a love of literature, they also made him yearn for the urbane, white man's civilization so many of them described.

His reading did, however, serve to improve his writing, as well as his sense of observation and his imagination. For weeks, some highly coloured reports were published in the *Sydney Bulletin* under the by-line Errol Flynn. The success of these made him think again about his financial state and as a result his attitude changed. He looked for other interests and most of these were ways to make money. Constantly, he thought about the gold he had given up. Or had he? He turned the idea over in his mind and decided to go after it again. The question was how?

Wealth was becoming an obsession. Coins jangling in his pockets were, as far as he was concerned, passports to success and acceptability. Without them, he felt rejected.

But the only coins he had now were halfpennies, not enough – even in New Guinea – for a pint of beer. As he turned them over and over in his hand, the thought occurred that even these contemptible pieces of dull copper could be worth more than they appeared to be. If, he thought carefully, he dipped them into liquid mercury, they might . . . just might . . . be made to look like shillings – coins, he knew, were as respected by the New Guinea natives as though they were sovereigns of gold.

Casually, Errol let the word slip so that it might reach the ears of one of the local chiefs: he had a miracle machine that could turn halfpennies into shillings – but only at the full moon.

It was full moon that night. Errol knew what would happen, and when the chief came calling after nightfall, he was fully prepared. The tall, dignified figure crept quietly into Errol's hut in time to see the young white man crouched over a cauldron, muttering strange sounds.

His eyes glistened as he watched what came next: coins were carefully placed into a tube and then, by the white man's magic, transformed into silver shillings.

The chief let it be known that he wanted to buy the machine and Errol just as clearly indicated his willingness to sell – for the price of forty tribesmen who would help him in his search for gold. A deal was struck and the chief went away happy in the knowledge that at the next new moon – it was too late for the magic to work this time round – he, too, would be rich from the proceeds of turning halfpennies into shillings. In the meantime, Errol and his forty "boys" discreetly vanished into the New Guinea dawn.

4

The Perfect Specimen

*He had a charisma like the great romantic
actors*
Vincent Price

Flynn made no fortune from his gold rush, although at one stage
it did seem that he could be striking it rich. In the mud-sodden
earth that his boys whisked around in their pans there did appear
to be just a suggestion of a gold-coloured substance. But there was
little enough of it to disenchant even the most optimistic prospector.
The time had come, Errol was now convinced, to move on, if for
no other reason than that the night of the full moon was fast
approaching. Errol knew that his friend the chief would soon recognize he had been duped and would send out his headhunters – the
head they wanted most being Flynn's.

Back at his plantation came a totally unexpected chance for him
to leave New Guinea and start afresh. He received a telegram from
a certain Charles Chauvel. He explained he was an Australian producer friend of Dr Herman Erben, the film maker for whom Errol
had acted as "pilot" on his voyage through the jungle waters.
Chauvel had seen the shots that featured the bronzed torso of Errol
at the helm and believed there was probably more to him that an
adventurous young sailor. Now he had a proposition for young Mr
Flynn.

The telegram was very explicit: there would be a fee of £50 with
all expenses paid, if Errol would take a trip to Tahiti and become
a film actor.

It seemed that Erben had been delighted with the filming he had
done in New Guinea. What was more, when the shots were run
through the projectors in his preview theater, he himself had noticed

how the handsome young man dominated every frame. Both Erben and his film editor had come to the same conclusion: young Errol was a fellow who ought to be grabbed before it was too late. It was fortuitous that only hours later Chauvel happened to mention he was planning to make a picture himself – about one of the great soul-stirring stories of the days when Britannia ruled the waves and her sea captains ruled their sailors with rods of iron: the mutiny on the *Bounty*. Erben suggested Flynn and when Chauvel saw the film his friend had shot could only agree.

Charles Laughton and Clark Gable were not even names to Errol Flynn at that time and it is quite possible that even they had not yet heard of the *Bounty* story – their own and now legendary version of the mutiny was still six years away. But Errol knew as much about it himself as if he personally had been cast adrift in the captain's boat, or, like his ancestor Midshipman Young, had gone with the rest of the crew on to the Pitcairn Islands. How could anyone with Errol's idea of adventure resist such an opportunity? Especially now with a tribe of cannibals at his heels! He didn't. He sailed for Tahiti immediately.

On the island's white beaches, Errol could not help but think he had chosen well. It was a paradise with sun, sand and women – even more beautiful than had been the native girls of New Guinea. His first meeting with Chauvel offered something that quickly stirred his imagination. The new film would be called *In The Wake of the Bounty* and Errol would, if he liked the idea, put on naval uniform and play Fletcher Christian – the role that would indelibly be linked in future with Gable, but which for the moment only conjured up memories for him of Midshipman Young and his sword.

In later years he was to say he was offered the filming job while working in Tahiti as a pearl fisherman, but this appears to have no more truth in it than did many of the other yarns he enjoyed spinning.

Yet he really did not see himself as an actor. He had not dressed up since the days when he was at home, competing with his mother for the loudest voice and the most sustained argument. Yet there *had* always been a temptation about the stage and now for the first time he had an opportunity to exercise it.

Flynn was not a dedicated movie buff. Certainly he had enjoyed going to the "pictures" when he was at school, if only because it had always represented a useful place to which he could take a girl. The back seats in the dark were as irresistible to him as they were to any other youth. But he had been away from what was fondly called civilization for a long time and a lot had happened in the cinema. Now that Al Jolson had shown that films could be made to talk, a veritable movie revolution had broken out, but he had seen none of it.

Now, however, he was invited to go on board a ship – which he had always enjoyed; dress up – which he used to think was good fun; and was being paid for it, too – which was an essential part of life. At a moment when the alternative was the clutches of a head-hunter, £50 was riches indeed.

Filming took three dull, uneventful weeks and by the time the rushes were ready, Errol was back in Australia, wondering where he was going next.

As well he might have done. The film was appalling, Errol's acting even worse. Yet in one somewhat prophetic speech, he had to say to a much older man: "The die has been cast, Edward Young." (Was this supposed to be his midshipman ancestor? The age and first name of the Mr Young in the picture could have been just one of a thousand inaccuracies.) "There is no turning back. The future holds the most awful adventure of all." With the sort of past that Errol had had, it seemed a fair prognosis for his own future.

If *In the Wake of the Bounty* was to make a lasting impression on Errol, it was a subconscious one. He had been surprised by the ease with which he took direction and learned his lines – as would be many a later director who heard about it – and, more important, he enjoyed the camaraderie of the film crew. Not in a long time had he been around so many white people, and that was vitally important to him. But the whole exercise seemed no more than another passing job.

The film itself would never have meant anything at all had not the name Errol Flynn come along to give it a place in the folklore of the film industry. The part of Captain Bligh, incidentally, was played by an actor called Mayne Lynton, whose fate was to be remembered even less than that of the film. It was not so much that the Laughton–Gable picture replaced this one in the story of the cinema or that in 1931, when the movie was made, Australia's studios had fewer exploitation opportunities than Hollywood's. *In the Wake of the Bounty* simply was not a very good film.

However, it was professional enough to introduce Errol to one fact with which he instantly felt sympathy: the one that said that in honour of the great god Publicity, you did not always have to tell the truth, the whole truth and nothing but the truth. He accepted as gospel that it was perfectly reasonable to pose with a young man whose back had been burnt by the sun, who carried a bundle of bananas on his shoulder and who according to the captions put out by the publicity department, really was called Fletcher Christian, a genuine descendant of the man who launched the *Bounty* mutiny. Errol did not believe it, but if the lie was one of the rules of the game he accepted that it should be so.

It did not over-impress Professor Flynn, however, who as if to demonstrate his displeasure, immediately presented Captain Bligh's sword to an Australian museum.

Incidentally, Errol was listed in the cast as Leslie Flynn. A print of the picture was to escape to Hollywood in the late thirties and be shown to a bunch of movie moguls, none of whom showed the remotest concern for the fate of the picture or offered to buy it. No one appeared to recognize Leslie Flynn either.

Back in Australia, Flynn spent his time visiting the local public libraries. He decided that he really had to try to educate himself, although never at the expense of sharing a bed with a beautiful girl. For much of the time he lived in a doss house, but starring in a picture he was convinced he would never see had made him think about his dignity. Perhaps, he finally reasoned, he ought now to go to Britain where his father's position in the academic world was constantly rising. He would – if absolutely necessary – even risk trying to make up to his mother.

Professor Flynn's career was certainly growing apace. Not only had he been a leading don at the University of Tasmania, but his knowledge of marine biology had been recognized by his government. It appointed him Royal Commissioner of Tasmanian Fisheries. But he too had not lost his spirit of adventure and when this urge combined with an opportunity to go back to the family roots, he and Marelle did not hesitate. In 1931 they sailed for Ireland, where Theodore had been offered the Biology Chair at Queen's University, Belfast, then the somewhat sleepy capital of Ulster. The Irish "troubles" were apparently over, and indeed would not recur for almost forty years. Belfast appeared to be the ideal place in which to follow his own peaceful academic pursuits.

Errol's own journey to England took months; there was no way for someone in his financial position to travel other than on a cargo vessel literally crawling across the world. But it did serve to broaden his mind. On the first stage of the voyage he met a young lady with the improbable name of Ting Ling O'Connor, who taught him two lessons, on both of which he would draw for the rest of his life.

The first consisted of demonstrating some fascinating intricacies of Oriental sex practice. But her other lesson was to have even more far-reaching repercussions. She explained that smoking need not stop at mere tobacco. Under her tutelage pure opium was to open doors for Errol Flynn that he did not even know existed and led to territories he longed to explore. He was still barely twenty-three and the thought that he could be doing himself everlasting harm never even crossed his immature mind. When he realized that Ting Ling could be transported – or at least claimed that she could be – into sexual ecstasies even more graphic than those he was experiencing himself, opium appeared to be the food of the gods. Certainly, it seemed to be answering all his own prayers. It also answered most of hers. When Errol awoke from his drugged slumbers, he discovered the loss of his wallet and every other thing of value he possessed.

For a time he sought a desperate solution to his problem: he volunteered for the Hong Kong Volunteers, which he has described as a local version of the French Foreign Legion. By sheer gall, he managed to make that merely a temporary period of duty. After doing little more than shining his boots to a mirror-like surface, spending most of his nights cleaning his other kit and day after day drilling in the humid Hong Kong heat, he escaped.

He took a boat to Shanghai, thanks to the captain accepting a piece of paper on which Errol had carefully stamped a wax seal.

It conveniently covered the line reading: "Not responsible for laundry left here over six months." Errol claimed the laundry list was his exit permit from the Army and the captain didn't argue.

The journey westward continued though a succession of brothels, doss houses and other sleazy establishments, avoiding tricksters one moment, seducing women the next. In India, a rickshaw-man showed his distaste for Flynn's inadequate tips by tearing through his stomach with a sharp knife, but as with his other near fatalities, he recovered sufficiently well to continue the trip scarred but apparently none the worse for wear.

Errol arrived in London with two shillings to his name, just enough for a taxi to the Berkeley Hotel where he registered and moved his belongings into a suite. This was one occasion when he intended to aim high. He explained his less than suave appearance by saying he had been on The Tour; and in the heart of what was still the Empire, there could be no more persuasive means of melting a true patriot's heart. He got his room.

The fortunate thing was that the moment for paying the bill never came. After two days at the Berkeley he was transferred, at the hotel's expense, to a private hospital room. He had convinced the hotel doctor he was suffering from acute appendicitis, and could not possibly concentrate on adding up a list of figures.

But he did not stay long. Errol escaped through a window when faced with an end even more drastic than the operation; his nurse suggested they get married. It was at that point that Errol decided to become an actor.

His experience in the *Bounty* picture was not really enough to do him much good. The film had not reached Britain. In England he was a man completely without reputation, which, considering some of his experiences in recent months, was not wholly a disadvantage.

As in all the cliché-ridden stories, he made the parade from one agent's office to another, advertised in theater papers and even thought of going back to New Guinea. In fact, it was a very serious thought. Only when a shilling – his sole remaining coin – landed heads instead of tails did he decide to remain in Britain. Then one agent conceded that perhaps Errol did have something to offer –

and suggested he contact the Northampton Repertory Company who were casting for their annual pantomime, *Jack and the Beanstalk*. As the agent said, the rep wanted a villain and Errol might be their man.

Errol agreed he would make a very good villain indeed and there was nobody around able to argue the point. Robert Young, the director of the company, clinched the deal. He asked Errol: "Do you play cricket?" and when Flynn replied "Yes" – as he always would because he knew on which side his next piece of bread was to be buttered – he had a job. The team lost its first game, but Errol was offered a place with the company just the same, at £3 a week.

Northampton was and is a town more famous for making shoes than for soaring to dramatic heights, but in those days people went to the theater in much the same way that they now turn a knob on a television set. Almost every place of a fairly reasonable size had a theater and apart from the bigger centers like Manchester or Glasgow most of them depended on a team of repertory players who cut their theatrical teeth in the small, usually seedy, playhouses constructed in the dying days of the nineteenth century.

Flynn was at Northampton for eighteen months, a time he seems to have enjoyed thoroughly, playing anything from Othello, which he admits was the worst in the company's history (this Moor of Venice had to die from a heart attack because the knife on which he was due to impale himself had got stuck in his cloak), to American gangster parts.

He even wrote a play of his own called *Cold Rice*, which was about the Raj in India. Strangely, this is one period in the developing life of Errol Flynn that appears to be bereft of vigorous sexual activity. Perhaps, on consideration, it is not so surprising. Having to learn a new part every week, rehearse during the day and play a different role in the evening left him little time to experiment. And the theatrical landladies – a breed of women who kept lodging houses that were aimed as much at preserving the morals of the theater as providing its actors with bed and board – were an obstacle to overcome. You could no more secrete a girl into a bedroom, let alone fumble with her skirts, without these secret agents knowing it, than you could refuse to eat everything they cooked.

Flynn, however, was being noticed by the young ladies of the town. Today, ageing matrons virtually swoon at the memory of the handsome creature on whom they used to feast their eyes in the same halls in which they now play bingo. And Flynn *was* handsome, with a magnificent physique which he found time to develop by playing tennis in the Northampton parks and by boxing in a nearby gymnasium.

For all actors, the square mile of London known as the West End is Mecca and Errol Flynn was no exception to those wanting to make the pilgrimage. When a talent scout from one London management called at Northampton – as he and his colleagues would do at every repertory company in the country – Errol was the man he picked.

If Errol imagined he was about to become a star, he had time in which to think again. London did not come easily. He was first advised to take part in the Stratford-on-Avon Festival, where plays due for a West End opening were given a try-out. The message was that if the plays did well there, then they would move on to the capital.

Errol was true to form. He went in not just feet first but with his arms and shoulders, too. His repertory experience had taught him he could learn two parts simultaneously. So why not act in two plays, too? He did, playing a Roman soldier in one and an Irish policeman in the other. He was the Roman in *A Man's House* by the celebrated playwright John Drinkwater and the cop in *The Moon and the Yellow River* by Dennis Johnstone.

The timing in Stratford had been perfect. He knew he could play the Roman in one play with plenty of time to change into his police uniform in the other. But in London it was not so simple. One evening he appeared in the Irish part wearing a toga. Neither he nor the plays lasted.

However, he had the luck of the Irish cop he was supposed to portray. Errol thought about making a career for himself in the movies. With the somewhat spurious experience of the *Bounty* epic behind him, he took a space in the British film trade papers – with a picture of his profile flanking a list of non-existent films in which he claimed to have starred in Australia. A scout from Teddington

Studios saw the advertisement and asked Flynn if he would like to pop round to see him.

The studio was making a series of "quota" pictures – to satisfy the law requiring every foreign-made film to be balanced by a home-grown product.

Errol was told to go to Teddington where he was to report to Irving Asher, head of the studios. As he waited in the corridors, a man in horn-rimmed glasses rushed by and then took a step back. "You're a big fellow," he said, peering at Flynn, who had already made up his mind to take this possible employment no more seriously than he had his qualifications for a New Guinea sanitation expert. "What have you done?"

"Want a list of my previous convictions?" replied Flynn flippantly. The man decided not to parry his attitude. "Come to my office," he ordered without making any noticeable change in his facial muscles. Twenty minutes later Errol emerged from the office with a film script and a contract. He was to report the following Monday and earn £20 a week.

Flynn's role has almost disappeared from memory like dust in the can in which the film was taken from studio laboratory to projection room. The picture was called *Murder at Monte Carlo*. In it Errol played a newspaper reporter sent to the gambling capital to investigate yet another "system" of beating the wheel.

Some of the footage of the picture was shot at the newly-opened Imperial Studios at Boreham Wood in Hertfordshire, now Elstree Studios. They were run in those days by Herbert Wilcox, who was to play an important part in the Flynn story twenty years later. "He was a natural," Wilcox told me shortly before he died. "Very puckish. He was charm itself. Not an actor in the usual sense of the term, he had almost got there through the letter box, but he was great."

Irving Asher certainly thought so. He immediately cabled Jack Warner at the Burbank studios just outside Hollywood: WE HAVE HELL OF PERSONALITY HERE SUGGEST SIGN HIM FOR HOLLYWOOD FILM. It was a message taken seriously. Warner cabled back: AGREE YOUR SUGGESTION.

Irving Asher gave Flynn £200 and told him to buy himself a wardrobe befitting his future station in life. To Savile Row Errol went and there ordered suits in the finest worsted and a coat of the softest camel hair. At Alan McAfee's wood-panelled establishment in Dover Street, the name Errol Flynn was added to the catalogue of customers whose feet shapes were preserved for posterity in their collection of personal lasts. Around these lasts were built a pair of riding boots, two pairs of black and white shoes and another in brown and white – all made completely by hand for the price of £5 apiece. Details of the transaction, and the lasts, are still held in the McAfee vaults. As we shall see later, they have reason to remember him.

Once more now Errol was travelling. This time, his destination was Hollywood.

5

The Adventures of Don Juan

He was just an incredibly, incredibly unique and one-of-a-kind man. You've got to give the man incredible points.
Sammy Cahn

It was a slow boat ride to America and as far as Errol was concerned at the time, the beginning of just another experience to add to all the others. He no more thought he was going to spend the rest of his life working in pictures than his parents expected him to allow the grass of Belfast to grow under his feet.

Errol had not seen the professor or his mother during all the time he was in England and it pained him to think he had so readily severed his family links. Not for a minute did Marelle think that letters betraying her own increasingly hostile attitude to her son could have anything to do with it. Errol felt he had been rejected at a time when he could have done with a soft, warm maternal shoulder to cry on and now he was not making any efforts on his own. As for his sister Rosemary, she was a virtual stranger.

For the moment, Errol was content with the knowledge that he would be having $125 coming in every week. For him 1935 did indeed seem to be the year of the oyster and more than it had ever been before, the oyster was the world.

Warner Brothers had no real plans for him yet, but they were bringing him across the Atlantic in style. They paid for his passage on the ss *Paris*, the pride of the French Line, and he did everything in his power to enjoy the experience. Within hours of checking in his baggage, washing the grime of the train journey to Southampton from his face and changing his suit, he was a recognized fixture in the first-class bars.

"The best champagne, sport," he ordered and emptied a bottle in what the unsophisticated youngster thought was true playboy style. Word of Errol's prospects had meanwhile been broadcast throughout the lounges and restaurants from one elegant passenger to another and it was easy to see why. His appearance was immaculate and his face handsome enough to make him the choice of any matron for her unattached daughter.

But he had his own ideas about this particular sport. The women he was interested in were those he spotted for himself and not the ones who looked his way without prompting.

In particular he found it very difficult to keep his eyes off two women who in the silky skin-hugging dresses of the day seemed to be exhibiting as many contours as were on the ship's charts. Looking was easy. As they promenaded from the open deck into the lounge, he would move his gaze from one to the other much like a spectator at a tennis championship. Acting on his impulses was another matter entirely. He was totally unable to relate to either of them.

Their attitude had a strange effect on him. He had not been known before to shy away from contact with beautiful women, but now that they were not proving to be particularly interested in him, he became uncharacteristically reticent. There was little more he could do than find out their names, which was not difficult. Both were celebrities.

One was Naomi Tiarouina, a Russian princess. The other, Lili Damita, a French film star who like him had been given a Hollywood contract. But hers was worth ten times more than his and she showed him the contempt that established performers frequently reserved for ambitious unknowns. When Errol threw off his inhibitions and asked her for a dance, she replied "Come back later", raising her pert nose so high in doing so that she succeeded in making him feel as though she had cast a spell and turned him into a dwarf. Errol spent the rest of the voyage nursing a bruised ego.

He arrived in New York, as much concerned about the flaws in his romantic make-up as he was enthralled by being in what at the time seemed to be the most exciting city in the world. The place, its skyscrapers and its fast-moving cars, made everything he had known before seem tame and provincial. His second meeting with the princess seemed to confirm that impression.

He was to claim that she removed all her clothes for him in her room at the St Moritz Hotel. It seems that they had been in an elevator together and knowing full well how he would react, she casually allowed the number of the room to slip out as she stepped into the corridor. When he accepted the bait, she introduced him to more than merely the delights of her aristocratic Russian body. As one kind of act was completed, she embarked on another – pummelling his naked back with a steel-bristled brush and drawing blood in the process. It was, he said later, his first experience of sadism. In a way, it was not to be his last.

In Harlem, a totally different kind of sexual experience awaited him – and one he never wanted to repeat. In a nightclub he danced cheek to cheek with a partner who made all the juices in his body cascade. At what he judged to be the appropriate moment, he guided the willing one to a dark corner and placed his hand on a smooth silk-draped knee, before gradually moving higher. That was when he realized that he had been spending the evening with another man. When he ran out of the building, he was not merely trying to avoid paying the bill.

He was not sorry to move on to Hollywood, an altogether slower, more casual town that seemed to be nothing more than a collection of studios and of restaurants occupied by people either working in the movies or simply waiting to work in them.

It was obviously a very unreal place, but since Errol never liked taking anything seriously, that suited him perfectly. When the Warner Brothers publicity machine told him they were making Errol Flynn an Irishman, he saw no reason to argue, particularly when they told him why. It seemed they considered it better to say that than to describe him as an Australian. As a publicity man told him: "Who's heard of this place Tasmania anyway?" Naturally enough, it was not allowed to end there. He was photographed wearing a policeman's uniform – all Irishmen were cops, weren't they? And it was in the bright Californian sunshine that he met a young lady who, he was informed, was his long lost cousin from County Mayo. A cousin by name, he insisted, of Suzy Goldstein, although that was not what the press were told.

It took several weeks before Mr Flynn from Dublin actually became a film actor in Hollywood. He spent those weeks dating pretty girls and playing tennis and swimming, all of which he was now doing to perfection. At the Los Angeles Tennis Club he was introduced to Donald Budge and they frequently played together. When a studio publicist heard that Errol was equally good at boxing, his inventive brain got to work. The result: from that moment on, he decided, Errol had been a member of the British Olympic boxing team that had competed in Amsterdam in 1928. It seemed a sufficiently long time before to ensure that the records would be unchecked, and check no one did. For years, Flynn would tell intrigued fan magazine writers about his experiences in Amsterdam, alternately winning either gold or bronze medals, and with no one bothering to contradict him. He did not recall the "interlude" in his autobiography.

Life in Hollywood seemed to be an uninterrupted diet of sport and wenching and of collecting his weekly salary check. But after a time even Flynn began to question not so much the morality of what he had been doing as the effect it was all likely to have on his future. Finally, the call he had been waiting for came. He was asked to report to the set of *The Case of the Curious Bride*. Jack Warner had a job for him after all. But any dreams of stardom he may have nurtured were short-lived.

Errol did not have a line to say in the picture and to call the part a "walk on" would be a travesty of the truth. More accurately, he was a "lay on", or perhaps a "lay down". He played a corpse on a mortuary slab. As the sheet was pulled back, the film's star, the now-forgotten Warren Williams, said: "That's him," and the cadaver's face was covered again. Exit Errol Flynn, film actor. Or so it seemed.

Actually, that is not quite true. He did in fact appear later on in the film, a Perry Mason story that preceded the Raymond Burr television series by twenty years. It was in a minute-long flashback scene. But it is as the corpse that he will forever be remembered.

His experience in *The Case of the Curious Bride* was followed by a slightly more auspicious role in *Don't Bet on Blondes*. In that he had all of four lines to say. He was not exactly proving to be an overnight sensation in the film business.

For the moment Flynn, who never imagined he really would be good at anything outside of the bedroom, the sports field or the open deck of a boat, had to content himself with his surroundings. And the surroundings seemed fine.

Errol looked right for Hollywood – a fair-haired Greek god of a young man with an air that said he was real, up-to-date and very approachable.

Few knew at the time just how much he did want to be approached, and as much by the studio executives as by starlets answering his call. He didn't care whether or not he became a great actor. But he did care about justifying his existence at Burbank as more than just a bedroom figure.

His reputation as a sport – indoors and out – had gone before him. People who met Errol were initially wary. But for them he had a disarming mechanism that went into action as if by natural instinct. For a man there was a firm handshake and a smile that said: "If I can do anything for you, *please* ask." For a woman there was a sweet look that promised strength and dependability, and if that told only half the truth, there was nothing to prove it. Any doubts were immediately put to rest by a compliment so generous yet so plausible that it seemed to have belonged in a bygone age. "I have heard so *much* about you," was all he had to say to a woman to make her feel beautiful and wanted. Never did she feel used by him.

When he met Lili Damita again, his manner was as effective with her as with anyone else. One story has it that they met again at the tennis club, Errol was playing in a championship and she was sitting in a box near the court. He directed the ball her way and this time she had no desire not to accept the invitation that she was sure came with it. When she threw the ball back to him her smile told him he would be welcome.

Lili was as ravishingly beautiful as he was handsome and had achieved her place in Hollywood thanks to a meeting with the same

Michael Curtiz who had directed Errol's debut on the mortuary slab. By now he was the town's favourite Hungarian, but in the 1920s he had been running a Paris girlie show. When his star was taken ill, he found a replacement in a youngster who auditioned for him at his club. She said her name was Lili Damita.

In Montmartre she was spotted by a French film director and before long became a big star in her own country. She was brought to Hollywood by Sam Goldwyn and her curves were a passport to all the big social occasions in town.

When she and Errol did get together, it was a case of instant mutual infatuation. Before long he was invited to share her bungalow at that famed hospice for the rich, the Garden of Allah. Lili was a firebrand who enjoyed exhibiting her body more than she liked talking, unless it was in one of the wild outbursts of rage for which she had become famous. These were usually accompanied by clawing nails and the throwing of whatever came to hand. To Errol, who always had an apt phrase for the moment or a name for everyone with whom he became involved, she was Tiger Lil.

So sensuous was Lili that the most virile men in Hollywood were constantly at her door; yet she always seemed to be surrounded by homosexuals. One night at a party at the Garden, she introduced the newly-arrived Errol to another stranger. "Fleen," she said, "meet David Niven."

Each of them spent much of the evening convinced that the other was queer.

Errol's relationship with Lili was altogether strange. When they were not actually removing them for more pleasant reasons, they seemed to be boring the pants off each other. Yet, even so, they decided to make something of their relationship. It was not long before they announced they were flying off to Arizona. To get married.

The news of the impending ceremony was broken by the *New York Times* on 19 June 1935. It gave a fair indication of the comparative status of the two parties of the marriage: "Lili Damita, French screen actress," it stated, "and Errol Flynn, a newcomer to Hollywood, announced tonight they would fly to Yuma, Arizona, tomorrow morning and marry."

Indeed, they did fly to Yuma the next day, in a plane piloted by a mutual friend, Bud Ernst. Flynn looked nervous when they walked into the chambers of Judge Ernest A. Freeman that afternoon. The only witnesses around were two court officials. Bud Ernst was going to be best man.

Errol tried to cover his feeling of awkwardness by asking the judge: "Can you marry us, sport?" Later the judge told reporters he understood the actor's enthusiasm. "I think I could fall in love with her myself," he said. Errol slipped on to Lili's finger a distinctive ring made up of a series of thin gold links.

He maintained the fiction perpetrated by Warner Brothers. He was born, he said, in Dublin. When it came to her signature on the register, Lili wrote the name on her certificate: "Lillian Madelein Carré." Both said they were twenty-six, which did not augur too well for their future. Lili was at least eight years older than her new husband. They left the judge's office hand in hand, an idyllic state of affairs by all appearances, but one that was not to last. Soon, they would squabble over the smallest detail – her hats, his love of oysters, a tennis match – and often in public.

Once when a friend happened to join them at what was plainly an inconvenient moment he tried to cover his embarrassment. He whispered to Errol: "You had better hit her again." In truth he was only partly joking.

Lili was heard to murmur: "You look horrible this morning," and Errol replied: "Thank you, my dear, I was just about to say the same of you." Even when insulting a woman, he couldn't lose the almost polite, gentlemanly terminology.

It takes not too wide a stretch of the imagination to think that Jack Warner had something to do with the decision that Errol and Lili should marry. By that time they had already moved from the Garden of Allah to a large house in the Hollywood Hills and in 1935 any news leaking out of stars "living in sin" could be calculated to have their films banned by a dozen or more do-gooding organizations.

The Flynns' life together never resembled anything quite as much as a marathon wrestling match. When they weren't fighting from a combination of pique and boredom, they were tying each other into ecstatic knots in bed. She was nightly earning her reputation as "Tiger Lil".

They were still the talk of Burbank, two exquisitely carved creatures who were welcome at any social gathering simply because they made everything around them look splendid and beautiful. But Errol plainly worried that she and not he was the star of the family, such as it was. That things were to change was due as much as anyone to the British actor Robert Donat. Donat had been all but signed to play the title role in a swashbuckling epic to be called *Captain Blood*. But just when things were looking settled, he dropped out, and said he wanted nothing of *Captain Blood* or Warner Brothers.

On reflection, Donat seems a strange choice for the role of the pirate captain, but it was a part for an Englishman and at the time he seemed to be the big white hope of the British film industry. However, from the earliest stages of the negotiations, it was clear that Jack Warner, a tough, somewhat crude man who epitomized the Hollywood mogul, and the suave Donat were not going to get along. Donat wanted more money and Warner was not prepared to pay him. They even fought on the transatlantic telephone, a rare and expensive thing to do in 1935. Finally, Warner was convinced he had to go elsewhere.

The heads of department at Warner Brothers were told to look for a Captain Blood. The search did not reach the scale of the public quest for a Scarlett O'Hara at MGM three years later, but within the confines of the Burbank lot, there had never been anything like it. Warner scouts roamed the mail rooms and the commissaries – those restaurants that were so peculiarly Hollywood, where men dressed as Indian chiefs consumed hamburgers at the same table at which girls in Hawaiian costume ate their steaks and looked over the contracts. The men all had the same duty: to search for the face that would fit.

One by one the faces they alighted upon were produced for director Michael Curtiz and one by one Curtiz rejected them. Using his favourite expletive, "sohn of a beetch", he let each and every one of them know exactly how he felt. Finally, someone mentioned to him the name Errol Flynn. Curtiz had heard little of Errol's acting abilities. As far as he knew, he just looked pretty good on a mortuary slab, although he heard he was better on the tennis court and had a reputation for being able to hold his own with Lili Damita. When he sent for Flynn, it was no more than one of many shots in the dark.

But that was how you made your name in Hollywood – and largely by scoring off other people. There may have been palm trees swaying in the breeze outside, and the executive suite offices in the studios may have been furnished in the best hide and mahogany, but the slopes leading up to them were often steep and slippery.

The contract system was said to make slaves of actors, but it gave them a security they would never quite feel again. Given their "freedom" twenty years later, stars were to worry about being washed up every time a picture finished. They would be afraid to take holidays lest they be forgotten. But not then. They worked because their contracts said they should and most of them tried to "sneak" leave whenever they could. For directors it was not quite like that. They were under contract, too, but were only as good as their last picture. If they failed, the word got around Hollywood next morning and a man who had been making first features one moment could be switched to travelogues the next.

To Curtiz, finding a Captain Blood became a test of his professional integrity. Should he fail, he would have the wrath of an ever more impatient Jack Warner to face.

Curtiz, however, could take Warner's chastisement better than most. He so mangled the English language with every phrase that it became a virtual impossibility to win an argument with him. Curtiz knew that and took advantage of it.

When Flynn walked into his office, the director sized up his visitor much like a member of the Jockey Club surveying a three-year-old. He decided he had a case that would be difficult to answer. He didn't waste words on the youngster, but just the same was confident his quest was over. Curtiz looked at Errol once more and then walked out of the room leaving him behind, waiting. At Warner's office, he threw open the door without knocking and announced: "I think so I have ze best man for ze job. Errol Fleen. He's a very good looking man, J.L., and you should let me make a test from heem."

Warner, who was feeling equally jaded by the exhaustion of the search, was willing to let anything happen now just so long as it promised to finish the whole business. "Make a test," he said totally phlegmatically. "You've made one of everyone else."

Errol went along to the make-up room, the wardrobe department and finally on to the sound stage, knowing full well what it was all for. There was the possibility of a starring role, and as far as he was concerned, that was what Hollywood was all about. If they made him a star, he was going to do his best. If they didn't, he'd play around at what he was given to do until he got fed up with it or until someone somewhere else came up to him with the message: "Mr Flynn, how would you like to earn a thousand dollars?" There was no itch to play Hamlet inside his soul.

Flynn was tested together with a fragile-looking nineteen-year-old girl called Olivia de Havilland. Curtiz for one was delighted with them both. He called other Warner executives in to share the moment of excitement with him. Warner's head of production, Hal Wallis, was equally thrilled. It was as if a cloud had lifted from above the studio. Yet, when Wallis saw Flynn the next day, he told him there would have to be changes if he fancied himself as a Captain Blood.

"I've seen the test," he said. "And I also saw those frills and cuffs and things you were wearing. Take my advice, you had better get rid of them. They make you look like a sissy."

That, at the time, was not such an outrageous statement as it now seems. If the rest of Hollywood was talking about Flynn the young stud, he was totally unknown to the public. And it was an age when film actors were desperate to prove their virility. Tough guys and even Robert Taylor were begging their studios to feature them in boxing pictures just to demonstrate their masculinity. Without hearing anything more, Flynn took hold of the costume he had worn and which was still in his locker and ripped off every piece of lace he could find.

He had heard the hints that the part might be his and now he felt sure it would be. But no one had told him so officially.

The news that made it certain came in a telephone call to Errol from his agent – Minna Wallis, Hal Wallis's sister. He and David

Niven were sunning themselves by the pool at the Garden of Allah. They had seventeen dollars between them. When Errol returned to his deckchair, a broad grin over his face, they decided to blow the lot on champagne.

Errol plainly enjoyed his new status. Girls smiled at him on the set, boys brought him coffee and Michael Curtiz spoke kindly to him about the way he saw the role. But if they all thought of Flynn – now that there was no lace on his cuffs – as epitomizing the virile male they had cause for second thoughts early on in the shooting. On the second day Errol fainted and had to be brought round by the studio nurse.

Later, doctors diagnosed blackwater fever. It was something Errol had picked up in New Guinea and which occasionally flared up without any then known medication being able to prevent it. This time Errol settled for a shot of brandy and went back to work. His salary was upped from $125 a week to $750.

But the Errol Flynn that Jack Warner saw in the day's rushes was not the man to whom he had so happily given the Captain Blood role. Flynn, he decided, was drunk. "No one drinks at Warner Brothers, Flynn," he thundered when Errol was brought to the presence. It was the truth. Since both Jack Warner and his brother Harry had ulcers, they were not going to let anyone in the studio enjoy what they so patently missed.

It was the beginning of a war between mogul and star. When Warner suffered a heart attack soon afterwards, he blamed it on to Flynn. But he recovered to fight him again, almost as if it were in spite of their relationship.

Captain Blood was a success. It was not the first version of the story. Vitagraph, a company bought up by Warner Brothers at the same time as they acquired the Vitaphone talkie system, had first made it in 1925, starring J. Warren Kerrigan. From now on, however, it would *always* be associated with Errol.

It was not just his good looks, but the way he handled a sword and duelled with that suavest of villains, Basil Rathbone (who seemed a villain even when he played Sherlock Holmes), that won over critics and paying audiences alike. When Flynn forced Rathbone to the edge of a precipice with the words: "So ends a partnership that should never have begun," he notched himself a place in film folklore.

The *New York Times* assessed the historic nature of Errol's first starring role with a review headed: A NEWCOMER ERROL FLYNN IN A HANDSOME FILM VERSION OF "CAPTAIN BLOOD" AT THE STRAND.

The paper's critic, André Sennwald, struck a note he would never be able to repeat. He wrote: "With a splendid and criminally good-looking Australian named Errol Flynn playing the genteel buccaneer to the hilt, the photoplay recaptures the air of high romantic adventure which is so essential to the tale." After complimenting Rathbone, who the critic said had an unfortunate habit of dying in all his pictures, he added: "Mr Flynn has an effective cast at his back. Olivia de Havilland is a lady of rapturous loveliness and well worth fighting for."

Flynn certainly did not look a sissy as Captain Peter Blood, the physician turned galley slave who became a pirate chief. Now he was being hailed as the only possible heir to Douglas Fairbanks, Senior.

Errol was ecstatic at the reaction of seemingly all Hollywood to *Captain Blood*. He was being acclaimed by everyone except Lili. For her, it was a disaster. At a party to celebrate the world premiere, she was in tears. "Congratulations," said a senior studio executive. "Overnight, he's a star." "I know," she said, "that's why I'm weeping. It's also the end of our marriage." The tears continued and she begged other guests: "Don't tell him how wonderful he was." Certainly, she was not a wife to bask in her husband's glory. Even when surrounded by reporters.

On one occasion, Errol was waylaid by pressmen. Both he and Warner Brothers were so pleased with *Captain Blood*, Errol told them, that more parts were lined up for him. One was going to be the lead in *The Charge of the Light Brigade*. Another was likely to be in *Anthony Adverse*.

"Do you like your work?" a reporter called out. "Certainly not," Errol replied. "I never did think that work was ennobling. I prefer ..." But as the *New York Times* recorded, "What he preferred may never be known. Miss Damita had shanghaied Captain Blood."

The differences between them were given frequent public airings, literally. Sometimes, they were embarrassing – such as when Lili drove to a nearby airport to await Errol's return from a short out-of-town visit. From the cockpit of the small plane he had chartered, Errol could see her waiting near the runway fence. He tapped the pilot on the shoulder: "Don't land here," he ordered. "Make for another part of the field – anywhere, where she won't see me." It was not long before he was having to make excuses about that. "A slight misunderstanding," explained a studio official who was used to saying such things.

As far as Errol and Lili were concerned, it was the beginning of the end.

Fights which previously had been mere diversions from sex had seemingly lost their fun. Now when Tiger Lil screamed "Fleen", there was a venom in her voice that was all too real and when Errol replied with a cool phlegmatic put-down like "Why don't you take a walk over the cliff, my dear" he really hoped she might do it. The items of household equipment they threw at each other only served to add a new dimension to the concept of their home breaking up. It was not the happiest moment for Errol. Once more, he felt rejected.

Finally, the two of them came to what they considered would be a civilized arrangement. Errol would move out, but the bedroom would remain joint territory to be used when the mood was mutually considered propitious. Neither of them had any doubt that there was a sexual compatability if there was not a domestic one. Curled up in bed together, they were of one mind as they were of one flesh.

Errol had to find a new home and someone to share it with him. His choice was David Niven. It was an arrangement strictly of convenience, lest anyone contemplate an entirely wrong idea. Errol was gregarious and the thought of living alone was too painful to contemplate, even if that did mean he could bring a different girl to his bed every night. Niven and he, they both agreed, had enough in common to safely contemplate life under the same roof.

In a place like Hollywood, the sort of stock from which one hailed was important. There were frequent jibes about the way the Jews stuck together, but they were no more cliquey than were the Hungarians, the Irish or the Anglo-Saxons. The English colony in the movie capital insisted on afternoon tea to go with their Saturday afternoon cricket matches. Niven was a Scot, Flynn was half Irish, but when it came down to it both were British and a couple of young men who had an instinctive love of good women, good food, good wine and above all, a good time.

They also had a mutual need of good conversation, of a much appreciated witty remark that they were able to top. Both were well read and needed the sort of cerebral stimulation each felt that the other could provide.

As far as the other part of their life was concerned, they early on came to a satisfactory arrangement. They would share expenses – with Errol paying the larger half in exchange for the bigger bedroom – at 601 N. Linden Drive, which they rented from Rosalind Russell. As Niven says in his masterly book of Hollywood reminiscences, *Bring on the Empty Horses*, he soon discovered something very clear about Errol – you could always rely on him. "He always let you down."

If David asked Errol not to mention a certain girl when another came to call, Errol could be counted on to greet her with his usual olde-worlde charm. "Hello, Joan," he would say pleasantly. "By the way, David asked me not to mention a girl called Betty ...' It was arranged that the bedroom in the apartment would be loaned to Niven should the need arise (that is, if he happened to have the more attractive girl at the more convenient moment). In which case, he would pay the bigger slice of rent that week.

At the time, Niven seemed destined to play out his Hollywood life if not as an extra, then certainly by portraying a succession of upper-class British twits. Meanwhile, Errol was well and truly established as Mr He-Man 1935, with the pristine Olivia de Havilland ever looking adoringly into his eyes. Certainly, she had enjoyed every moment of *Captain Blood*, if only because her introduction to Errol Flynn seemed to the innocent beauty to be a meeting with Adonis. She instantly fell in love with him, although she did not dare think the love would ever be returned.

"There was an instant attraction," she says today. "I thought he was the most beautiful-looking man I had seen in my life."

If the love had been returned, it would not have pleased Jack

The young Errol Flynn – before fame, moustache and Hollywood.

The very first Flynn film role, in the British-made *Murder at Monte Carlo*.

Errol standing by the plane which took him to his first wedding – to Lili Damita.
Next to him is his friend, Bud Ernst, who piloted the plane.

Lili Damita and Errol in 1935. They were the most stunning pair in Hollywood – especially when they displayed a similar taste in tailoring. Note the initials on the car door.

The film that made Errol Flynn a star. With Henry Stephenson and an unsuspecting Olivia de Havilland in *Captain Blood*.

Errol usually looked his best in uniform – and never better than in *The Charge of the Light Brigade*. With him in this scene is Patric Knowles.

Warner at all. The last thing Warner wanted was to have a carefully nurtured marriage floundering around him. It would have had a disastrous effect on Lili's ego.

As if to assuage both her and the Warner stockholders, the studio rushed Errol and Lili into a picture together: It was no more than a two-reel short called *Pirate Party on Catalina Isle* and was probably most notable for the appearance of a certain young man called Archie Leach who had just changed his name to Cary Grant. But it did keep the names of Errol Flynn and Lili Damita in the public eye and provide an excuse for them to spend the night together.

Errol did not play in *Anthony Adverse* but Warners' promise of *The Light Brigade* picture was honoured. They would have been idiots had they not looked into their contractual commitments and decided to take the fullest advantage of them. The combination of Flynn, Curtiz and the kind of films the director was so good at making was too good to resist.

Curtiz also decided to add David Niven to the cast list, which turned out not at all badly for Niven's literary future as well as for his acting potential. It was during the shooting of this picture that Curtiz called for a group of riderless steeds with the immortal words "bring on the empty horses".

The locale of this Light Brigade charge had mysteriously been altered from the Crimea to the North-West Frontier of India. The troops did manage to get to the Crimea just in time for the charge itself, if nothing else, to be enacted at the right location. As handsome as Errol had looked in Captain Blood, in his Light Brigade uniform he was nothing less than devastating. The film had some moments that were notable for him too, such as the time he took part in a leopard hunt from the howdah of an elephant which, on sitting down, felt "like the earth subsiding underneath us".

But mostly it was the animals who had a rough time in the film. Several horses broke legs and backs when the script called for the gallant band of troops galloping to their deaths to go down with their mounts. They did, indeed, go down to order, thanks to a trip wire tied to their forelegs. When their riders pulled the wire, they simply collapsed.

In *Bring on the Empty Horses*, Niven tells of another hapless horse, the one that carried Flynn in the charge. As he says, Errol was very sure of himself. He knew he was worth more than the salary he was getting. Certainly more, he thought, than the extras over whom he was constantly lauding his status.

One of these lesser players decided the time had come to teach Errol a lesson. He leaned forward and wiggled his lance through the unsuspecting beast's back passage. The horse reared and Flynn fell.

"Which one of you sons of bitches did that?" David Niven recalls Errol asking quietly. "I did, sonny," said one extra. "Want to make something of it?" "Yes," Flynn replied, "get off your horse." Errol proved he was not a man to trifle with. As Niven says in his book, the extra was "taken to the infirmary ten minutes later and Errol's stock rose dramatically".

There were times when Flynn seemed to be never better than in the role of the amused bystander. He was very good at laughing at another's misfortune. When David Niven provided him with the spectacle of an ice pick neatly fused to both a block of ice and one of his fingers, Flynn suggested his friend keep it that way until their two girlfriends had had an opportunity to enjoy the scene, too.

An early foray into water-skiing left Niven equally distraught and Flynn just as entertained. They had read about the sport taking on in the South of France and thought what a good idea it would be to introduce it to California. Errol was nobody's fool. He would stay on board the boat – a newly-bought schooner which Flynn decided to call the *Sirocco* in memory of happy days in New Guinea – Niven would take to the skis. It was an arrangement that seemed to please them both, except that Errol had his hands caressing the exposed bosom of a girlfriend and his mind was certainly not on the other activity then in progress. Casually he broke the rope and sailed off to take tea with Ronald Colman whose own yacht was moored nearby. As for David, he had to use one of the skis as an improvised raft and make for land as best he could. When Niven told him he had been all but eaten by a shark, Errol replied: "Jesus, I wish I'd seen that."

Flynn's own performance on the set was becoming less amusing. He now knew he was considered a star but was behaving like a spoilt prima donna.

He would turn up late for shooting and then forget his lines. Curtiz was totally thrown by his behaviour. "Sohn of a beetch," he roared. "What a bum you are! I picked you up from a corpse and made you into a hero" (that was another of his favourite phrases – his actors were always bums, heroes or sissies). 'And now from a hero I'll put you back to a corpse and you'll be a bum again."

Irving Rapper, who was an assistant director on the *Light Brigade* project – and went on to be the celebrated director of *Now Voyager* and other films – told me he discovered that beneath Errol's poise was usually a considerable amount of sweat. "If you scratched on the surface it was usually fatal," he said. The insecure Flynn, stripped of his bravado, was never sure he would make it.

After the film, Flynn embarked on an even more bitter attack on Jack Warner, whom he called every then unprintable name he knew. With a crowd of male cronies surrounded by a mount of empty brandy bottles, he let off steam about a gentleman who was always one kind of bastard or another, but invariably a Jewish one. "Jew" became a term of abuse as vitriolic from his lips as any of his other expletives. He did it so often that a group of Hollywood people began to associate his comments as much with Fascism as with simple anti-Semitism, and although he never knew it himself, he was soon to become the subject of an anti-Nazi investigation. Until now, it has never been made public. Its findings were inconclusive but in some circles the mud stuck. Despite late attempts at changing the image, to many a Hollywood liberal. Flynn remains the archetype reactionary. To others, he was simply a rabid anti-Semite.

Flynn himself thought Jack Warner was exploiting him and demanded more money. When Warner refused, Errol flew off to Bermuda in a fit of pique. Naturally there was a girl at his side and, later, in his bed.

For the moment, the studio could reflect that their star was probably worth a raise. The *New York Times* commented:

"The Frères Warner may not give a hang for history, but they do know how to turn out a smashing and spectacular adventure film. *The Charge of the Light Brigade* which has taken what will unquestionably prove to be a long-term lease of the Strand is the 1936 model of *Lives of a Bengal Lancer*. Like its magnificently melodramatic predecessor, it is a virile and picturesque saga of blood and empire in India with the usual treacherous Amir lurking in one corner, the immaculately heroic Lancers in another and in the middle ground a splash of leopard hunt, native uprisings and outpost massacres."

The reviewer was conscious, as his opening words must have confirmed, of his cultured readers. The facts, the writer decided, had to be put straight: "Do we hear a startled protest that the cavalry charge celebrated by Alfred, Lord Tennyson occurred in the Crimea not in Suristan! Hear it we do and we hasten with the reassuring word that the Warners, bless 'em again, have not been caught napping over a book of movie boners. They have remembered it although barely in the nick of time."

As for the *Charge*'s star, *The Times* said: "There can be no fault with Errol Flynn's portrait of the dashing Major Vickers with Patric Knowles as his brother, Olivia de Havilland as the attractive but thematically unnecessary officer's daughter ... David Niven and E. E. Clive. *The Charge of the Light Brigade* is a grand movie."

When Jack Warner saw that the first box-office figures for *The Charge of the Light Brigade* confirmed the critics' approval, he offered Errol a new deal. He couldn't afford to part with him. It would prove to be a recurring story.

So would be Errol's relationship with Tiger Lil. He seemed to be using her now as a bedmate to add a particular spice to the girls he was dating and bedding on the side, alternating her with a Warner starlet, a secretary, a waitress or whoever presented herself and her body at the right moment. To adapt a phrase, their life together was one big brawl. But every time there was talk of divorce, more rumours followed of a patch-up in the marriage. This was not altogether surprising, for when Lili talked of the sort of alimony she would require, she sounded like a cash register listing its annual takings.

When even Errol seemed to accept the situation, and think seriously of divorce, she threatened suicide, only to hit him over the head with a champagne bottle when he appeared to weaken and agree to stay with her. Naturally, most of their rows were over his other girls. One breakfast time she stood in front of a Welsh dresser filled with expensive plates. "You can't do this to me, you sonofa-bitch, Fleen," she shouted. "You're my husband. I'm your wife and that's it."

Errol's reaction was simply to go and collect his own bacon, muttering something about her trying not to upset herself too much. Upset she was and showed it by emptying the entire contents of the dresser, piece by piece, in Errol's direction. All the plates missed, with Errol in his blue dressing gown fending off the missiles with a tray. Eventually he grabbed his warring spouse and the morning ended as it always did in the best Hollywood domestic comedies: in a long clinch in which their lips seemed to part only to draw breath.

In the few moments that the sweetness of Lili's temper matched the expression on her face, she could tell a Hollywood writer: "I do not depend on Flynn for the things women usually expect of their husbands." True, a conventional loving husband who always brought home his salary check, he was not. She complained that he was inconsiderate and always late, which she considered typical of his whole casual approach to responsibility. But what worried her most were his girls. One of the women Errol did not take to bed was the one who said she was madly in love with him – Olivia de Havilland. Born in Tokyo, the descendant of a family who came to England with the Norman invasion of William the Conqueror and related to the de Havilland aircraft clan, her upbringing – like that of her sister Joan Fontaine – was that of the perfect lady. It is not difficult to see that, to her, Flynn's roistering behaviour was a revela-tion. On the set of *Light Brigade* as in *Captain Blood*, he teased, flattered, and teased her again. She once asked a Hollywood writer what he thought of Flynn. He said that if Olivia were his sister, he would see to it that she stayed home with mother.

Errol did have other things on his mind. He had begun writing – sending off more pieces to the *Sydney Bulletin*, this time from an altogether different jungle to the one he had described in New

Guinea. He also wrote dozens of letters to the editors of the Los Angeles papers, and for them produced a couple of short stories and even some poetry.

He also began writing a novel. He said it would be largely autobiographical, a book he had planned for about three years. "I'm going to be my own censor and cut a great deal of it," he explained at the time. "If I were only an author, it would be all right. But if it appeared as I had intended, now that I am a movie star, people who disapproved of the book wouldn't come to see me. I'd have all sorts of societies for the prevention of this and that on my neck."

Certainly, he was now taking his writing seriously. There was only one real hazard to prevent him doing it for a living to the exclusion of all else (women and booze apart, that is), the telephone. "If you leave it on the hook ringing constantly," he said at the time, "or if you cut it off, you wonder what the heck you are missing."

In 1937 his book was published. It was called *Beam Ends*. Longmans, Green published its 241 pages for $2. It turned out to be very autobiographical, indeed, centered on a voyage of a narrow-beamed 50-foot wreck of a cutter in which its crew covered the 3000 miles from Sydney to New Guinea. The story ends in a shipwreck. The *New York Times* commented: "Up to the time of the shipwreck, the story is told in a tone of recklessness and irresponsible gaiety which suits the adventure."

The book had unexpected international consequences. Adolf Hitler banned it from Germany, "because it is not suitable to be read by young Nazis". An ironical deduction, considering the investigation still going on into Errol's alleged Hitler sympathies.

The same year Flynn decided to see something for himself of the kind of life the Nazis were trying to export. The Spanish Civil War was now fully into its stride and Franco's Fascists were anxious to establish a Berlin in Madrid. Errol was not so much concerned with the political repercussions of the war as the one word it seemed to spell for him: adventure.

The idea to go there and see it all for himself came to him when one of his old New Guinea cronies turned up with a cargo of monkeys, which he said he was going to sell to American laboratories. When the friend suggested that he and Errol should go on to Spain, it was an idea Flynn could not resist despite the vocal protests of Jack Warner.

They announced they were on the Loyalists' (anti-Franco) side – it was the only safe one to take at the time – and Errol was going to play war correspondent. Afterwards, his activities appeared somewhat more suspect. Ernest Hemingway said that as far as he knew Flynn merely crossed the French–Spanish border for a few yards and then went back again. One writer suggested that Errol should have taken a Warner Brothers PR man with him.

Suspicions were made only more acute when the local newspapers reported that Flynn had been killed, and then amended their reports to note that he had simply received minor bullet wounds while caught in the midst of a burst of machine-gun fire at Madrid University, then the center of the city front. The *New York Times* said that the people of Madrid did not know whether to be resentful or amused at being "adopted" by a film star who never turned his back on publicity.

The Defense Junta thought it important enough to issue an official statement. Colonel Fernando Redonda said sharply: "For whatever good it may do, this is to make it known that neither in the Defense Junta nor in the section of operations has notice been given of the film actor Errol Flynn's being wounded on the Madrid front or that on any occasion he has been authorized to visit the university city front or any other part of the capital."

Errol himself continued to play the hero, repeated that he had been in the thick of the fighting and embroidered his tales to talk about his exploits with a beautiful girl called Estella. He probably figured that if he could get a native girl in New Guinea, how much more necessary was it for him to show his prowess in the midst of a conflagration with Latin female company. No witnesses confirmed his story, but it would always make good listening.

Part of his narrative dealt with the friend who asked for a nine o'clock call next morning. A call that was totally unnecessary. According to the story they woke to see a hunk of masonry fall from the building across the plaza, followed by another slice of brickwork next door.

"What's that?" Errol asked the reception desk. "It's nine

o'clock," he was told. "The Fascists always shell that building at nine."

Errol claimed he was finally given the red-carpet treatment, because word got out that he was a courier delivering $1 million to the Loyalists' cause from Hollywood sympathizers. "To say this news made me nervous is the understatement of the year," said Flynn when he reached this stage of the story. "I figured they'd think I'd spent the money or stashed it. So naturally I'd be shot. Such matters can be hard to explain in war time." But then the truth according to Errol Flynn, accompanied by a glass of whatever did you good and a pretty woman, was usually difficult to explain.

The stories gained momentum all the time that he was there. Even James Cagney announced that Flynn was going to photograph the war and that he had a sizeable part of Hollywood behind him in his sympathies with the Loyalist cause.

It would have been reasonable to think that Flynn went to Spain simply to recuperate from the effects of three films churned out on the Warner Brothers' assembly line and shown on his return. Two of them, considering the circumstances, were passable. The worst was the first of these, *The Green Light*, which had Errol as a surgeon who believed in behaving honourably. That says enough about it.

The Prince and the Pauper, with the Hollywood boy twins Billy and Bobby Mauch, was much more notable. It teamed Errol, too, with Alan Hale, who was later to become very much part of the Flynn set. It was based on the famous Mark Twain story of the young Prince Edward swapping roles with a beggar.

Another Dawn was even more interesting, and not just because he co-starred in it with the beautiful Kay Francis. It was the first of a veritable flood of pictures to feature Errol Flynn wearing a contemporary military uniform, this time fighting for King George V in the Sahara desert. It is interesting to note that while Errol was being feted as the all-Hollywood boy, he seemed invariably to be cast as an English gentleman.

There were a few embarrassing moments in the film, notably on the occasions Errol fell off his horse. Some of the extras decided this gave them an excuse to repeat the teasing he received in *The Charge of the Light Brigade*.

Nobody doubted Flynn's capabilities as a flirt or a charmer. On the set of his next film, *The Perfect Specimen*, Errol arranged for an additional piece of equipment to be installed alongside his chair: a private telephone. He would use it in between takes and when other members of the cast were idly chatting or munching sandwiches he would make dates, holding the receiver in one hand and caressing with the other the fingers of his co-star, Joan Blondell. While he waited for his chosen date of the evening to come on the line he whispered compliments into Joan's ear. As he planned his assignation on the phone, he told Joan that she was so beautiful but – he knew – unattainable for him. The way he said it always sounded convincing.

Joan would sometimes go to the *Sirocco* with Errol for the weekend, but always just as a member of his party. Every Friday he would have a different girl as his date for the yacht, invariably the one who an hour or so earlier had been shown discreetly into his dressing room.

The Perfect Specimen was not a brilliant film. Errol played the heir to his aunt's estates who for the first time was being shown the big outside world by a newspaper reporter – Miss Blondell, of course. Nevertheless, he managed to give everyone on the set the impression that he was trying hard to do a good job and that, contrary to most people's beliefs, was indeed an actor. When he sidled up to Allen Jenkins in the picture's boxing sequence, even Michael Curtiz was prepared to be convinced. A fight with Errol at any time could be an intimidating experience. But when, like now, it was written into a script and his partner was not the sort of man Flynn was, it was likely to be devastating. He was not so much acting as playing a role in real life.

In this film, Curtiz tried to persuade Jenkins not to duck every time Flynn swung a punch in his direction. He pleaded with him not to be frightened. "Arlen, Arlen," said Curtiz in his best Hungarian English. "He wouldn't hurt you. Don't pull back." But every time Flynn aimed in Jenkin's direction the smaller, older man ducked. Finally, Jenkins announced that he was seeing reason. "All right," he told Curtiz, "all right, I won't duck. I'll try again – but if Flynn hits me, I'll break your goddam nose."

"Print the last one," shouted Curtiz.

Strange then that Flynn put up with a lot of the more demanding trappings of film making. He would tolerate seemingly endless hours of costume fitting. With a bottle in hand and a ribald story on his lips he would entertain a coterie of friends and fellow cast members while Orry Kelly, one of Warner's top designers, patiently pinned a sleeve here, a lapel there. Kelly had a reputation for being the studio's gay, but Errol liked him enormously. If Kelly told him that a fussy, almost effeminate style suited him, Flynn – despite Hal Wallis's earlier strictures – took his word for it and was rarely proved wrong.

Errol never tried to run away from nonconformity, so that his association with Kelly was always a happy one. Certainly, he was never attracted to homosexuality himself but neither did he despise those who were. For the same reason, he saw nothing wrong in experimenting with drugs, first the opium to which he had been introduced by Ting Ling, then its various derivatives. At this stage he did so in such minute quantities that he was convinced it would never have any serious effect.

He felt the same way about drink, although already he was drinking very immoderately. It was playing a very important part in his life. When he had first gone to Hollywood, he drank beer, seemingly, by the barrelful. Then he switched to champagne and martinis. He tried whisky for a bit, but turned soon to brandy, and the occasional variation.

With Joan Blondell he would escape from the other members of *The Perfect Specimen* crew and go out into the country and drink glass after glass of Pimms Cup instead of eating a more solid lunch. He went back to work in the afternoon without slurring a word. Later at a studio party, he saw Ann Sheridan slipping something strong into a tomato juice. "What's that?" he asked. "Vodka," she replied. He tried it, liked it and decided it was for him. Without the tomato juice.

He was back living with Lili now for another one of their now-we're-together-now-we're-not periods. Whatever else, Errol was a good host and Lili the perfect hostess, even if the entertainment they provided was frequently in the form of a spirited duet, to the accompaniment of more broken plates.

But it was always a pleasure to be a guest in their luxury home. How could it be anything else? Not only was the food excellent and the drink plentiful, but they were waited upon by some of the finest servants in California. And if they just felt like sitting down and talking – and even some of the Flynn set enjoyed that – they had the most tasteful furniture on which to do it.

Even so, anyone who knew Flynn well knew that he cared more for his boat than he did for his home. In December 1938, he proved that his love for the *Sirocco* could never be as impermanent as his association with a girl.

The United States Government got to hear some stories and started investigating. Mr Norman Neukom, Assistant United States Attorney, said he had heard that not only was Flynn's yacht worth $25,000 but it was 60 feet long and weighed 31 tons. The problem was that Mr Flynn was still a foreigner and aliens were not allowed to own any craft that was more than 20 feet long and which weighed in at more than 5 tons.

"I've never heard such nonsense, sport," said Flynn to his lawyer, and went away for another weekend. But it was serious. He had to change either his boat or his nationality. Before long, he gave instructions to the lawyer to start putting in his application for citizenship papers. If the choice was between his boat and his British (Empire) nationality, then the boat had to win.

The boat more and more became the center for Flynn's fleeting love affairs – he rarely wanted them any other way. Since Lili was no more than a port of call, the fact that she detested sailing was never any drawback.

The act of getting his women on to the deck of the *Sirocco* was planned to the minutest detail. Errol and David Niven together – and later on individually when they went their separate ways – were developing around themselves a group of friends who shared their stories, their drink and, when it suited them, their women, too.

Errol's friends would be deputed to bring the girls to the mooring in a fleet of fast cars. When the young ladies sauntered across the gangplank, usually in the latest of casual wear and giggling as they held hands with each other, they knew exactly what was expected of them.

They were told there would be moonlight swimming and lots of long, cool drinks (laced with whatever was currently believed to be the best aphrodisiac). Then, it was to the bunks, with Errol having first choice of both maiden and sleeping accommodation. If the girls performed satisfactorily and let it be known they enjoyed sailing, they would be invited to cruise with the men the next day. If for any reason they were neither satisfactory bedmates nor games partners, they were driven back to their Hollywood homes with a polite smile and a kiss from their host.

The lifestyle of Flynn and Niven was very much a meeting of kindred spirits. They called their beach home, which Flynn used whenever he and Lili were apart, Cirrhosis-by-the-Sea, a name Niven was to use again for another bachelor pad. They launched every new affair with a bottle before bed, usually with the pair of them choosing the booze while their girls brought the food.

The sort of love affairs others boasted about would never have sufficed as more than an hors d'œuvres or at most a dessert to Errol. He had every opportunity to indulge himself. He no longer insisted on making the first move. Women believed that if he noticed them, their own chances of success in films would be vastly improved. Starlets would waylay him – the terminology is not inappropriate – on the way from the commissary to his dressing room, and he never sent them away. Secretaries would come into the room ostensibly with a page of notes, and then close the door behind them, casually undoing their blouses and letting their skirts fall to the ground as they did so, while Errol sat on his couch admiring the view.

On more than one occasion, a girl would spot him in a bar and as easily as he drank his vodka, remove her brassiere with the same movement she used to unbutton her dress. Young women found ways of stripping so no one else could notice – just so long as *he* saw what was going on. Some of them did it for the sheer thrill of exposing themselves to the man all women columnists said was the most attractive in Hollywood (somehow it did not matter if they thought so themselves; just knowing other people did was enough).

It didn't matter to Errol that he wouldn't be able to do anything to advance the girls' career prospects. He found reneging on promises as easy as making them in the first place.

Errol was like the little boy always chosen to captain the football team for no better reason than that he owned the ball. In Errol's case, he was convinced he was the possessor of an irresistible animal magnetism strong enough to ensure he always got his own way – and because he could control the ball, the rules of the game were the ones he made for himself.

His contempt for the accepted standards of morality was matched only by his lack of concern for the feelings of the women who fleetingly entered his life. The child who hated his mother had turned into a man who could not believe that a girl available for a night was also a person with emotions and feelings of her own. He sought variety in bed companions because it had become a habit to do so and, like most habits, the more it was indulged the greater the need he felt to move on to someone else.

He was the polygamous male incarnate, who by natural instinct knew which girls would succumb to his advances and which would be simply a waste of his time and energy. He did not care what happened to them once they had served their purpose. Probably quite genuinely he felt he was doing them as much a favour as they were doing him.

Not since he had posed as the Irish cop had Warner Brothers felt the need to build up Errol's image. He was one of the few Hollywood stars who lived every minute of his day the way that his public expected him to live it and without any help from the publicity department. If people knew about his image, it only made it that much easier for him to get the girls who were never in any doubt as to the role they were expected to play in his life.

He did not think a woman could enjoy the more serious aspects of his life – his growing interest in art and writing, his ribald sense of humour and his need to drain a bottle at a single sitting. What he assumed to be the superior male intellect needed the stimulation of male company. When a woman did come along whom he could take more seriously, she was the one whom he respected and did not try to take to bed. It was almost as though he believed having sex with a woman outside marriage somehow defiled her mind.

But he was not happy. If Lili had provided him with more than just sexual fulfillment, it is possible he would have settled down. As it was, he had to continue to chase, knowing he would never be satisfied.

There was always a steady supply of willing and very able young ladies in the small nightclubs that proliferated at the time around Hollywood Boulevard. Into these, Errol would stroll like a visiting potentate. It was in one of the boulevard dives that he saw a girl smiling as he made his way past her table. "Hello, Errol darling," she purred. Flynn looked down, smiled too and then kissed her bare shoulder as his right hand casually pawed the breast that she seemed to be presenting for his attention. "You look lovely tonight," he whispered. "Call me soon."

He did not care that the girl was not alone and that her escort looked as though he had just won the Hollywood Rose Bowl single-handed. "You filthy bastard," said the man. But he didn't have time to finish talking. Errol, with his cigarette holder still in place, punched the fellow so hard that he flew across the room like a paper dart. Flynn took out his cigarette just long enough to kiss the girl appreciatively on the lips. Later he insisted that he hardly knew her – "just another ship who passed in the night". But then he never wanted to disappoint a lady for whom he had no responsibility.

To be fair, there were often men who wanted to smash into Errol Flynn just as there were women who wanted to go to bed with him. A night out in a Havana café ended with Errol blowing into a pair of sore red fists while a fellow customer who had dared challenge him was taken off to hospital. Meanwhile, almost everyone else in the place seemed to be slugging someone.

In 1938 Errol had a bout with the Irish polo player Aidan Roark, who was now assistant to Daryl Zanuck. Roark should have known better but when he called Errol a "Northerner" it was like calling a Catholic a Protestant, or worse.

It happened at a cocktail party given for Mrs Jock Whitney, wife of the man known as the Technicolor King and who would later become Ambassador to the Court of St James's and owner of the New York *Herald Tribune*. The fact that Flynn was not Irish at all did not seem to make much difference. He knew Roark intended an insult and that was enough. When the polo player added a few choice comments about Errol's acting prowess, Flynn took off his jacket and said forcibly: "We'd better settle this right here."

Roark was floored by a perfect right hook. When he shakily got on to his feet, Errol punched him again. The polo player rose just long enough to see a friend aim a right at Flynn's jaw and then he went down again. This time he stayed down for twenty minutes.

An assembled crowd of Hollywood personalities were not sure whether to be shocked or to cheer. Everyone had heard of Flynn's fighting ability but this was the first occasion he had used it to effect at a Hollywood party, an occasion that was always more important as a shop window in which to be seen than to actually be enjoyed as a social evening.

"He made some fly remarks about me," said Errol afterwards. "I'm sorry it happened. It was just one of those unfortunate affairs. Some remarks were too pointed. That blow was my final answer to Mr Roark," he added, "and was punctuated with discernible effect by remarks which I considered highly offensive."

Meanwhile, Errol's father thought much the same about his son's fighting activities, which increasingly were getting into the newspapers. Theodore wrote to his erring son complaining that he was besmirching the family's honour. While he was about it, he took up another matter that had been concerning him: "Why don't you write to your mother?"

Errol wrote erratically to Belfast, and when he did his letters were always addressed to the "pater" whom he idolized. But he didn't feel comfortable writing to someone to whom he could never relate. His mother had always seemed a void in his life.

When he took time to think about their relationship, he wondered how if she of all people could find no love for him, he had any chance with anyone else. If no one did care for Errol Flynn for his own sake why should he bother about anyone else's sensibilities?

At the age of twenty-nine Errol Flynn, who could have any girl he wanted, knew he was totally unloved. Needless to say, Warner Brothers had less affection for him than anyone. But they did know he was very much a commercial property. In September 1938 they presented him with a new contract. From now on he would get $3,600 a week and twelve weeks' holiday with pay every year.

Errol had threatened to start taking the same sort of action with Jack Warner – whom he now more politely called "Sporting Blood" – as he had already done with Aidan Roark. The award made him one of the highest-paid male stars in the world, in the same bracket as Gary Cooper, Ronald Colman, Clark Gable and Robert Taylor.

Now Warner had plans for his new super star. He wanted him to aim his venom at new targets. This time using an arrow.

6

The Adventures of Robin Hood

*Here was really a wasted life. He could
have gone down with Kean.*
Herbert Wilcox

A Hollywood studio is never a more exciting place to be in than
when it has an expensive, attractive new product about to shoot.
It is the talk of everyone in the place, from the producers, directors
and actors down to the boys carrying messages or the girls making
cups of coffee.

The new sets are discussed in the studio cafeterias, the costumes
are the talk of the ladies' powder rooms, the way the leading man
was chosen is the subject of gossip that runs from chair to chair
in the barber shops and in the make-up rooms.

When *The Adventures of Robin Hood* went before the Warner
Brothers cameras at Burbank in 1938 it was *the* topic on everyone's
lips, although perhaps three or four other pictures were being shot
simultaneously on adjoining lots. There was also a distinct interest
in how Errol Flynn would behave in the star role.

The studio had been toying with the idea of the picture for more
than a decade – ever since, in fact, the coming of sound when
Warners first decided to re-make one of the most spectacular epics
of the silent screen. Douglas Fairbanks had in those days turned
The Robin of Locksley legend into most people's idea of the
definitive outlaw.

But now Errol Flynn was being asked to create it all over again
for an investment of $2 million – a colossal sum for the time, but
as history has shown, one that would be recouped over and over
again.

Jack Warner himself knew the importance of the picture he was shooting. He wanted all the latest technicolor techniques to be used to their fullest advantage. He demanded of his director – William Keighley – that he convey all the romance, glamour and action of one of the most famous legends in English folklore. What he asked of Errol Flynn was that he look his most handsome and cause as little trouble as possible, particularly not to make life difficult for his leading lady, Olivia de Havilland.

He knew about the torch that Olivia carried for Errol and he also worried about the speed with which Flynn, with one unthinking gesture, could douse it.

He had good cause for concern. Flynn marched on to the set on his first morning an hour late and for days afterwards every scene had to be reshot half a dozen times before a complete line of remembered dialogue could assemble itself on his lips. When the rushes were shown the next day, however, it was clear he had been the right choice for the part. He looked splendid.

Errol was never better than when rescuing his Maid Marian (Olivia). He teased his way through an assortment of retakes, kissing Miss de Havilland far more ardently each time than would ever have been allowed to get through the Hays Office – the film industry's own censor, whose main task was to be sure that their pictures got the widest possible showing without risking the ire of any one of a long list of organizations who at the drop of a shoulder strap would have a movie banned.

But the rest of the film looked dull. "It's no good, sport," Errol told Hal Wallis. "I can't make anything of a part that sends me off to sleep." It was probably the only time that Errol took a role seriously enough to worry about the way his picture was shaping up.

Other people worried with him, particularly Alan Hale, who had been chosen as "Little John" – a part he had played in the Fairbanks film and one which he would recreate yet again in a 1950 re-make – and Eugene Pallette as Friar Tuck, perfectly cast since the original Friar just had to have looked like him.

The film looked wooden whenever Errol had to try his skill once more fencing with Basil Rathbone, who was prepared to look evil as Sir Guy of Gisbourne but had little chance to do so.

Wallis came to the inescapable conclusion that Keighley had to be replaced. An audible sigh of relief greeted the news that a new director had been chosen. Relief from everyone except Flynn, that is.

"Here we go," said Errol when he heard the news. "I think we'll be having some fun." Michael Curtiz in charge of another film meant trouble for Flynn.

Once in harness he not only studied every movement in front of the camera, he watched intently as Errol was given still more fencing lessons and as he was coached in archery by a wizard of the bow and arrow, Howard Hill. When Hill scored a bull's eye, Flynn sidled up to Curtiz, slapped him on the back and said: "Good, wasn't I, sport?"

The Hungarian muttered "sohn of a beetch" and tried to ignore the interruption. But the picture was moving and that was what he needed – if only Errol had not been there to spoil things. He was not simply upsetting the director. The big star was showing a distinct lack of concern for his fellow players, who by now knew better than to try to make things difficult for him.

Robin Hood was shot in the height of a California summer, not the hottest temperature in the world to wrestle with, but difficult enough if, as in those days, you augmented even the brightest sunlight with the strongest artificial lighting that the technical department could provide. When you added to your performers' discomfort by locking many of them in heavy armour, there was little to choose between playing in a film and working in a sweat shop.

It was in those circumstances that Errol Flynn took it into his head to be later than usual. He had either found a secretary anxious to bestow a favour or he had got stuck into a bottle of cognac; certainly he was very late and tempers were badly frayed.

"Who do you think you are?" called one man from among the crowd of assembled unhappy extras. It was the cue for the Flynn charm. "I'm so sorry," he said, and it was difficult at that moment not to believe him.

Jack Warner, who had been called on to the set by anxious accountants totting up the gradually increasing costs of it all, muttered a string of obscenities and told his wife he was sure he was on the crest of another heart attack.

When shooting finally got through that day, Mrs Warner told Irving Rapper, now dialogue coach on the picture: "I can't wait to get to our boat in France. All I hear all day are the arguments between Jack and Errol Flynn and Errol's lawyers."

Warner called Flynn to his side and told him: "Either you start behaving or you're fired."

"Sorry, sport," said Flynn in his most irritating cool manner. "I think I have a contract."

Fortunately for all concerned, he did. *The Adventures of Robin Hood* was all that anyone had ever hoped it would be. Even now, nearly forty years later, it still seems the perfect version of the story and the best film of its type ever made and Errol, the only possible incarnation of Robin Hood.

Everyone connected with the film looked good – Rathbone, de Havilland, Pallette, and Claude Raines as a superbly underplayed Prince John.

The *New York Times* summed it up when the film was finally released: It was, the paper's Frank S. Nugent reported: "Payment in full for many dull hours of picture going." And he added:

"A richly produced, bravely bedecked, romantic and colourful show, it leaps boldly to the forefront of this year's best and can be calculated to rejoice the eights, rejuvenate the eighties and delight those in between. ... In Errol Flynn Sir Robin of Sherwood Forest has found his man. A swashbuckler from peaked cap to pointed toe.... Mr Flynn is not the acrobatic Robin Douglas Fairbanks was some years ago. He doesn't slide down tapestries or vault his balustrade with the Fairbanks père's abandon. But he moves swiftly when there's need and Guy of Gisbourne rues it."

Even so, in October 1938 the London *News Chronicle*, following on tributes beginning "Here's richness', said:

"In these glowing excitements Errol Flynn is really too good looking if anything, as Robin Hood. It was very wrong of me, no doubt to be reminded so much of a principal boy in pantomime but such was the effect of his lithe beauty. Mr Flynn strides through the part with an engaging humour. His voice, however, lacks the commanding quality one would associate with a leader of men. In this respect he is not the equal of Basil Rathbone."

The *Daily Herald* also took the pantomime theme, but was kinder.

"The story is handled as it should be, as a pantomime subject glorifying physical prowess. Robin Hood's single-handed escapes from the midst of enemies are as wildly incredible as the accuracy of every arrow shot by his merry men, but who cares? It is not history but the legend we are enjoying."

Indeed, history was rewritten to a considerable extent, although much of the story was taken from contemporary ballads. But the studio was right not to allow a few mere facts to intrude. Perhaps the *Sunday Express* said it all: "Robin Hood is a boyhood hero and what Warners have done best is to keep the picture refreshingly boyish."

It would be stretching the imagination to say that Errol himself was either boyish or in any way refreshing, except when he boxed or played tennis. He was spending more of his leisure time now with a growing circle of men whom he considered shared his own extra-sexual interests – getting drunk, telling jokes and, in their more sober moments, discussing the world of letters and art.

It was another sign that Errol was feeling insecure. He had done such a lot in such a short time, but he had mastered very little. Errol Flynn was not the best actor in Hollywood, or even among the better ones. And although he enjoyed writing, he was quite obviously not going to win any Pulitzer Prize. He had grown to love art, but he couldn't do anything with a paintbrush himself. For that reason, he chose to mix with people who had scored in those fields. After being introduced to the artist John Decker, he felt honoured that the painter treated him as a friend.

Decker had a reputation for painting the way-out, and before long he would shock a number of the more literate Hollywood set by painting the face of W. C. Fields on to a portrait of Queen Victoria that was to be hung at Chasens Restaurant. But to Flynn he could do no wrong.

Errol felt much the same way about John Barrymore, so brilliant an actor, so articulate a man, and it seemed, one who had so much in common with himself. Both had a strong love of booze and of the English language and both a contempt for much of what they were being paid to do. Nevertheless Barrymore was much more highly regarded as an actor, at least until drink washed away his self-respect, and by then he considered much of the stuff he was required to recite on the screen to be beneath his dignity. When Barrymore's memory went, he had "idiot boards" placed in front of the camera so that he wouldn't have to clutter up his mind trying to remember such unworthy material. Both too, loved boats, and when Barrymore could no longer afford to keep one himself he would inveigle an invitation on to the *Sirocco* whenever the opportunity arose. Other people would be sent packing if Errol thought they were using him, but Barrymore always merited special privileges in Flynn's eyes.

Another member of the set was Alan Hale, also a roistering Irishman but one who had proved on the set of *Robin Hood* that he not only knew what to do with a bottle of the hard stuff but could talk intelligently, too.

The group met so often – usually at Decker's house – that they gave themselves a name. They were the Olympiads. Word of their activities spread through the film colony, seemingly put about by a press agent who felt he had something to gain by making the Olympiads sound like keen art connoisseurs who rarely allowed a drop of drink to sully their deliberations. One day, Edward G. Robinson, by then the owner of one of the finest art collections in California, let it be known he wanted to join. The idea was laughed out of Decker's Bundy Drive home. Errol said later that the reason for his exclusion was that the *Little Caesar* actor – a fellow member of the Warner Brothers' stable – took himself too seriously. There was a more probable one: Robinson was a Jew.

Had he been allowed to join, they might have felt inhibited in their discussions on their favourite *bête noir*, Jack Warner, who, nevertheless, was still keeping Errol Flynn very much before the public eye.

When *Robin Hood* was duly pronounced sensational, Warner and his ever efficient number two Hal Wallis decided they had to put Errol Flynn and Michael Curtiz together again. For both of them, *Four's a Crowd* was a fairly nondescript picture on which their contract said they had to work.

The difference was that Curtiz put as much into it as he had into *Robin Hood*, turning a dull story into a madly funny situation comedy, with the help of Olivia de Havilland and Rosalind Russell. Errol, meanwhile, in the part of the PR man building up the image of a mean millionaire, did what he was always to do when bored with a project – he showed his boredom.

Only when he had got into the final stages of the picture, when he could see for himself some of the fruits of all that had gone before it, did he start working hard. Until then, he was a caricature of the undisciplined artist. When Curtiz ordered "action" and Flynn didn't feel like acting, he just wouldn't. Yet he never argued with Curtiz. He would usually smile and say: "What the hell. Let's just have a lot of fun." He simply didn't think his work was worth taking seriously.

The more that Curtiz pulled out his hair and muttered insults in Hungarian following the essential words "Sohn of a beetch" the more Errol laughed and tried to get him to change the subject. Curtiz would even start reciting Shakespeare but all Errol would do in return would be to sidle up to him and say: "I've got a great story for you, sport."

If Errol were the *bête noir* of Curtiz, the name calculated to send shivers up and down the spine of Jack Warner was more likely to be that of Bette Davis. She had a spirit of independence about her that worried Warner every time she was assigned to a new picture – although he appreciated her power at the box office.

A call from his own office one day in 1937 seemed likely to change all that. Warner had had a discussion with David O. Selznick, an independent producer who was working on a big new project with his father-in-law Louis B. Mayer, boss of MGM. As a result of that meeting, Warner was now making Bette an offer: "MGM want us to loan you out to play Scarlett O'Hara in *Gone With The Wind*."

He was not being particularly generous. The money MGM would

pay Warner Brothers was likely to be thousands of dollars more than
Bette received under her own contract.

It was an offer which on the surface was likely to make for the
sweetest of truces between Warner and his star. Not only would
it give her a chance to get away from Burbank, it was a part she
coveted above all others. Everyone knew of MGM's search for a Scarlett, and the public had already indicated that Bette was the one
they wanted for the role. As part of a publicity campaign for the
film, MGM had announced they were seeking nominations from
cinema-goers – and Bette came up top of every poll in the country.

There was, however, a snag. A condition of the deal was that Errol
would play Rhett Butler. And the little that she knew about Errol
told her they were not going to get along. She made it perfectly
clear that she didn't think he was suitable for the part. The result
was that Selznick said he wouldn't take the one without the other.

"Oh, if only I could have played it with Gable!" she said years
afterwards (in a commentary to her biography *Mother Goddam* by
Whitney Stine).

Warner was not pleased at her refusal to take the part. As a result,
he showed his displeasure by ordering her to play opposite Flynn
in his next picture. This was *The Sisters*, directed by Anatole Litvak
and billed as co-starring Bette Davis.

Errol always claimed that Bette was unreasonable to him, putting
him in intolerable positions, constantly dominating him – a woman's
position Errol liked as little in the studio as he did in bed. Miss
Davis has since said that he was a liar. She claimed she was delighted
to have the opportunity of playing with the young Mr Flynn, about
whom she had heard so much. She also saw the funny side of a
film listed as "Errol Flynn in *The Sisters*" – not so funny, however,
that she didn't later insist that she be given equal billing.

The movie was about the three daughters of a druggist caught
up in the San Francisco earthquake. Two endings were shot for the
film. In one, Bette Davis marries her employer, Ian Hunter; in the
other she goes with Flynn. The reactions of preview audiences were
studied and it was quite clear that the customers preferred seeing
Bette with Errol. The alternative version was discarded.

Years after that Bette Davis told me it was only when she saw the film on television that she realized how good Flynn was in *The Sisters*. One of the film's big problems was that Anatole Litvak was not the right director. It needed a totally different, more expressive, more mobile touch.

The *New York Times* was not sure how to take *The Sisters*. "The story of how Bette and Errol try in vain to make a go of it down in San Francisco is the burden of the film and there are moments perhaps when it may grow a wee bit burdensome, especially when Mr Flynn is trying to look as if he believed in his despair."

Some people put it stronger and said Errol's acting in *The Sisters* left a lot to be desired. All he wanted to do was to have a good time and show how much gloss he could put on the more serious side of acting. As Irving Rapper says: "Bette was granite and a highly disciplined woman." So granite strong that she didn't trust any director to make films that would show her as anything but the star in full control of everything.

But it was Errol she trusted least of all. She resented the girls who waited for him off the set. If she suspected that a continuity girl had her eye more on Flynn than on her clipboard she would complain and, says Rapper, walk off the set. It didn't worry Errol. At five o'clock he was on the phone, arranging his dating schedule for the night if not for the next week. You always knew when he had had a good night. He turned up in the studio the following morning looking very haggard, usually the worse for drink; but at that stage in his career no one was ever sure whether he was drinking to forget the night before or simply to help him to remember what he was supposed to do next.

Errol enjoyed being seen with pretty women almost as much as he liked and needed to be with them himself. Flynn without a beautiful girl on his arm felt as undressed as he wanted to be a short while later. She certainly boosted a frequently depressed ego.

He did, however, have one much more constant companion than any girl – one to whom he was a lot more loyal than he ever was to a woman – Arno, the dog given to him by Hollywood producer friend, Robert Lord. Everywhere that Errol went, it seemed that the dog would surely go too – to the studio, to nightclubs and to the *Sirocco*. Flynn lavished on Arno all the absolute devotion he could never show to a woman. But that did not mean that women were any more reluctant now to offer their services than they had ever been in the past.

Certainly, if Errol was in trouble, there was usually a woman at the bottom of it all. When he disappeared with one for more than a week, he used his absence as an excuse for a neat piece of blackmail.

He sent a message to Jack Warner saying: "I'll be glad to return if you pay $25,000 into my account in return for a treatment I have just done on the story of the White Rajah of Sarawak."

It was his one way of revenging what he considered to be the shabby treatment of a studio that would never pay him what he himself considered to be his fair due. He had worked on the treatment with a studio publicity man. The studio paid up, but never made the film. It was fortunate they didn't. Flynn had lifted the entire thing from a magazine article. As Hal Wallis has said: "He would make demands, disappear and then have the top brass in the studios apologizing to him for causing so much inconvenience!" Just occasionally he acted out of less selfish motives.

About this time, Errol chartered a private plane to rescue a sailor on board the *Sirocco*. The man was suffering from an acute appendicitis. The yacht had been let out on charter, but Errol still felt responsible. The sailor, Roy Hayes, was taken off the boat in a launch and had then to be driven fifteen miles to the field where Flynn, with the help of a pilot, had landed. On arrival in Hollywood, Hayes was taken to hospital for an operation. "Just the spirit of adventure, sport," Flynn told a friend afterwards, as if he couldn't himself accept that even this once he had done a good deed without an ulterior motive.

As far as his public were concerned, the best possible deed from Errol Flynn would have been to make a succession of pictures like his next vehicle *Dawn Patrol*, a film that had so much going for it that it deserves to be remembered as a classic of the period.

Once again, Errol shared the honours with Basil Rathbone, although this time there was no fencing. Instead, they were both kitted out in the fetching uniforms of the Royal Flying Corps and David Niven was on hand displaying his own unique British public school tragi-comic elegance. As for Flynn, he looked superb in uniform, and his role as an air ace who finds the bottle as comforting a partner as is his plane was, to say the least, perfect casting. One paper described it, not unfittingly, as his best part to date.

Certainly, *Dodge City*, his next film, paled against it. How could it do otherwise when Flynn was told to forget about being British and not even pretend to have been brought up on the rarefied atmosphere of San Francisco's Nob Hill? *Dodge City* was a Western and in it Errol wore a stetson – even if he was playing an Irishman. Of course, it all could have been much worse had not Michael Curtiz yet again been the director who was as careful as ever to pick up the pieces of havoc wrought by Flynn's casual attitude to working on a film for which he had no more affection than he would for a bottle of milk. There was also the additional saving grace of Olivia de Havilland, maturing now with a sense of self-confidence that was dulled only by the behaviour of Errol. One morning when he had nothing better to do than contemplate lines for which few writers would want to take responsibility, he saw a dead snake lying a rock's throw from the camera. He picked up the moribund reptile and stuffed it into one of his fringed pockets.

No one saw either Errol or the snake, until the moment came for the assistant director on the set to ask Olivia to go and change for the next scene.

Dutifully, Miss de Havilland walked into the canvas hut that served as her dressing room, picked up the dress she was to wear and then let out the kind of shriek that in other circumstances would have been the delight of her director. Curled up in the panties set out for her change of clothes was four feet of dead snake. She hoisted her hooped skirt, charged out of the hut, raced down the hill and plunged into the lake close by: from the bushes at the side of Olivia's dressing room came the sound of Errol Flynn's raucous laughter.

Olivia, who admits she would have wanted to marry Errol had the opportunity presented itself, never felt quite the same about him again.

Nothing much happens in *Dodge City*. Frank S. Nugent reported in the *New York Times*:

"Just a shooting scrape, a cattle stampede, a murder, a couple of street fights, another murder, a bar room brawl, a runaway, a few more street fights, another murder, a lynch mob's attack on a jail, a fight in a burning caboose and a few dull things like that. Errol Flynn skips through a debris as the frontier marshal out to restore law and order and Olivia de Havilland is as pretty as ever – prettier in fact since she is in Technicolor – as the miss who pretends to despise him for having shot her brother."

The fact was that Errol seemed to "skip" through most of his film work. Usually he was having a great time, teasing the girls, laughing with the guys and telling the director how much he admired his work. Being so affable, how could anyone complain about his acting? Everyone knew he didn't take it seriously. He never pretended that he did.

Up against Bette Davis again, however, he would have been wise to have changed his tactics. But he didn't. The result was that one of the most important pictures in his career began in a spirit of ill will and – if you take his word for it – violence.

The Private Lives of Elizabeth and Essex had Miss Davis playing the Virgin Queen, establishing the "fact" that Elizabeth must have looked as much like Bette Davis as everyone now knew that Robin Hood looked like Flynn. In this picture he played Essex.

After her experience with *The Sisters*, Bette was reluctant to work again with Flynn, which is putting it both mildly and kindly. But the project itself proved irresistible. It was to be based on the play *Elizabeth the Queen* which had been an amazing Broadway success for the Theater Guild, starring Lynne Fontanne and Alfred Lunt.

Miss Davis accepted everything she was told about the marvellous opportunity now being offered her – except the part about Flynn. Warner executives still talk about the persuasion they had to use to team them. Maxwell Anderson's verse dialogue was superb, they told her. She herself would be the only one who could possibly make Elizabeth come alive. As for Flynn ... to the female customers he represented visual poetry. "We need his glamorous image," they told her. Finally, she just had to agree. But that did not mean she was convinced.

Seemingly, every other day she would express doubts that verged on pronouncing a veto, and risked suspension by the studio as she did so. But even she had to admit that the opportunities the part appeared to present were too good to throw off.

"I was tempted to do it," she was to tell me. "But Errol was not right for the film."

One of her reservations was based on Errol's insistence on having Maxwell Anderson's rhythmic blank verse rewritten. "I can't remember lines like that," Errol told Michael Curtiz, who was once more suffering as Flynn's director, and there was little he could do but oblige and get the lines rewritten. With the alternative of presenting audiences with Anderson's poetry or Flynn's looks there was just no contest. The box office had to win.

Another of the things Bette disliked was the change of title. It was *The Sisters* situation all over again. Errol was not prepared to laugh at the funny side of billing that read: "Errol Flynn in *Elizabeth the Queen*." As it was, Bette got the top line in the credits.

On the set, however, he kept a respectful distance from his co-star and – if *My Wicked, Wicked Ways* is to be believed in this instance – she was the one to cause the problems. To Bette now, it amounts to a typical example of the Flynn imagination getting the better of the situation, and the worse of the relationship between them.

But as Errol tells it, she made life hard and tough for him, quite as hard and tough as he had ever been accused of making the existence of extras and bit players in earlier films.

For one thing, Errol alleged that time after time he had to walk down a seemingly endless carpet to face not Bette Davis, but a stand-in. He objected to his co-star being granted that particular privilege while it was he himself who had to walk all that way in heavy armour and under blistering lights. Then, when she did finally mount her throne, she greeted him with a powerful slap across the cheek – a slap made all the harder by the heavy rings on her fingers and the expressions on the faces of the hundreds of extras who seemed to enjoy every humiliating minute of it. When he went to her dressing room to complain, he said she told him – without inviting him to sit down – that she was unable to "pretend" anything. A slap had to be a slap. His reaction, he recalls, was to throw up.

He claims to have got his own back by striking her so hard on the behind that she leapt at least two feet off the ground. Miss Davis says that all these stories are fabrications of the Flynn imagination. As if to emphasize her feelings for Flynn, she told Whitney Stine, author of her biography *Mother Goddam*, that every time she and Errol shared a scene she would close her eyes and imagine it was Laurence Olivier who was with her.

The years have softened her view somewhat. In 1975 she told me, "You could say all you liked about Errol and yet when he walked into the room, you'd tell yourself 'I'm crazy. This isn't true. He's enchanting.'"

Elizabeth and Essex was to be the first of two films in which Bette Davis played the Queen. As she said: "There was a reincarnation here somewhere. I had a feeling for this woman. I had read everything in the world written about her."

If Errol was unhappy about Miss Davis, the critics were equally unhappy about his own performance, and with the change of title. Frank S. Nugent in the *New York Times* reported:

"After seeing it yesterday at the Strand with Bette Davis playing it the way she has, we still think 'Elizabeth the Queen' is the way to describe it. It's Queen Bette's picture just as surely as Mr Flynn is a good-looking young man who should be asked to do no more in pictures than flash an even-toothed smile and present a firm jaw line. His Essex lacked a head long before the headman got around to him."

One line in the film, said Nugent, Errol recited "with the sincerity of a small boy apologizing to his teacher for throwing spitballs".

That sort of comment did not appear to worry Errol at all. Yet there was at this time the same vacuum in his spirits after a bad press as there invariably was following an unsatisfactory night with a girl – and, though he told no one, often his women friends did leave him feeling particularly empty.

The stories published in the papers, however, indicated he enjoyed every minute of his bedroom activities and he saw no reason to give any other impression. Certainly few of the reports about the company he kept and the frequency of the changes being rung were incorrect.

If Professor Flynn continued to be embarrassed by them, he did find the time also to bask in his son's reflected glories. In June 1939, Theodore, now Dean of the Faculty of Science at Belfast University, together with Marelle and their daughter Rosemary, paid their first visit to Hollywood.

He may have hoped that Errol would cool his behaviour for the visit. If so, he was disappointed. The younger Flynn didn't relax either his drinking or his womanizing for their trip and when the professor paid a surprise visit to his son's dressing room, surprise was the right word. He found a young lady, stripped to the waist, in the process of helping Errol out of his trousers.

It certainly was no place for a nice girl like Rosemary and at nineteen she was completely unimpressed by the things she saw and heard.

"I am on holiday with mother and am not interested in film tests," she said when reporters asked her the inevitable question. She added: "I like Errol's films but a career like his does not appeal to me at all. People think, I suppose, that because my brother is a star that he could help me to get parts. I'm just not interested. My studies are more important to me."

She could have observed, however, that outside of the studio Errol and Lili were yet again playing the lovey-dovey married couple. For a time they were living together, but it did not last. They were too alike in spirit to have any kind of lasting relationship, rather in the way that he and Marelle could never exist under the same roof together. He would continue to try, but Errol and Lili were still like an electric power point wired to the wrong terminals.

In Hollywood sparks flew again between Errol and his mother, too. This time they argued about stories that Errol planned to renounce his British Empire citizenship.

Britain and its Empire had gone to war and David Niven and a number of other British subjects announced they were packing their bags for the old country and were going to volunteer to fight. Errol kept very quiet.

Then, in July 1940, the Marquis of Lothian, Britain's Ambassador in Washington, dashed off an appeal to British exiles to come home and join up. Among them was the acting colony in Hollywood. It was stressed that there was nothing in the Military Service Act to order British citizens living abroad to come home and Errol was an Australian. But his name was on a list that included Alfred Hitchcock, Laurence Olivier, Ronald Colman, then already forty-nine, Charles Chaplin, fifty-one, and sitting out his second war in California, Victor McLaglen and Ray Milland. The Ambassador said that anyone over thirty-one need not regard himself as a priority case for an immediate comeback. Errol decided that let him nicely off the hook. He was exactly thirty-one.

While other members of the British Hollywood colony went back, Errol stayed – and to his mother's disgust talked about becoming an American.

It was the end of Errol's friendship with David Niven, who was about to become a front-line officer. As far as Errol was concerned, the only fighting he would do would be either in the studio or on the floor of a nightclub.

A duel of wits – and swords – with Basil Rathbone in *Robin Hood*.

Face to face with Bruce Cabot in *Dodge City* – he was the man Errol came to regret describing as "the nearest thing to a brother I ever had". In the center is Victor Jory.

Errol the Elizabethan courtier. (Above) with Flora Robson as the Queen in *The Sea Hawk*. (Below) with Bette Davis in *Elizabeth and Essex*. Miss Davis and he didn't get on at all.

With two of his closest friends, Alan Hale and Guinn ("Big Boy") Williams, in *Virginia City*. Nora described them as his "drunken buddies".

With Olivia de Havilland. Unrequited love in *They Died with their Boots on*.

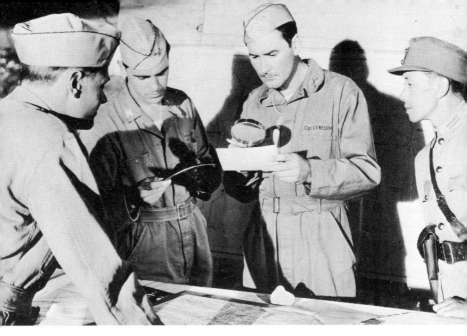

Trying to look interested in *Objective Burma*. Errol had no idea how much trouble was brewing for him over the film. With him in this scene are William Prince, Warner Anderson and Frank Tang.

They called him Don Juan, and *The Adventures of Don Juan* was certainly perfect casting. Viveca Lindfors sits on the throne.

7

It's a Great Feeling

*Someone put a demon in him and the
demon probably paid off.*
Herbert Wilcox

Lili continued to mention the idea of divorce, and Errol continued
to talk her out of it. The unarmed combat between them seemed
to have its interesting side and it was still a lot cheaper than paying
alimony. But he didn't bargain for one unexpected consequence.
In late 1940, Lili announced to a startled gossip writer that she was
pregnant.

The idea of Errol Flynn embarking on parenthood threatened
to play havoc with his image and for a man like Errol that was not
something to be taken lightly. Even Warner Brothers' press department, which normally revelled in such glad tidings, kept remarkably
quiet about the event.

As if to demonstrate that he was still a playboy able to deliver
everything expected of him, Errol left the mother-to-be at home
and took off for Brazil, where on arrival he was mobbed by fans
in the grip of orgasmic hysteria. An avalanche of between 6000 and
7000 women and girls broke through a police cordon and tore at
Errol like a pack of hungry wolves. Every visible button – and the
invisible ones on his trousers had always been popular targets – was
wrenched from his clothes before a police back-up squad could sur-
round and rescue him.

From Brazil he went to Buenos Aires where fighting of a rather
different kind threatened to be even rougher. The newspaper *El
Pampero* was less than kind about his acting prowess when they reported his arrival. Flynn, said the paper – which had been displaying
a marked pro-Nazi stance – was "suffering from synthetic courage".

Errol challenged the editor to a fight. "Your articles are like those of Goebbels," he said. It was a perfect opportunity – at a time when public opinion in the United States was swinging Britain's way – to show how misguided were all those suspicions about his pro-Nazi sympathies. "Come to my room, we will lock the door," he challenged. "If you open it before I do, I'll kiss the ground three times before your office. If I leave first, then you can publish in your paper that for once a Nazi hero had the courage to meet a contender on an equal basis."

His challenge was ignored. Nobody doubted that Errol had been serious. Other people blustered and then escaped when the opportunity arose to call their bluff, not Errol. But that test never came. Another one did. When he returned to the States, he announced finally that he was becoming a citizen.

Mrs Marelle Flynn now made her row with her son public. She said she was shocked at the news, although it seemed tame compared with some of the other stories that were reaching her. Her patriotic pride was hurt. "I can't understand it," she said. "He is essentially British."

Later on, she muted her attitude and wondered whether she was being quite loyal enough to Errol. "I cannot imagine why there should be so much fuss about this," she told reporters. "If Errol were at home he would most certainly have joined up by now. But he decided to take out American citizenship papers long before a war was even threatened. He has to pay both British and American income tax and this costs him thousands of pounds every year. His decision will save him a lot of money."

The matter was allowed to rest for a time and Errol did his best to prove that he was not running away from anything. He announced that he was going to help British evacuees to settle in California and that he would raise money for Britain's war effort by embarking on a coast-to-coast tennis tournament. Some people said that was a very nice way to raise money. Fortunately, they did not ask what he was going to wear for the occasion. When Errol and his actor buddy Bruce Cabot, who had been with him in *Dodge City*, played a foursome with two magnificently endowed girls about this time, they all did so stark naked.

The story of that game did not get into the newspapers, but almost every other thing involving Errol Flynn did. Some of the things published about Errol he did not like at all. When *In Place of Splendour*, a book sub-titled *The Autobiography of a Spanish Woman*, appeared in September 1940, he sued for libel because it alleged he had gone to Spain during the Civil War simply to get newspaper publicity. The matter was settled out of court.

He was getting into the habit of suing people now, and of being sued. Flynn's agent Myron Selznick, brother of the famous David O. Selznick, sued him for not paying his commission. Flynn countered that not only had the agent been unable to get him a raise, he had had to engineer a $600-a-week increase for himself. He told the court he needed about $14,000 a month on which to live. He wanted to have $6000-a-week salary released from the attachment which he gave 10 per cent of all he earned to Selznick. Errol said he could not afford to keep paying the money. "It is excruciatingly expensive to be a movie star," he maintained in a signed affidavit.

A typical monthly expenses chart read like this:

> Home expenses $1200
> Phone and telegraph $60
> Automobiles $150
> Boat $400
> Payments to Lili $1000
> Personal expenses $1000
> Doctor and dentist $150
> Interest $135
> Insurance $500
> Publicity, professional and business expenses $4000
> Taxes $5000

Above all, he had appearances to keep up.

Judge Albert Riss agreed. He said that a film star had a station to maintain higher than that of mere ordinary mortals and that he could see Errol needed at least $12,000 a month on which to live. The judge dissolved the attachment. Clearly Jack Warner wished it had been as easy to dissolve *his* attachment to Flynn, and to Humphrey Bogart, too, for that matter.

The two actors appeared together in *Virginia City*, which is now often confused with *Dodge City* but was a lot worse. Both Warner and Michael Curtiz – who swore he could not take another moment of the "sohn of a beetch's" laxity before the cameras – decided they had had enough. Jack Warner screamed "You're fired" at both Flynn and Bogart – who was still not a star but was quite as undisciplined as Errol – but he had to admit they both had watertight contracts.

"You'll lose a fortune if you do get rid of us," said Errol, trying to put on his most sympathetic tone, and went away with his new chum for a few doses of liquid refreshment. In the studio bar, they planned a way of getting Mr Warner out of his financial predicament.

"It's easy," said Bogey, "all we do is set fire to one of the stages and that bastard collects the insurance."

"Excellent idea, sport," said Flynn and together they went looking for a can of paraffin and a box of matches. They actually got as far as striking the first light, when an alert technician spotted a smouldering bundle of props and called the studio fire brigade. Their part in the affair was never discovered.

Unfortunately, their roles in *Virginia City* were. It was a Civil War story with Flynn playing a Union officer, Miriam Hopkins pathetically miscast as a saloon singer, Bogart as a Mexican bandit who lost his accent as frequently as his quarry, and Randolph Scott adding the only apparent touch of Western professionalism.

Scott says now that he liked Flynn a lot when he got to know him on *Virginia City*. The thing that impressed him most was the fan mail with which Errol was deluged. It came on to the set by the sackful and almost everyone there would swarm over the letters, reading the outrageous offers of undying love being made by young girls. The critics felt slightly differently. "Mr Flynn is about as mobile as a floor-walker," said the *New York Times* in reviewing *Virginia City*.

If Errol did not appear to worry about the critics, Warner did. They decided that if nothing else, he would be one of the standard-bearers in their own fight for democracy.

Alfred Duff Cooper, the Minister of Information in Churchill's

Cabinet, had been telling the Hollywood moguls that they would help their British customers if, once in a while, they produced a film that would stir their patriotic instincts. In 1940, Harry Warner, Jack's elder brother, sent the minister a note saying he had just the thing to warm the cockles of his heart, and it was about to cross the Atlantic.

This was another story about Queen Elizabeth and once more Errol Flynn was the male interest. But now, there were no antics between the Virgin Queen, played this time by Flora Robson, and her supposedly devoted servant. Errol had the title role of *The Sea Hawk*, which most people took to be Sir Francis Drake under an assumed name. It gave him plenty of opportunities for fighting with his fists and for fencing as a swordsman of class. After one scene in which he had summarily dismissed a dozen "enemy" troops, he walked behind the cameras, sighed with relief and said, "Gosh, I don't think I've been braver than that."

The whole story was something of a fraud, too; for instance, it was set thirty years before the time of *Elizabeth and Essex*, and it suggested that Britain fended off the Armada in exactly the same terms as it was currently giving the two-finger sign to the Luftwaffe.

It certainly pleased the *Daily Express* which decided it put the case for England "nearly as well as Mr Churchill would do".

Like *Captain Blood* the film was based on a Sabatini novel, although by the time it came to the screen there was little but the title left of the original story. Nevertheless, *The Sea Hawk* ranks as one of Flynn's best ever efforts. Two full-scale ships were used in making the picture, which also conveniently managed to take advantage of a number of sets used in *Elizabeth and Essex*.

The relationship between Flynn and the lady who is now Dame Flora seems to have been extremely amicable, although most of the glamour interludes were between Errol and the beautiful brunette, Brenda Marshall.

Bosley Crowther of the *New York Times* plainly liked *The Sea Hawk* more than he liked Errol Flynn: "Yes sir, mates," he wrote, "the Burbank Brothers are really giving us some action this time – one of those old-style film epics which, back fifteen years ago, when Douglas Fairbanks was the Black Pirate and Milton Sills was a 'Sea Hawk' too, they labelled spectacle films. ...."

He liked the parallel between the recent Munich period and the vacillation of a Queen Elizabeth who found it difficult to decide "between a policy of appeasing Philip of Spain [and] building a fleet to oppose his growing Armada".

"Of course," he went on, "it is all historically cockeyed and the amazing exploits of Mr Flynn, accomplished by him in the most casual and expressionless manner, are quite as incredible as the adventures of Dick Tracy. But Flora Robson makes an interesting Queen Elizabeth...."

Flynn followed this demonstration of British patriotism with more work waving the American flag, this time as another of the heroes of the Civil War, Jeb Stuart. It was mostly notable for the appearance of Ronald Reagan as George Custer – who was not yet a general – and of his own old sidekicks Alan Hale and Guinn (Big Boy) Williams, both of whom had appeared in *Dodge City* and *Virginia City*.

Footsteps in the Dark, which followed in early 1941, seems to be justified by nothing more than the fact that Errol, Brenda Marshall again, Ralph Bellamy, Alan Hale and Allen Jenkins were all on the payroll and had to be put to work. It was an inept comedy directed by Lloyd Bacon.

If Errol looked uncomfortable in many of the scenes, there could be good reason: Lili had given birth to a son, while Errol was out sailing in the *Sirocco*. With baby Sean now making his presence known, Errol was beginning to feel that the years were catching up on him. He made up his mind they would not win.

At a ceremony in New York, Errol was allowed to make amends for all those times that he had played a cowboy hero. With Mayor Fiorello La Guardia in attendance, he was made an honorary Sioux Indian. There was no particular reason for the ceremony. Certainly Errol had no great feelings about the way Indians were treated in his or anyone else's movies – few did at that time, except for occasional real Indians and those in Central Park appeared to have no hang-ups in that direction.

To Mayor La Guardia, however, it was a chance to gain a handful of ethnic votes and for a politician who was quite as much a show-man as any film star, some great publicity. Errol was happy to join in and get his share too. First, genuine members of the tribe made him take off his shoes "because it is not right for you to come among us in white man's shoes". Then he slipped into a pair of moccasins and stood on a couple of blocks of wood while a ceremonial leather coat was draped around his shoulders, on top of his over-coat.

"Do you come here with a pure heart?" asked the chief, who either was speaking with forked tongue or didn't know much about Errol Flynn. "I hope so, I hope so," lied Errol, at which point the chief swung at him with a tomahawk.

"I only hope that the paleface will not take away my land now," he stammered. He was not joking, for there was no telling what punishment Lili still had in store for him next time he had a raise.

His audiences had reason to be happier than he was himself. *Dive Bomber* brought back his glamour image and was helped both by Technicolor and by the direction of Michael Curtiz, who against his better judgment had been persuaded to direct "just one more" Flynn picture.

He had, as usual, good reason to curse and mutter about his star's behaviour. As always Errol arrived late on the set and sometimes couldn't be found at all. "I think you'd better try his boat," Fred MacMurray advised Curtiz on more than one occasion and, yes, that was precisely where Errol always was. "I was prepared not to like him," MacMurray told me, "but he turned out to be the most charming guy."

Every time he finally surfaced, Errol would go up to his fellow actors and tell them with a pleading look in his eye: "I'm so sorry I have kept you waiting. I *do* hope I haven't caused you too much inconvenience." The way he said it, no one could possibly think they *had* been inconvenienced. "He was quite a fellow," adds Mac-Murray.

More than 150 actors, including Flynn, Bellamy and MacMur-ray, had a lengthy stay with real airmen at the US naval base at San Diego, men who in those months prior to Pearl Harbor saw about as much value in having the film people with them as they

did in their military activities. Two naval officers were assigned as
technical advisers.

The film also introduced a lady who would face the familiar para-
dox of co-starring with Errol Flynn – driven to despair one moment
and then overwhelmed with his unique charm the next.

Alexis Smith was tall, beautiful in a way that displayed as much
character as sex appeal, and anxious to prove – as all young actresses
wanted to prove – that she could be a woman of dramatic power
when given the right lines to say and the correct position in which
to say them. In *Dive Bomber* she had a close-up to look forward
to that she just knew would get her noticed, and, possibly in the
space of two or three minutes, make her a star.

She waited for that glimpse of stardom patiently. Finally, it came.
Curtiz said "Action" and at that moment Errol Flynn walked
straight across her path and into frame. He epitomized the cliché:
he stole the scene.

Alexis was distraught. She ran to her dressing room, tears welling in her eyes and convinced her opportunity had been lost for
ever. She went home that night in a fit of deep depression.
When she returned the next morning, she felt worse still – until
she walked into her dressing room and saw a note in front of
her make-up mirror. It was in an envelope bearing the words
"Errol Flynn". Inside, on his own personal stationery, Errol had
written a note of apology, so sincere in appearance that if she
wanted to be angry, she could be so no longer. "It was that Errol
Flynn charm," she explained to me, telling the story for the first
time.

The only person who never seemed susceptible to the magic ingredient was Curtiz. His days on the set seemed taken up with coax-
ing Flynn to perform much as a mother had to persuade her child
to smile for the nice photographer. There was little that could take
his mind off the awful responsibility he bore to make Errol appear
the actor his audiences believed him to be. Only one thing could
– the appearance of royalty. Then, at the very mention of a royal
personage's name, Curtiz would virtually come to attention and
click his heels.

Irving Rapper told me the story of one such incident which conjuresupa pictureof Ruritania in Burbank and of Errol Flynn dancing on the sidelines like a thwarted musical comedy juvenile.

Rapper, still Curtiz's protégé, heard that the Archduke Otto of Austria was on the Warners' lot after having been to see a fellow art connoisseur, the Edward G. Robinson who had not been good enough to join the Olympiads.

Curtiz flushed with excitement when he heard the news. "What you say?" he asked, getting more aroused with every word. "What you say ... Otto from Austria is *here*?" The way he asked the question sounded as though he had just been told of the Second Coming.

Rapper told him he was and added casually: "And he says he would like to meet *you*."

"What, sohn of a beetch, bring him here. . . . He's such a wonderful person." As Rapper tells it, the whole studio was abuzz, Curtiz's excitement having been transmitted like a telegram.

When the Archduke arrived, Curtiz did not know what to do with himself. "Your Majesty," he said, using the wrong terminology. "When you were boy, I was young photographer and I took your photograph as I ran after your carriage. It was most beautiful face what ever existed in whole of Austria–Hungary."

The Archduke was suitably impressed. So much so that Curtiz felt obliged to introduce him to his players, beginning reluctantly with Flynn, whom he did not think deserved the honour, and who never sincerely respected anyone but himself. "Well," Errol told the royal personage, "you must enjoy yourself in this town." (He did manage to avoid calling the guest "sport".) "Come and have a nice evening with us. We have Doris Duke coming." Which, as Rapper says, was a pretty silly thing to say to an archduke.

Otto said he could not come but Errol, who did not like to be disappointed, insisted. Finally, the Archduke succumbed, accepted the invitation gracefully and was told the time he had to arrive. That evening, a chiselled-toothed gentleman clicked his heels at the Flynn home and introduced himself. He was Otto's equerry and had come in place of the Archduke.

Such things rarely were allowed to happen to Errol Flynn. When they did, he felt once more like the child expelled from the party for tipping the other children in the fountain. He had to get his

revenge. Wisely, Curtiz kept out of his way. But he spread the word
of how unreliable Errol was and all the Warner executives knew
that to tangle with Mr Flynn was to bring them into troubles which
they could all do without. But they talked about him. He was the
favourite subject for conversation both within the confines of the
studio building and in their homes. The stories they told in the privacy of their own dining rooms and in bed were not the sort of subjects with which to regale strangers in polite conversation.

Errol, of course, knew who they were and the things that they
said. He had made a mental list of the executives he disliked most.
When the right moment arrived, he would have his own back. As
usual, he chose his own way. He invited a group to dinner – men
and women who possibly had in common only the fact that their
host hated them all even more than they disliked him. Each one
of the wives had gone to the Flynn party voicing disapproval but
convincing herself that to turn down the invitation would be to harm
her husband's career.

On this evening, however, they were all overwhelmed. Flynn was
more good-looking than they had ever imagined. His manners as
he flattered each one of the fat and ageing women were superb. His
next but one film title had just been announced as *Gentleman Jim*,
but that night he was Gentleman Errol – until it came to serving
the dessert. Then, one by one, the women blanched as their husbands choked over the claret and cigars. The waitresses, the same
girls who up to then had served everything so perfectly, came into
the room and delivered the peach melba in front of the guests stark
naked.

Nudity at Hollywood parties was the big talking point of the age.
Important and not so important visitors to the movie town would
beg for an opportunity to get on to the guest list of these affairs.
There was little concrete evidence to go on, but rumours there were
aplenty that the most beautiful girls in films attended as many
parties in the buff as they did in their coutured finery.

On one occasion, a foreign diplomat inveigled himself into Errol's
house for a party which he had been told would be in the nude.
As he rang the bell, an exquisite little blonde with the sort of
upturned pointed breasts Errol was known to favour came to the

door naked. The visitor was delighted. "Would you come with me to the undressing room?" she pouted. He couldn't wait.

Having completely disrobed, his pot belly shaking with excitement, the door of the main lounge was opened and the guest announced. He found a crowded room awaiting him – but every other person there was fully dressed. That night the diplomat proved a medical theory: he blushed from his toes upward. Errol enjoyed this experience immensely, roaring so loudly that his immaculate teeth looked in danger of rattling.

There would be no more parties given by Errol and Lili. In August 1941, Tiger Lil, with baby Sean in her arms, left him once more and finally in November she asked for a divorce on the grounds of Errol's cruelty.

It was finalized in April 1942, with the garnishing of some highly punitive alimony. Lili had told Superior Court Judge W. J. Palmer: "He used to pay more attention to his yachts than to me." And she added: "He wanted to be free and did not want a wife and child. He would be away for two or three months at a time but seldom took me along. As a matter of fact, Judge, my husband was on the boat while I was in the hospital last May giving birth to our child."

Judge Palmer approved a property settlement under which Lily received $1500 a month for as long as Errol's salary remained in the $180,000-a-year class and a minimum of $9000 a year if it ever fell below the $180,000 yardstick. But there was worse to come. Not only was Lili awarded custody of baby Sean, but half of Errol's property too, said to be worth $150,000.

As if to show that he wanted to start anew, Errol built himself a bachelor home high up on Mulholland Drive, one that would be untainted by any Damita association. He called it Mulholland House. It had everything he needed, all on one level, including a master bedroom suitable for his favourite mistress with a mirror over the bed. The bar was specially constructed so that it could dispense all the brandy and vodka he might need at a given moment. It also had its own riding ring outside. He called it his "playhouse".

He was, however, desperately unhappy. Lili's "desertion" seemed to signify failure on his part and he really didn't think he had behaved so badly to her. Once more he felt rejected. He could, however, still enjoy the occasional film review. *Dive Bomber* had just been released, and the *New York Times*'s Bosley Crowther declared it shed a great deal of credit on Warner Brothers who were following up their medical epics about Louis Pasteur and *Dr Ehrlich's Magic Bullet* with this study of aeronautical medicine. It was the best of the new wave of "service films" to date. "Never before," he said, "has an aviation film been so vivid in its images, conveyed such a sense of tangible solidity when it is showing us solid things or been so full of sunlight and clean air when the cameras are aloft." As for the story, it was a "necessary evil". And Errol? He played the surgeon "with his usual elegance, looking very dashing and romantic in a variety of uniforms and behaving with solemn dignity in moments of stress".

More dignity, certainly, than some of Flynn's latest antics with young women. The variations he employed never failed to amaze the people who knew about them. One night at a New York hotel he saw a redhead who stirred all his instincts. "I must have her, chum," he told a friend who was with him that night, and invited her to his room for drinks. She came.

The next day he bought her a nurse's uniform to wear. Like many men, Flynn thought nurses particularly attractive. They also had a purpose. In those days it was not always easy for a man, even a top film star like Errol Flynn, to get a girl into his room. A nurse helping an invalid was a different matter.

The girl, as he put it, was a good sport. When some friends joined him in the room, he asked the girl to be even more of a sport – run him a bath. She did so and took off all her own clothes to do it. When she came back into the suite's lounge, it was to invite the astonished friends to watch her giving Errol his bath.

He frequently was outrageous in hotels, and not always solely with women. In Chicago he decided to justify his reputation as a wild man. He passed a pet shop window displaying three lion cubs. "Just the thing to impress the public, sport," he told the owner and bought one of them. The cub was about a foot and a half high and, Errol reported afterwards, did not seem to like him very much. But it was fun to walk through the streets of Chicago, the cub on a leash. The pair walked as far as a luxury hotel while passers-by stared incredulously. Through the plush carpeted entrance of the hotel Errol walked, right through the reception hall, and up to the desk. "My name's Flynn, my good man," he said to the man on duty behind the heavy wooden counter. "Do you have a registration for me?"

"I'm afraid not," said the man. "Right," said Errol. "Check this for me, I'll be back soon." With which he walked out the way he came in, minus the cub. He often wondered how long the hotel clerk stood there holding the leash. Had he returned, he may have got involved in yet another fracas.

A bust-up with a gentleman called Jimmy Fidler was one he could not avoid and which had more lasting repercussions than most. It could have broken Flynn completely, had Warner Brothers not wanted to protect their investment quite as much as they did.

It happened soon after the only really big loss in Errol's life, that of his dog Arno. After years as a Hollywood fixture, Arno jumped overboard from the *Sirocco* and vanished. When its washed-up body was identified, Errol could not bear to look at the dead remains of a friend that had meant so much to him in life. He buried its collar in his garden at Mulholland Drive.

Fidler, always anxious to find a new angle on the people upon whom he thrived, reported in his column: "Errol Flynn, whose love for his dog Arno has been much heralded, didn't even bother to go get his body when it was washed up on shore. That's how much he cared for him."

That, no matter what anyone else thought of Errol, was quite patently a lie. For a whole day Errol went looking for Fidler. Finally, he spotted him at the Mocambo nightclub. All the anger welling in Flynn was compounded by the other things Fidler had been writing about the British colony in Hollywood because somehow these, too, had struck a raw nerve.

Fidler was known as an arch-isolationist whose aim, it appeared, had been to keep America out of the war. He had testified before a Senate committee only a week before on the need to avoid, as he put it, "intervention". He had been extending his arguments to include the effect British influence was having on Hollywood, which was aimed, he said, at getting America into the war. He alleged an attempt had been made to bribe him with $2500 to give a good review to the movie *The Prisoner of Zenda*, and he said that people in Hollywood had been trying to force newspapers to drop his column and radio stations to no longer relay his regular talks. Fidler had not mentioned Flynn in his testimony, but the committee had been told by Senator Clark of Idaho that the film *Dive Bomber* was "pro-war propaganda". It all upset Errol as though he had personally been attacked in every line.

When he saw Fidler he struck him forcibly across the face with his open hand. "I won't dignify you with a closed fist," he muttered and Fidler went down with a thud, while the assembled diners sat incredulously watching what looked like being the best cabaret in Hollywood.

Flynn shouted to the prostrate Fidler: "You told the Senate one lie too many." Marlene Dietrich with her right leg bandaged following a recent fracture saw it all. "Get me out of here," she cried. "They'll break my ankle again." French actor Jean Gabin carried her out, missing what everyone expected would be more fun.

Mexican actress Lupe Velez, who had long been a Flynn admirer – he, in turn thought she had one considerable attribute, the ability to make her breasts dance independently of each other – jumped up and sauntered around Errol carrying a bottle of tomato ketchup. "Geev eeet to heem, beeg boy," she shouted, at which point Mrs Bobbie Fidler got up from the table and gave it to Errol on her husband's behalf – with an oyster fork. She stuck it in Errol's ear and drew blood. Errol didn't know what had hit him, but he was impressed.

"I admire that in a woman," Flynn, nursing his ear, told Bobbie, who ran a local dress shop. "Bless you, you've got the bravery to try to defend your husband. Which is more than he wants to do for himself."

Fidler decided to do his defending elsewhere: in court. He sued Errol for assault. Judge Cecil Holland concluded that he had little more to do than make Flynn promise not to punch the writer again. "I did not punch him," said Errol. "But I did slap him. A slap is a bigger insult than a punch."

Fidler didn't seem as happy as Flynn to see the case settled. He issued a statement saying that Errol had published one falsehood after another following the Mocambo brawl and that Flynn's real complaint was that he objected to Fidler writing about his accompanying a ballet dancer to the airport. Which to anyone knowing anything about Errol Flynn would have been tame stuff indeed.

Meanwhile, Jack Warner was having apoplexy about the whole affair. Insulting the press was the one thing that even a Hollywood mogul never did. Call your stars anything you liked. That was all right. Swear at your directors, castigate your producers. All right, too. But the press – they're your bread and butter and should be treated that way. Fortunately, and remarkably, Fidler said he bore no grudge and later Errol went as far as to describe their relationship as one of close friends.

There is no record of Errol actually losing any of his fights, but in truth he did not always bring his opponent to the floor simply by using his fists. More often than not, his success was due to a comparatively easy foot movement: he would lever his heel down over his adversary's instep and force him down.

The fights and the other aspects of his way of life were taking their toll, although at first he would not recognize it. In September 1941, Errol collapsed in the elevator of a medical building. He had been on his way to have a check-up after recently feeling ill. The doctor decided that Flynn was suffering from "nervous exhaustion".

A lot of nervous energy certainly had been expended on having a good time. His evening drinking sessions with his crowd of male buddies were quite as exhausting as his activities with starlets and secretaries. He was always looking out for something new, and frequently coming away dissatisfied.

When he read a book – and reading was his only "quiet" passion – about cockfighting in the Caribbean, he told John Decker: "Say, sport, why don't we get a couple of birds and let them bite the heads off each other?" When Errol had ideas like that, they had to be fulfilled. For weeks, Sunday night was cockfighting night at Mulholland House, although the police never got to hear about it.

Soon after the Pacific fleet was decimated at Pearl Harbor bringing

America into the war, stories about certain actors' "cowardice" became popular cocktail hour gossip. Errol was their main target.

Yet none of his detractors knew that he did volunteer for Army service, and had been rejected by the medical board. He was told he had an "athletic heart". He was not too dismayed by the news but the medical authorities were. They called him back, and again he was rejected. He was examined five times altogether. Finally, Flynn was given some stunning news: not only was his heart affected, but his lungs were in a poor shape, too. "You've got perhaps a couple of years to live," said one of the doctors.

Two years? He believed it no more now than would anyone who knew anything about the reputation of Errol Flynn – and that reputation certainly would not allow him to talk about it. But if it were true – and could all those doctors be wrong? – he was going to live out those years to the full.

8
The Edge of Darkness

*I don't remember how many times he said
he was in love.*
Raoul Walsh

It was a daunting prospect, just two years to live. The five doctors
had headed five different teams and the man they selected as their
spokesman confided to him: "We couldn't understand how you
could jump around on and off all those ships and kill all those Indians and yet not pass your physical. That's why we had to go into it
so closely."

The only person he told about the virtual death sentence was
Raoul Walsh, the then sixty-year-old film director who had a reputation as the cracker-jack "man's director" of Hollywood, a fellow
who could make feeble actors seem good and good actors great.
Before a misguided jackrabbit had crashed into the windscreen of
the car in which he was travelling on a film set in Utah, gouging
out his right eye, he had been an actor, too, playing John Wilkes
Booth – Lincoln's assassin – in D. W. Griffith's *Birth of a Nation*.
Now he wore a black eye patch, which always gave him the air of
the swashbuckler, even when directing John Wayne in *The Big Trail*
and James Cagney in *The Roaring Twenties*.

He and Errol were about to work together in a film called *They
Died with their Boots on*. It was clear that someone had to take over
from Michael Curtiz. The Hungarian had had enough and said so
frequently. It was not that the "sohn of a beetch" had done anything
more outrageous than before. It was simply that he had not changed
and Curtiz was no longer going to be swept up in the wash of Errol's
charm.

From the moment they had first met, Flynn's relationship with

Raoul Walsh was totally different. They instantly liked each other, shared both adventures and drinks, and Walsh was never unwilling to apologize for his younger friend's behaviour. To people like Flynn, Walsh was not just another director, but a "regular guy". He was a man's man on whom the star could lean a troubled head when he needed to, a quality essential for any pal of Flynn's. He became part of the Flynn set and before long would be its virtual leader. He called Errol "the Baron". Flynn called him "Uncle", and never was there a more appropriate nickname. When the news of his "4-F" rating came from the medical board, Errol went straight to Walsh. "Uncle," he told him, "I'm going to live two lifetimes in the next two years." From that moment on, his daily drink intake was doubled or trebled. Sessions knocking away the "hard stuff" were spiced with puffs first of pot and then of pure opium. Before long, he discovered that using a hypodermic and a dose of cocaine made him feel better than ever. The strange thing was that it did not appear to be having any serious effect on him. He was quite obviously beginning to enjoy his two lifetimes.

The snide comments about his escaping from military service were brushed off with a shrug. Sometimes he would tell girls he had been clever enough to puncture an eardrum to get out of serving. What they thought didn't appear to matter. Least of all did he worry what other members of his rabble-rousing set thought. They could usually be relied upon to be even more outrageous. One morning John Barrymore called at Mulholland House at four o'clock "for a little drink" and stayed for three weeks. There was nothing Errol could do all that time to persuade him to leave.

Barrymore once told him, with more than a little truth: "You look as if you might be my illegitimate son. Was your mother ever in America?" Errol replied that he did not think she was. "Must have been in England then," he said, and drifted into a drunken sleep.

In May 1942, Barrymore, the "Great Profile", died, the result of being "in like Flynn" for years before Flynn was born. Doctors diagnosed cirrhosis of the liver, and then gave a virtual catalogue of other diseases: kidney failure, chronic gastritis, ulceration of the oesophagus, hardening of the arteries and chronic eczema. John

Decker, completing the triangular relationship, was with him when he died.

Errol was deeply disturbed at the news. Perhaps he saw a foretaste of what he knew would sooner or later be in store for himself. Perhaps it was merely the sadness of losing an old friend who liked nothing more than to quote Shakespeare one minute and talk about the women he had seduced the next.

Flynn used to ask him: "Was there really an affair between Hamlet and Ophelia?"

"Only in Cleveland," said Barrymore.

Subconsciously, Errol would find himself imitating Barrymore, even on the film set. Raoul Walsh used to tell him on the set of *They Died with their Boots on*: "You're Flynn, not Barrymore."

For all his shortcomings, Errol needed to look up to other people, even to worship them. He still adored his own father, though he saw little of him. In some ways Barrymore was a surrogate father, if not quite his illegitimate one. Like the professor he was brilliant, with a God-given talent, and had let the world see it.

Errol saw in Barrymore's drinking and in his Irish pedigree a past life of his own. When told of the once great actor's death, he was as deeply touched as he would have been had the professor passed away.

It was in that mood of mourning that Errol heard about the last minutes of his idol. John Decker had sketched the dying Barrymore, one of the most moving works he ever produced. He had then gone on to take care of the funeral arrangements – because Lionel Barrymore, John's brother, had been too distressed to think about them. Decker was a loyal but not over-generous friend, so he arranged for the body to be taken to the Malloy Brothers Funeral Parlor where the rates were cheaper than in any of the Beverly Hills establishments.

That job having been done, he moved on to Mulholland Drive to tell his friends about the moment of death.

Errol was brought to tears.

"Uncle," he said to Walsh, who with a coterie of their "gang" had gathered at Mulholland House for an informal wake, "I can see the old fellow sitting there now and telling us about his wild adventures." He then blew his nose, swigged another drink and went out to meet a girl at a Beverly Hills hostelry, called "The Cock and Bull", leaving Walsh and the rest of the crowd behind in his house.

While Flynn was away, Walsh had an intriguing but morbid idea. "Why," he suggested, "don't we bring the old boy back here?" Eyes that formerly had been red now sparkled.

Three of the assembled "mourners" drove to Malloy Brothers, a firm well suited to what Walsh had in mind. The director knew that one of the brothers was a small-time actor in his sixties who could be relied upon to go along with anything Walsh suggested. Mr Malloy agreed to "lend" Walsh the body for a couple of hours.

With the undertaker's connivance, the mortal remains of John Barrymore were bundled into a car driving off in the direction of Flynn's house. It was not an easy journey. Rigor mortis had already begun to set in and it was difficult to bend the corpse's legs.

When they arrived, Flynn was still not at home. But his Russian butler Alex was there to let in the motley band. He didn't like what he saw. "He doesn't look well at all," said Alex, peering closely at the body, but still not quite sure exactly what it was he was looking at. "He looks bad." He still didn't know how bad, but before long he made up his mind.

"I think he's dead," he whimpered and started to back away.

"Nonsense," said Walsh. "Just dead drunk. Get him a drink!"

Without Alex's help, Walsh and friends managed to get the cadaver into a sitting position and placed it in what Barrymore had been used to thinking of as his usual spot.

Soon, Flynn bounced in looking much happier than when he had left. "Hello, boys," he said – and then screamed.

He continued screaming as he dashed out through the french windows and hid in the oleander bush on the patio.

It took several minutes before he was able to compose himself and walk back in again. "You big bastard," Errol shouted at Walsh, who was doubled up in hysterics. "Get him out of here! We'll all end up in San Quentin."

Happy that their job was done, Walsh and his pals took the body back to Malloy's where the part-time actor was waiting anxiously.

"How did it go?" he asked.

"Fine," said the one-eyed bandit.

"A shame I didn't give him a better suit," said the undertaker.

Later, Errol could joke about it all as much as Walsh. Nevertheless, as he sat in the chair used by Barrymore both in life and death he would lament: "It was not the correct way to say goodbye to John."

While the shenanigans of the Barrymore passing were at the time private, the public were about to see the results of the first Flynn–Walsh partnership, *They Died with their Boots on*, about Custer's last stand and one of Flynn's best efforts to date. It still looks good today although many of the facts were changed to protect the Warner Brothers' bank balance.

To get him to play the part of General Custer, Walsh had first to convince Errol that it was a role to take seriously, and not to upset Olivia de Havilland with whom he once more co-starred.

Not irritating Jack Warner was another matter. Half way through the picture, when it was quite clear that shooting had gone beyond the point of no return, Errol sat himself in his dressing room surrounded by a useful supply of vodka and refuse to budge – until he got a raise. It was about this time he heard that his naturalization papers had come through and he was now a citizen. That being so, he made it clear that Warner's skinflint behaviour was no way for one American to treat another.

Errol got his raise and filming continued. So did Lili's alimony demands and those of the Internal Revenue Department. In September 1943, the department asked for $121,858 to be deducted from Errol's salary in unpaid taxes.

That salary was about to be earned from the title role in a charm of a film laced with as much blarney as a caseful of Irish whiskey – *Gentleman Jim*, about the legendary Irish-American boxer, Gentleman Jim Corbett.

Alan Hale was with Errol yet again, this time playing his father. Ward Bond was John L. Sullivan, the world-heavyweight champion whose title Corbett took, and Alexis Smith starred as the beautiful but rather haughty society lady who loves the "Gentleman" rather more than she is prepared to admit.

Errol was good in the picture, good as an actor and good as a fighter – he didn't want to use a double for the scenes in the ring since he thought he could box better than any stand-in possibly could. That he *was* good was thanks in no small way to Raoul Walsh, who was again the director.

Once more, the "one-eyed bandit", as Flynn liked to call him, had to talk him into the part; not into actually playing it, he was happy to coast along with anything he was given, but into how it had to be played. "I persuaded him," Walsh told me, "that Jim was a great idol of the American public and it would be terrible if he did it wrong."

As usual, Errol was the life and soul of the studio party, arriving late, drinking too much and charming his way through one indiscretion after the other.

Alexis told me she enjoyed every moment with him. Except one. It was while working out in the ring making *Gentleman Jim* that Errol collapsed, clutching his chest. Doctors diagnosed a mild heart attack. "Don't tell anyone, sport," he asked the physician who gave the verdict. Alexis, however, did get to hear about it. She pulled him aside and said kindly but firmly: "It's so silly, working all day and then playing all night and dissipating yourself. Don't you want to live a long life?" Errol was his usual apparently unconcerned self: "I'm only interested in this half," he told her. "I don't care for the future."

Shooting stopped for days but all that the studio would say was that Errol was suffering from fatigue. He was, however, bad enough to be taken to Los Angeles' Good Samaritan Hospital and then flown on to Baltimore so that he could enter the Johns Hopkins University Hospital there for a complete examination.

He promised the doctors that he would give up some of his more strenuous activities. But in return, all they could tell him was that the Army doctors had been right. They did add, however, the little touch that his lungs were in as bad a shape as was his heart and like the heart they could give out fairly soon.

Just occasionally after that, Errol did wonder about the future. Once sitting in Mulholland House, overlooking the twinkling lights of Hollywood, he confided to a friend: "I've paid in a zest for living. Sometimes the futility of it gets me down."

Gentleman Jim was futile in almost nobody's eyes. As the London *Evening Standard* commented: "How can a film set in San Francisco in 1890 fail?" The paper's critic Mary Hunt added: "Errol Flynn ... assumes the tone and manner of the character very well.... You need not know the finer points of boxing to enjoy this picture. In fact, I have a sneaking feeling that you will appreciate it more if you do not. You are swept into the atmosphere of good times and gaiety and can boo and whistle with the spectators at the ringside."

The *Daily Express* said: "Errol Flynn smooths [Gentleman Jim himself] down and dolls him up in this story, but when he gets in the ring he delivers the goods to an incredible effect."

Errol couldn't deliver the goods in uniform, but Warners thought they could make him sound patriotic just the same – and patriotic to his old country.

In a picture called *Thank Your Lucky Stars*, featuring almost everyone on Warners' books, Errol sang a song called "How I Won the War". He was dressed as a cockney and his accent was thick enough to sound as though he were ordering a half pint of jellied eels.

A lot happened between the completion of this and his next film, *Edge of Darkness*. Like a fountain of trouble it all seemed to cascade around him on the set of the latter picture with the arrival of a party of unexpected visitors.

It was not unusual to have guests on the set. Unlike some stars, Errol usually welcomed them. After all, to turn them away on principle would be to turn away the chance of meeting a pretty girl. But there was nothing attractive about any of the three men who presented themselves at Burbank early in 1943. The director Lewis Milestone was sufficiently concerned to button-hole Errol while no one was looking. "I think they are policemen," he said.

9

Don't Bet on Blondes

He was one of the most absolutely delight-
ful, irresponsible guys I can remember. He
couldn't be more charming.
Walter Pidgeon

It was the most traumatic moment of his life. Ever since he had first been able to shock the other guests at a children's tea party, Errol had lived unconventionally. But somehow not even the experiences in New Guinea matched what was happening to him now.

When he met the strangers on the set, he blanched. There and then he was warned he was going to be arrested and that whatever he said would be taken down and used against him. The charge: statutory rape.

The officers began to unravel a story that at first Flynn had difficulty in picking up. Then, slowly, the pieces began to fit, but very awkwardly.

It had all begun, he was told, when he had met a young girl called Betty Hansen. Betty who? Remembering the name was the most difficult part of the ordeal at this stage. When you had spent the best part of your life taking practically anonymous women to bed, it was never easy to place exactly who had been called what. Miss Hansen certainly had not been one to remember. So who was she? He protested he could not remember her at all.

When he was shown her picture, there was little about her that he found attractive. Her face looked plain. From the photograph, it appeared she had no breasts at all. For a time he was genuinely puzzled. And then he said something for which he was soon to be very sorry.

"You mean that frowzy little blonde?" he stammered. As he said in his autobiography, that did it. Miss Hansen was so deeply offended when she heard about the comment that she pressed on with her allegation that Flynn had taken her into a bedroom at the home of sportsman Freddie McEvoy, had laid her down on the bed and after removing first her jumper and then her bra, had undone her trousers, pulled down her panties and had intercourse with her.

The charge, repeated the police, was *statutory* rape. No one, least of all Miss Hansen, alleged that he had taken her by force. But the operative word was the one before "rape". Statutory rape meant that Betty had not just been a partner in sexual relations but an under-age one at that. The charges were being filed against Errol at the local Juvenile Hall where young girls were taken when they were considered to be in need of care. That in itself didn't altogether worry Errol at first. After all, as he let slip in another unfortunate and unguarded moment, when he went to bed with a girl he did not usually ask for a birth certificate. The difference this time was that he denied even fondling Betty Hansen. "All she did was sit on the arm of my chair," he told the policemen as they scribbled everything he said, hoping that they really would be able to use it all in evidence against him.

Within minutes of his arrest Errol had regained his composure. As Lewis Milestone told me: "He was suddenly like a man of steel." The director asked him what he was going to do. He said: "I'm going up to Jack Warner's office, put my feet on his desk and say: 'You've got a very expensive piece of property here in me. Protect it.'"

At first Errol had called up Robert Ford, a young Irish lawyer whom he knew. It was Jack Warner's idea to bring in Jerry Giesler, a man whose very presence in a court of law could appear to make the bricks in the walls shake. "You've got to help the guy beat this rap," Warner told Giesler without too much ceremony. The lawyer agreed to try, which meant there was likely to be some excitement on the way.

At Juvenile Hall, the first damaging evidence was read to Errol and his lawyer. The girl, in a statement read by Dorothy Palas, the juvenile officer, had said that a man friend of hers offered to introduce her to Errol Flynn, which was an invitation no girl was likely to turn down.

She was working at a drug store at the time. "I had always admired [him] on the screen," she said. "I asked my boss for time off. He refused to let me go." As a result, her friend told her to quit her job and come anyway – because "Flynn would get me a job".

They went to the McEvoy estate uninvited, she said, "but they seemed glad to see us. Buster Wiles, Flynn's friend and stunt man, asked us to stay for dinner."

Meanwhile, she said, the man who had brought her to the estate had gone away and come back with another girl. He had previously told Betty to take a drink, "and I did." She added: "After dinner we went into the living room. Flynn began showing me attention. He told me he was very fond of me and would get me a job. He asked me to go upstairs with him. Flynn disrobed and then assisted me in taking off my clothes. I protested against what he did to me then, but I did not struggle very hard."

Despite this apparently damning evidence, Giesler appeared to justify his reputation. The case went before the Los Angeles Grand Jury and was thrown out. There was, the tried and true citizens of the city decided, no case to answer. Now officially, according to the law books, that meant little. The Grand Jury may think one thing, but they were not the custodians of law and order and there was nothing to prevent a district attorney from saying he was going to carry on fighting. In practice, as anyone with even an elementary knowledge of the law knew, that was not usually the way things worked out. When a Grand Jury said "No", that was, in effect, that.

Needless to say, Errol breathed a heavy sigh of relief. "Just another young dame trying to cash in on my reputation, sport," he mumbled to Fred McEvoy and went home to open a bottle of champagne.

The news was worth the champagne bottle Errol and McEvoy opened to celebrate. But the very idea that he could appear before the Grand Jury at all worried him. Finally his mood got the better of him. "To hell with Christ!" he shouted. McEvoy objected to the blasphemy. "To hell with God, too," cried Errol. Soon he would have something to cry over.

The next day, 16 October 1942, two more policemen called at Mulholland House and announced they had a warrant for Flynn's arrest. Despite the decision of the Grand Jury, the District Attorney was going ahead with the prosecution.

At the police station, Errol was fingerprinted, and placed next to a murder suspect on one side and a man charged with kidnapping on the other. Both said they were innocent. When they asked Errol what he was in for, he just said that he was innocent, too.

Later, in court, he was formally charged with the statutory rape of Betty Hansen on the night of 27 September. She was sticking to her allegations and had now given even more detailed statements of her clothes being removed one by one by Errol then told of being raped not just by him but also by three other studio employees.

The DA, Mr John F. Duckweiller, said he believed her. "The jury obviously ignored the evidence," he said. "It doesn't matter whether she consented to these acts or not. She's under age. That's statutory rape under California law."

"I'm bewildered," stammered Errol as he left the court on $1000 bail. "I can't understand it."

The offenses took place, Betty had alleged, at the St Pierre Road mansion home at Bel Air shared by McEvoy – he was once an Olympic bobsled champion – and actors Bruce Cabot and Stephen Raphael.

Betty was, in the American phrase of the period, a homely girl and the defense was going to make as much capital out of that as it could. She appeared in court without make-up wearing the brown denim uniform that girls held at Juvenile Hall always wore. Betty Hansen had been sent to the Hall because she had been picked up for vagrancy, staying in sleazy hotels by herself. She said she had been directed there by a strange man but he had not gone there with her. Neither had he even touched her sexually.

A difficult ordeal was now before her. Under California law, the accuser had to confront the accused. Meeting Errol that day, she was plainly not at ease. The police made no obvious effort to help her.

"Is this the man?" she was asked directly. "Yes," she replied in a barely audible whisper. Pressed by the policeman to state what Errol had done to her, she murmured: "You know what I told you." But he persisted.

"Did he," asked the policeman, "have an act of sexual intercourse with you?"

"Yes," she said.

That, the DA decided, together with her statement, was enough to get Flynn sent down for years.

The State's case would be that Betty was just the sort of girl whose drab life would allow a man like Errol Flynn to do whatever he wanted with her, for whom his immoral fondling would be an adventure she would remember for the rest of her life.

Charged with Errol had been the three Warner Brothers' employees alleged to have "attacked" her after his own assault – Armand Knapp, eighteen, Morrie Block, twenty-two, and Joseph Geraldi, twenty.

Betty had said that she was one of three girls who had gone to a tennis party at the Bel Air mansion on 27 September, brought there by two Warner Brothers' employees. She had alleged that Flynn was there and that after tennis she had gone to sit on the arm of his chair. They had dinner together and after the first course Betty announced she was feeling ill and wanted to go to lie down. None of this was disputed.

The differences arose when she said that Errol went to the bedroom with her, stripped her and told her she had a "nice fanny and nice breasts". That, she said, was before the statutory rape. She was just a month past her seventeenth birthday. Yet, as Errol was to maintain throughout the next painful weeks, weeks that would turn Hollywood into even more a focus of public attention than usual, he had no cause to ask her age. Certainly, he maintained, whether or not she was eighteen never came into it, because he had not done anything to her. He was not remotely interested in a girl who had no more conversation than she appeared to have good looks.

One of the strongest points of the DA's case was the way in which Flynn had reacted when he heard about the charges. Not only had he called her a "frowzy little blonde", but he had said: "My God.

This is the most horrible thing I have ever heard of. I hardly touched her." *Hardly* touched her. Not the sort of phrase calculated to swing a jury your way.

The case against Errol was strengthened still further when, without warning, two more charges of statutory rape were brought against him. Not this time with Miss Hansen, but with another "minor". And one whom this time Errol readily admitted he did know – although, he stressed, only in one sense of the word.

Peggy La Rue Satterlee was just the sort of girl to whom he would have enjoyed whispering sweet nothings while exploring her well-shaped body. But he did not know that she was still only sixteen. Neither did he admit he had touched her. However, the appeal of the type was undeniable.

She had worked as an extra in *They Died with their Boots on* and had been one of those girls who gazed ecstatically into the eyes of the star at the end of a day's shooting. She had, more importantly, been one of those girls whom he had decided to date and take on board the *Sirocco*. It was there that the rape had taken place, she alleged.

By the time of that trip Errol had developed a new technique. He would not always contact the girls whom he wanted as night-time companions himself. More often than not, he would get someone else to do it for him. On this occasion the call, through an intermediary, had gone to Peggy.

A few weeks later Peggy came home and told her mother that she had been raped. The police were informed and a woman doctor was called to give an internal examination. She confirmed that Peggy had indeed been raped.

"Who," the police officer in charge of the case asked her, "was responsible?"

"Errol Flynn," she replied. But strangely, the matter was dropped. Perhaps it was all put down to a juvenile flight of fancy. Flynn did not even know the allegation had been made. Now he *was* told, but it would take a little while longer before a hearing could be arranged and so his bail was extended.

He went back to work filming *Edge of Darkness* with Ann Sheridan, but for days he couldn't work and this time neither Milestone nor Jack Warner tried too hard to persuade him to do so. They had a lot of money tied up in the film, but there was no point in haranguing Flynn when he was so obviously down. Besides which, there were other problems worrying the studio. All over the country Flynn films were being booed by audiences. Every time newsreel shots were run, cries went up of "draft dodger". Milestone tried to cheer him by saying: "You know you really are a good actor." He replied: "Don't be silly."

In his way, Errol respected really competent actors, many of whom he knew would never become star material but who with a seemingly magic lilt to their voices could make words come alive in a way that he was never able to do. He did not put himself in their class and that is why he so rarely tried. Often enough when everyone else thought he was concentrating only on a girl or a glass, he would walk over to a bit player to compliment him on a speech well delivered or a movement smartly executed.

He did have more faith in his writing ability, however, and much of the time that dragged so interminably on the set of *Edge of Darkness* he was scribbling.

"What's that?" Milestone asked.

"Memoirs," he replied.

When the court hearing finally got into its stride on 2 November 1942, Betty Hansen told Deputy District Attorney Tom Cochran that she was a movie-struck girl of whom advantage had been taken. She said she had stayed at the party at McEvoy's house because of the talk of her getting a job in films. She did not want to be there.

Under defense cross-examination, she told of her rows with her sister Patricia Marsden and agreed that she had gone to live at the hotel to which she had been directed by the strange man. The Giesler line of defense leading to attack was becoming clear. Betty was not the homespun girl she claimed to be; after all, a man had found her the hotel, a "man I met on the street". Giesler did not try to suggest that she went to bed with him.

Then came Giesler's unexpected breakthrough. Yes, she agreed, she usually did tell people she was eighteen, because that was the age she needed to be before she could get herself a job at the drug store. And, she said, she sometimes called herself Ronnie Hansen.

Just before the end of the preliminary hearing, *Life* magazine
photographer Peter Stackpole gave evidence that Errol had told him
he was being made the victim of a "shakedown".

Stackpole had been on board the *Sirocco* on the night of the
alleged statutory rape of Peggy Satterlee. He had taken photographs
of Peggy – one of which was in colour – which Errol had said he
was going to caption "five thousand dollars".

"Did Flynn ask you to destroy the photos?" asked Cochran.
"No," said Stackpole, "at one time I said I was willing to destroy
them but he didn't insist."

On 6 November Errol Flynn was sent for trial at the Superior
Court. The preliminary trial judge had agreed with the DA that there
was, after all, a case for him to answer. After being released once
more on his $1000 bond, Errol said: "The DA has had the ball so
far. But when I get it, the picture will change. My ultimate vindica-
tion is all that counts and I have complete confidence in the essential
fair-mindedness of the American majority."

On 23 November Errol pleaded not guilty to all charges at the
Superior Court. The hearing was then adjourned until 14 January
1943. That day, the road leading to the courthouse was jammed
with crowds, all waiting to get a better view of this Bluebeard Errol
Flynn. Inside, the marble-walled corridors were equally crowded,
so much so that the police and lawyers working there had to fight
their way in and out of the courtroom itself. There, every public
seat had been taken since the building first opened that morning,
mostly by women who had come both to glimpse their handsome
hero and to gloat at the evidence. Not a few of them left court offering imaginery services to an invisible Errol. "You can take me to
your bedroom any time you like," shouted one who had to be
escorted gently from the courthouse precincts by an usher.

Betty Hansen, wearing a grey sweater and a green floral skirt –
chosen by the defense to make her seem even more mousy than
usual – was the first to go into the witness box.

Errol shuddered as he looked in her direction, doubtless feeling
that the whole allegation was an affront not merely to himself as
a citizen but to both his taste and his very manhood. Seducing a
girl like Betty Hansen did no good whatever for his image.

Betty told Mr Cochran that on the day they met, she and Flynn had shared the same chair and that later she had moved on to his lap. During dinner, she confirmed, she felt ill and went to lie down on a divan, accompanied by Errol.

"He said he was going to take me upstairs and lie me down because I was sick," she told the lawyer.

"What did you reply?"

"I said it would be all right." And, she admitted, she and Errol had gone upstairs together and he had taken her into a bedroom, a room with two beds.

"The next thing he done," she said – the bad grammar was another point in the prosecution's favour – "was to sit me down on the first bed closest to the door."

What, the prosecutor wanted to know, happened then?

"I said I did not want to stay up there. I was feeling all right and wanted to go down and stay with the others. And then he said to me: 'You don't think I would really let you go downstairs, do you?' and I said, 'Yes I do.' I was sitting there and the next thing he done was to walk to the door, and I heard a click and I did not know whether he was locking the door or what."

It was then, she said, that he started undressing her. Betty said she allowed him to interfere with her clothes because she thought that he was just being helpful. The innocent image was building up steadily and effectively.

"He said he was going to put me to bed. And he said he would come right downstairs afterwards and all, and so I thought that was the idea of undressing me and putting me to bed."

"So," asked Cochran, "he undressed you, removed all your clothing?"

"Yes, sir," she replied. "Everything except my shoes."

The judge, Leslie E. Stills, seemed to be having difficulty in hearing her. "Speak up, please," he ordered. She promised to do so.

Her voice was louder when she told Cochran what happened next. "The next thing he done," she said, "was undress himself. He removed everything but his shoes."

Errol with his shoes on! A nice one that for the gossip writers. And also for the publicists of Warner Brothers – if they could turn

away the antipathy that was building up all the time to Errol Flynn
– for when the public was reading of Errol's alleged sexual activity
in shoes, Warners were releasing his film *They Died with their Boots
on*.

Cochran wanted to emphasize the enormity of what had happened. "How were you dressed when you went up there with Mr
Flynn?" he asked.

"I had a sport shirt on, slacks, shoes and stockings." And he had
removed them all. "What undergarments?" Cochran asked.

"Brassiere and panties."

Were the two of them sitting or lying down when it had happened?

"Lying down. The next thing he done," she said after some
embarrassed fencing around, "well, he had an act of intercourse
with me."

The words seemed strange coming from a girl like Betty Hansen
except that it was the kind of phraseology likely to be adopted by
the police in their questioning and she could have remembered it.

It was a strangely innocent age in matters of public morals.

"Do you mean . . ." asked Cochran, "that the private parts of Mr
Flynn were inserted in your private parts?"

"Yes I do," she replied. Afterwards, she alleged that Flynn had
told her to go to the bathroom.

Before she went home that night, she added, Flynn had kissed
her. "He said he would phone me the next night at seven at my
apartment. I asked him if he was sure he would, and he crossed
his heart and said so." She never saw him again until the confronta-
tion at Juvenile Hall.

Under Giesler's cross-examination she confirmed that there had
been no disturbance while she was with Flynn. Neither had she
raised any objections to his behaviour.

He wanted to know if she really had had no idea that Errol was
going to try to have sex with her. "He said he was going to put
me to bed," she repeated.

"Now, when he took off your panties, did you still have no idea
about what was going to happen?"

The process of belittling the witness had begun in full force. The prosecution had demonstrated that she was like the girl next door. Now the defense was trying to prove that even the buck-toothed girl next door knew that a man did not take off all a girl's clothes without having some sort of ulterior motive.

She told him again that she thought Errol had still only intended to put her to bed.

"You did not think then about sexual intercourse?" probed Giesler.

"No, sir, I did not."

That being so, he asked, when did she think about it?

"When I had sexual intercourse with him."

"You mean," Giesler went on, "it wasn't until then that you had your first suspicion that he was going to try to do it with you?"

"That is right," she replied.

"Up to that time you just thought – well, this kindly man is helping me to undress and take my things off so I can lie down because I was sick at my stomach?"

"That is right," she repeated.

At this stage, it was clear where Giesler was going. He was saying in almost as many words that Betty had learned a phoney story but was just a little too dumb to find a way out of it.

Did Betty object when Flynn locked the door behind him? Yes, she said, she did, "because I didn't think he needed to lock it for just putting me to bed."

"And when he commenced to have sexual intercourse, then you knew what he was trying to do?"

"Yes," she told him.

Giesler asked her if she had objected to intercourse. She said she had. "I objected to him being on top of me like that."

But, he said, she had earlier protested that she had no objections. "Why did you object? It was intercourse then, wasn't it?"

"No, sir," she insisted.

He moved ahead in the questioning. "It was before the intercourse began that you objected?"

"Yes, sir," whispered Betty.

"But you had no objections to the intercourse itself?"

"Yes, sir, I had no objections."

He asked her more about her leave-taking of Errol that night.
"You say that Mr Flynn kissed you?"

"Yes," she said emphatically.

"Did he hold you in his arms tightly?"

"Oh, yes."

"There in the presence of the others?"

"Yes."

"Did he kiss you or did you kiss him?"

"He kissed me."

"You did not kiss him?"

"I kissed him back. Just one smack."

"You mean it was not a lingering kiss, it was one of these quickies?"

"It was not lingering."

Betty might have then felt she had acquitted herself well. But Giesler was to get tougher with her.

"Miss Hansen," he said politely, "do you remember after you were taken to Juvenile Hall that you told the officer there that it was easy to get money in this sucker town?"

Cochran objected instantly to the question but the judge said that the defense attorney should go ahead. Betty was stunned: "I never said that. I certainly never did."

Giesler asked her if she had had intercourse with the man who had introduced her to Flynn. She said that she had not, although he had tried several times to do so.

At the end of that day's hearing, Errol was jostled by a crowd of women who besieged the doors of the courtroom. One woman fought her way through the mob to kiss his hand. Another snatched the handkerchief with which he was wiping his brow. "Please," she begged in a high, whimpering voice, "please autograph it for me."

The next day Giesler took the questioning still further. Had Betty, he asked, disrobed in front of two men "to prove that you were a true blonde?"

She said that she had not.

She repeated that when it came to the love-making with Flynn, all that he wore were his shoes. Not slippers, she insisted in answer to another apparently irrelevant Giesler question. "And he kept them on all during the time the alleged sexual act was occurring?"

"Yes, sir," she replied.

"Now how long did the act last?" he asked.

"About thirty minutes."

"And during that entire time he was on top of you?"

"Yes."

"Did it pain you?"

"Yes it did."

"Did you scream or cry?"

"No."

"Did it hurt very much?"

"Not very much."

"During that time did he say anything to you?"

"Yes."

"What did he say?"

"He said ..." This time her reply was less audible or confident than the early answers. Judge Stills asked her to raise her voice.

"He said I had a nice pair of breasts."

"Did he say anything else?"

"Yes," she replied, "he said I had a nice fanny."

Now Giesler was ready with his strongest argument so far. Was it true that Betty was being held at Juvenile Hall for, among other things, being involved in an act of sexual perversion?

There was uproar in the court, and a buzz from the public seats. All the protests of Mr Cochran were now to no avail. The judge ordered Mr Giesler to proceed.

"You hope to be released when this trial is finished and not be prosecuted?" he asked her, but she did not reply other than to nod and even if she had, her answer would have been lost in the general hubbub.

"Think carefully, Miss Hansen. Did you not admit under oath before the Grand Jury that you had performed two acts of sexual perversion with a man?"

After the judge had again overruled Cochran's protests Giesler once more put the question, this time spicing it with one additional detail.

"Did you not testify before the Grand Jury that you committed an act of oral sexual perversion with a man while in a motel room?"

"I did," she replied.

"And, Miss Hansen, did you not admit having committed another act of oral sexual perversion with that same man on another occasion at your residence?"

"I did."

Nobody had suggested that the man was Flynn. The innocent witness needed no explanation of what oral sexual perversion meant and Giesler realized that the fact had registered with the jury. Would such a girl also not know what a man was planning when he undressed her?

To complete his cross-examination, Giesler asked if she had been charged with any offense relating to perversion. She said she had not, although she knew it to be a crime. The man involved, she confirmed, had been charged.

After Betty had sat down, Lynn Boyer, the singer who had been with her at McEvoy's house, was called to the stand. She said that she had heard Flynn answering when she knocked on a locked door.

He had told her, she said: "You can come in if you want to, but I am taking a shower."

"Did you hear anything else on the other side of the door?" Cochran asked her.

"Yes. I heard a laugh or a giggle." It was, she added, a female voice. She knew it was Betty Hansen's.

She was asked about the couple's farewells to each other. She remembered seeing Errol kiss Betty on the lips.

On 15 January 1943 it was Cochran who produced gasps from the public section of the courtroom. He it was who up to then had been fighting the case as if it were the only thing in life that mattered. Now he asked Judge Stills to say that everything that had gone before had been a mistrial.

He said he had affidavits signed by prospective jurors who had been excused before the trial began. These accused two of the chosen panel members of "obtaining their positions by deceit and perjury".

One of the affidavits, from a woman, alleged that before the trial started she had met juror Elaine Forbes, who had told her: "I just must get on that jury. I don't know what I will do if I don't get on that jury." She had also said that she would never convict Errol Flynn. The affidavit said that Miss Forbes had feigned illness so that she would not be called to serve on any jury before the Flynn case came up.

Another woman's affidavit said that Miss Forbes told her: "If we get on the Flynn jury we will fix it, won't we?" She said that one other juror, a Mrs Lorene Boehm, had said: "I am for Errol Flynn in a big way."

By 18 January both prosecution and defense had had a chance to assimilate what the affidavits had alleged and agreed that the trial should go on. Elaine Forbes, secretary to a radio network executive, was excused. Mrs Boehm was allowed to continue as a juror.

The story now switched to the other leading lady in the case, Peggy Lee Satterlee. The alleged offense had occurred, she said, about eighteen months before in Balboa, on the boat. She had gone there with her sister Mickey and with Errol's friend Buster Wiles. There were other girls aboard and Flynn was there, too. Errol had called her "JB", short, she maintained, for "Jail Bait", as though even then he knew he were courting trouble. A name, the prosecution obviously believed, calculated to push the defendant directly into prison.

She had also seen Errol, she said, on board the boat in August 1941. Only the crew was there at that time. On the second night of the voyage – on the first one, she had been left alone in her stateroom – Flynn, in his pajamas, had come into her room. She was wearing a slip and a pair of panties.

"He sat on the edge of the bed for a minute," she said. But she couldn't at that moment produce everything that the prosecution wanted her to say. Her voice was soft and her throat obviously dry. The judge offered her a glass of water.

When, once more, she was asked precisely what had happened, she said: "He got into bed with me. And he completed an act of sexual intercourse, I guess."

"What, if anything, did he do to your clothing?"

"He pulled them down. He pulled my underwear down and pushed my underskirt up as far as my navel."

Cochran again went into the seemingly unnecessary detail of confirming what intercourse meant – "inserting his private parts within your private parts?" – and asked whether she resisted him.

"Well, I resisted at first," she said. "I mean I did not fight or anything. I just told him that he should not do that."

On the night of the return trip, Flynn invited her down to his stateroom, so that she could look at the moon. "So I got up on the bed, the one on the right side, and I looked out through the porthole."

She said she thought that she did see the moon and before long he had pulled her down on the bed again and had taken off her clothes. Once more, they had intercourse and this time there *was* a struggle. "I kicked and I knocked the curtain down. I fought him," she said.

When Giesler's turn came for cross-examination, he asked her why she had not struggled or tried to shout for help the first time.

"I thought about it," she said, "but I did not think it would be worth it, because the people on the boat were all his friends."

"I see," he replied.

Then his tactics began to take shape. "Miss Satterlee, when you decided to look at the moon through the porthole, did Mr Flynn carry you down the stairs?"

"No, sir."

"He didn't pull you or drag you down the stairs?"

"No."

And then he added: "You say that when you tried to get down from the bed Mr Flynn pushed you back on?"

"Yes."

Giesler wanted to know about her state of mind at the time. "You were pretty mad then, were you not?"

"Yes."

It was the beginning of a volley between them.

"You were angry?"

"Yes, I was angry."

"Very angry?"

"Yes."

"When you get that mad you can fight pretty hard?"

"Yes, I was fighting pretty hard."

"As hard as you could?"

"No, not as hard as I could because I was trying to fight and trying to think at the same time."

"I see. Now, Miss Satterlee, did you cross your legs?"

"I don't remember."

"You don't recall crossing your legs?"

"No, I don't. When something like that is happening to you, you do not remember everything."

She told Giesler that since the matter had come to trial, she had stayed at hotels or in the homes of policewomen.

He asked: "Have the lady officers treated you well, taking you to shows and out bowling and on a trip or two?"

"Yes, sir," she replied.

Giesler went on: "Has anything been said to you, Miss Satterlee, about getting you a job when the trial is over?"

"Yes, sir."

That was the point when Giesler pulled out all the stops. He asked her if she had had an operation. She said that she had.

"You know that the operation you had was a criminal act, do you not?"

"Yes, sir."

Peggy Lee Satterlee, still sixteen, was revealing that she had had an abortion, resulting from an affair with another man, not Flynn.

"Miss Satterlee," Giesler went on, "did you ask the District Attorney's office not to prosecute the man involved with you?"

"Yes, sir."

"And did you ask them not to reveal his identity?"

"Yes."

"And did they promise you that they wouldn't prosecute that man if you testified in this case?"

Her answer was drowned in more noise.

The strangeness of the times was never more evident than when Peggy admitted that a forty-three-year-old Royal Canadian Air Force Group Captain, Owen Cathcart-Jones, paid the rent on the apartment that she shared with her sister, Mickey. He had asked her to marry him and had called her pet names.

"What were the pet names?" asked Jerry Giesler.

"It sounds kind of silly," she answered, "but he called me his strumpet."

"I think she must mean crumpet," interrupted Mr Cochran.

"Oh no," insisted Peggy, "I mean strumpet. It is some kind of English muffin."

In further evidence, she admitted that she held a driving license that gave her age as eighteen.

Peggy's sister and mother were called to the stand and asked about money received from Cathcart-Jones. Mickey said she had had small amounts.

A woman police surgeon confirmed that she had carried out an internal examination of Peggy after her mother had taken her to the police station and agreed that it all pointed to the girl having recently had sexual relations.

Cathcart-Jones himself said he had been Peggy's boyfriend, but had never had intercourse with her.

Finally it was the time for the defense to make up its case and the first witness was Errol Flynn. Giesler was plainly worried about the possible effect on the jury of Errol's failure to be in the Armed Services. So the first question was: "What is your draft status?"

"It is indefinite," Errol replied, "pending the outcome of this trial."

"What is your draft classification?" he further asked, brushing aside objections from Cochran which had been overruled by Judge Stills. "4-F," Flynn replied.

He was asked what was wrong with him. "I was told I was in a run-down condition," he replied.

"What were you ailing from?" enquired Giesler.

"I don't know." Even at a moment so desperate, Errol was not going to damage his public image by saying he had a bad heart and was not expected to last out the decade.

He said he had been feeling "off colour" during the voyage of the *Sirocco*. "Feeling very bad. Maybe the drinks we had made me feel a little better. I don't know."

He said he did not know what quarters Peggy had occupied. He had not kissed her on the voyage. "Not even lightly?" pressed the prosecution. "Not lightly or heavily," he replied.

That matter cleared up, Giesler asked whether he had ever called Peggy "Jail Bait". Errol said that he had not. Nor had he called her "San Quentin Jail", another name that had come up in the prosecution's case. Nor, as Peggy had suggested, did he "lace" her milk with rum.

He said that Peggy had come aboard after arrangements had been made for a date with her by Jim Fleming, his stand-in. He knew that the photographer wanted her and another girl to model for a *Life* magazine piece.

About the night on the boat, Giesler asked: "Did you go over to her bed and pull the covers down and pull her underclothes down and have an act of sexual intercourse?"

"I did not."

With Giesler's careful schooling, Errol insisted that it would not be possible for Miss Satterlee, nor indeed for any woman lying on the bed in his stateroom, to see the moon through the porthole.

A statement made by Flynn was read to the court. This said that he had had something else on his mind during the voyage: the loss of Arno. It was the trip on which the dog had disappeared.

As for Betty Hansen, he said it was impossible to lock the door of the room in which the offense was alleged to have taken place, because the lock had been broken for more than a year.

At that, the State called a rebuttal witness, a police chemist who said that scratches had been found on the shank of the lock of that door and that filings that matched the scratches had been seen on the carpet below. But, he agreed, he could not tell how long before then that the scratches had been made.

Errol said in his evidence that he had not asked Betty Hansen to sit on his lap, nor had he gone upstairs with her.

"Did you get into bed with her and perform an act of sexual intercourse?"

"I did not."

"What, then, about her allegations?"

"False. Absolutely false."

He had not had intercourse with either girl at any time, he repeated.

A soda fountain assistant, Mona Mervyn, was called in to say that Betty Hansen had told her about her hopes of one day meeting Flynn and, as a result, of getting a job in the movies.

A sailor on the *Sirocco*, now a Corporal L. Oliver, said he recalled no disturbance during the trip in which Peggy Satterlee was a passenger. Flynn, he said, was at the wheel throughout the journey home. "Did you hear Mr Flynn say jokingly or otherwise that Peggy had *attacked* him?" asked Giesler. "No, sir," said Oliver.

When McEvoy himself came to give evidence, he denied that at any time did Errol go upstairs at his Bel Air home. He and Flynn had played tennis from between two and seven thirty. Errol had then changed and joined the rest of his guests for drinks. Dinner was at eight thirty and Errol left soon afterwards. Yes, he said, Betty had left the table feeling ill during dinner, but Flynn had remained.

The real bombshell of that day came when a former bellboy at the Hollywood hotel where Betty had stayed – "as often as three or four times a week" – said that she told him about the party, but had specifically said that she had not been intimate with Flynn.

The trial had by now become an international talking point, seemingly a subject on every family's lips just as soon as the youngest children were packed off to bed. What was more, it was having some fascinating by-products.

In Washington a Senate committee's hearing was getting an unprecedented following. Hundreds of people queued for admission to the meetings that would decide whether or not the President's choice for Minister to Australia would be approved. His name: Edward J. Flynn.

"Most of the people who went along were disappointed young ladies," said a guard at the Capitol gate.

At the same time a youngster called William S. Buckley, one day to become a right-wing Republican United States Senator from New York, was setting up the American Boys' Club for the Defense of Errol Flynn, so giving a large chunk of support for the Flynn case.

Meanwhile, Mayor La Guardia appealed to the newspapers of

New York to "tone down some of the disgusting details" of the trial that had been filling their columns. He was doing so, he said, not as mayor "but as a parent seeking to avoid publication of such matters in a way offensive or dangerous to impressionable young minds". The National Federation of Catholic Students appealed for newspapers to ignore the hearings, and in the same resolution decided to condemn the practice of birth control.

The place where the trial was being talked about most of all was in the Los Angeles courthouse itself. It was the one subject of conversation in the small shops and kiosks inside the building. At the cigar stand facing the main elevator, a pretty blonde teenager called Nora Eddington chatted about the hearing with her customers and watched admiringly as the still handsome figure of Errol Flynn entered and left the elevator. She couldn't be sure that he noticed her, but there was something about Nora that made its mark on practically everyone who gave her more than a passing glance; her legs. They were the sort of limbs that always made a girl's stockings look more as though they had been sprayed on than were actually hooked to a suspender. When Buster Wiles became a customer, the conversation turned naturally to Errol. He said little about his relationship with the star: merely, in fact, that they were friends, or that he worked for him. If Errol had noticed her himself, he had, Buster told her, neither said so nor given any instructions to say it for him. Wiles was, however, carefully laying the trail. There was a lot about the girl behind the cigar counter that appealed to Flynn. She had little or no bust, but at this stage in his life Errol during his man-to-man chats was showing greater interest in girls' legs than in their breasts.

There are not many men who, when fighting for their very existence – and if he lost this case Errol knew he was washed up professionally and in every other way, too – would devote their nervous energy to the idea of picking up women, yet Flynn was very much thinking along those lines. "But," he told Buster, "*you* must do it for me. Not just yet though."

Perhaps that separated Errol Flynn from other men. Yet he had moments when he reacted as others would, and perhaps with greater cause. Although few people knew it, he was still living out his death sentence. On the doctors' reckoning, he now had just a few months to go. When he thought about that for any length of time and when not even the vodka or the drugs which he surprisingly still kept to a minimum would deaden his depressions he thought of those months and wondered if they were worth wading through. Why not end it all now?

One night he loaded the revolver which was always kept for possible use against an armed burglar and aimed it towards his head. He didn't have the courage to pull the trigger. The next day in court, when the DA made his final speech, Errol wondered again about that gun. But he did no more than wonder.

Back in the witness chair Flynn told the Assistant District Attorney, John Hopkins, that he did not know how old was either Peggy Satterlee or Betty Hansen.

When he came to review his case, Cochran was noticeably tougher than before in his description of Flynn, a man with a high IQ who was an undoubted ravisher of innocent young women. He admonished the jury: "Don't be misled by this man. Don't be misled by his accent, his polished manners and his apparent good breeding. This man is an actor who is paid to give good impressions. There is only one way to find out what this man really is. And that is by studying the laws this man has broken."

He told them that there was only one issue to decide: "Did Errol Flynn have sexual relations with these girls? Nothing else is really significant. You must not think about the possibility that they may have wilfully submitted to Flynn. The law under which we are trying Flynn is designed particularly to protect underaged girls. Under this law, they cannot – and I repeat, they cannot – give their consent to sex attacks!"

For Flynn, he insisted, there was only one suitable place: "This man is a sex criminal. One of the lowest forms of criminal the courts ever come in contact with. A man who preys on young girls! This man must be – and will be – sent to the state prison where he belongs."

It was up to Jerry Giesler, of course, to show that that was the one place to which Errol did not deserve to go. He did so in the way of the master that he was. One of Giesler's main points as far as Miss Satterlee was concerned, was that she could not possibly have had intercourse on a bed and seen the moon through the port-hole at the same time. He told the judge he might ask his permission to take the jury on to the *Sirocco* to prove that point; there were sniggers in the jury box at that, but he did not elaborate.

He was not there, he said, to smear the reputations of the two girls involved. "Smear these girls? I cannot smear them," he said almost sarcastically. "I regret to report that these two girls smeared themselves long before I ever heard of them and they ever heard of me! You heard their own testimony regarding their reputations." One of them, he reminded the jury, had taken part in an illegal act of sexual perversion, the other had had an abortion – this time he was not afraid to use the word.

He summed up Peggy Satterlee's attitude – or rather what he saw that attitude to be – by quoting an imaginary conversation in which she is supposed to have said: "If I testify the right way, maybe nothing will happen to Mr X who caused me to have my abortion. And if I testify the right way, they won't put me in jail either."

As for Errol: "He must not be sent to prison because of their lies. It is your duty to free Mr Flynn and return him to his proper place as one of filmdom's brightest stars. And I know in my heart, as you do in yours, that you will set him free."

The judge, in his summing up, reminded the jury of the strange circumstances of this particular trial. "You must," he said, "regard the testimony of the girls with care and caution. It will be your duty to convict the defendant even should you determine that these two girls invited any acts which may have occurred."

At eleven fifteen on the morning of 5 February 1943, the jury was asked to go out and consider its verdict. All day the jurors deliberated while Errol desperately tried to keep sane, talking almost incoherently about the studio and his boat while Jerry Giesler, with the benefit of years of experience behind him, tried to keep the conversation steered that way – any way, in fact, other than towards the hearing.

Inside the jury room the panel weighed up the pros and cons. All except one admitted they had doubts. The exception was the man who throughout the trial had sat in the number three place in the jury box – Mr Loren B. Curtis. He marked his first ballot "Not guilty" and was not going to be swayed from that for the rest of the time he was in the room.

At nine forty-five, all the jurors agreed they had to be locked in for the night. There was still too much at stake to "rush" a verdict.

So far, they had had six or seven ballots among themselves. By this time they were ten votes to two for acquittal. The two holding out were Charles Boyd and Homer F. Jacobsmeyer. Both said they knew in their minds which way the case should go but needed further discussion.

Most of his time in court, in fact, until the jury had gone out, Errol had sat calm and cool as though it were just another part. Now, at about ten thirty on the morning of 6 February, his courage appeared to have deserted him even more than it had on the day before. Finally, there were three strident buzzes on the bell outside the jury room. It meant only one thing, they were ready with a verdict. For the next half hour, Flynn chain-smoked, lighting a succession of cigarettes none of which he more than partly finished.

Finally at eleven nineteen the jury filed into its box and the foreman Mrs Ruby M. Anderson said yes, they had a verdict on all three counts.

Errol leaned forward nervously as Mrs Anderson handed in the verdict, written on a small piece of paper, to a bailiff who then gave it to Judge Stills. The judge inspected it carefully, but no facial expression was visible to give any insight into what it contained. Then he passed it to the court clerk, who read the verdict on the first charge: "Not guilty." The news was greeted by a roar of obvious and enthusiastic satisfaction from the public seats. The judge had to bang his gavel angrily before the people would be quiet.

All was total silence when the verdict on the next charge was about to be read. Again: "Not guilty." The smile on Errol's face was growing broader. Then came the third. That, too, "Not guilty." The only noise now was from Errol's table.

There was no need for the man who had been on trial to conceal his emotions. From the chair, he patted Giesler on the back and shouted loud enough to be heard throughout the courtroom: "I feel like whooping."

Then, he jumped from his seat and rushed over to Mrs Anderson. It was the first time in all those weeks before the court that he had felt free to walk – or run – wherever he wanted to go. From the foreman, he went down the line of the jury benches, shaking hands with every one of the smiling jurors as he did so.

Peggy Satterlee and Betty Hansen had meanwhile diplomatically left the courtroom, never to be seen in public again. Betty was sent home to her parents in Lincoln and kept quiet about the whole affair.

Peggy was distraught at the news – and bitter.

"They just sat there and looked at him adoringly," she said of the jury. "Just like he was their son or something. They never did believe he was guilty. I don't know what I'm going to do. Here I am two days less than seventeen years old and I feel like a broken old woman."

She went back to her mother's home at Applegate, California, where she was to have another year in high school.

The judge said he was pleased with the verdict.

"The evidence was evenly divided and there was sufficient evidence to warrant a verdict for the people or for the defendant. But viewing all the circumstances of this case, I feel the jury brought in the correct verdict."

"Justice has prevailed," said Jerry Giesler. "We are thankful for a fair and impartial judge and jury."

But what of Thomas Cochran, who had said everything was so sewn up that he and his colleagues were overruling the recommendation of the Grand Jury? "It was my duty to prosecute the case," he said. "And I did so just as honestly as I could."

Many people saw the trial as a political stunt that went wrong and it certainly had about it the smell of a reactionary California establishment trying to fight its biggest taxpayers, the "uncouth" people of Hollywood.

And what about Errol now? Warner Brothers were certain that the verdict could only make him a bigger star than ever. Asked for his reaction now that the gruelling twenty days were over, Flynn replied: "My confidence has been justified in essential American justice. I really mean it. I didn't become an American citizen for nothing. The fair play I received during the trial proves that. I want to thank all those who stood by me during the trial."

Now he could start thinking in earnest about that little girl with the lovely legs at the cigar stand.

10

Green Light

He admired pretty things. He liked to look
at beautiful things – and beautiful girls. He
was a very shy person who had to have
someone to break the ice for him.
Nora Flynn Black

Once Errol had realized that it was all true and he was free at last,
life had both to continue and to return to what he considered to
be a normal pace. That meant more champagne and vodka to drink
and more new girls to take to bed – with one difference: he had
made sure that from now on there would be no problems about a
lady's age. Before he would so much as say "hello" to a girl in future
he would ascertain first that she was at least eighteen.

A few years earlier, he and David Niven had stopped their car
outside a girls' school so that Errol could admire the landscape
as the nubile maidens left for the day. Then, when a policeman
had warned them to move on, he had shrugged and laughed. Now
he would not dare to be seen in the vicinity of such an establishment.

Indeed, he would always – rather than just occasionally as before
– use friends to get over those tiresome introductory details. Buster
Wiles became more of a stand-in than ever.

On the set of *Edge of Darkness*, buzzing with excitement as Errol,
relieved of his courthouse worries, stormed through its final scenes,
Buster waited patiently in the harsh glare of the studio lights while
Lewis Milestone was getting ready for his redeemed star. Then he
would go to wherever Flynn sent him to chat up the girl of his boss's
choice.

From the first, Errol had got Buster to work on the blonde at the cigar stand. "But go carefully, sport," he told him. "Don't give her too many ideas just yet." Without admitting it to himself, there was something about Nora Eddington that made her seem worth more than a night's fling. While the preliminaries with Nora were being worked out, he had other girls to take to bed, but she was the one he wanted.

Buster did his work well. Every day for the six weeks that Nora worked at the cigar stand, he went along to talk to her. They became very good friends. The name Errol Flynn hardly even crept into their conversations. She had told him a lot about herself, that she was half Mexican, that her parents were divorced, that her father was an assistant sheriff – even that didn't put Errol off her scent – and, most important of all, that she had just turned eighteen.

One day Buster said: "Let me have your telephone number." She gave it to him without thinking too much of the possible consequences. "After all," she told me, "he was so much older than I was. And I had a steady boyfriend in the Marines."

As for Errol, his impact on her was practically non-existent. Once he had stopped coming to the courthouse as a celebrity in the midst of a legal battle she had lost interest in him. "I was not star struck," she says now. "It was the very last thing. I couldn't even have told you the colour of his eyes or of his hair." More important, she was now engaged to her marine.

In the meantime Errol had reason to think about other things. The months were passing, it seemed, more rapidly than ever and Raoul Walsh, the director of his first film since the court case, *Northern Pursuit*, knew it. He tried without success to get Errol to think about his health and to toe the line. But every day Flynn came into the studio the worse for wear, suffering from the combined effects of alcohol and of women with whom the term sleeping was a euphemism. Sleep was the one thing he was not getting.

In the picture, Errol played a German-speaking Canadian Mountie being used to penetrate a Nazi spy ring at Hudson's Bay. It was difficult for Walsh to get Errol to show any enthusiasm for the role, which was hardly surprising. It was one of his most

pedestrian to date. "I would hustle him through and shoot a scene
without him knowing it," the veteran director told me.

One day, however, Errol could not be "hustled through". On the
set of *Northern Pursuit*, he collapsed yet again and was rushed to
hospital. There, it was firmly diagnosed that he had tuberculosis.
But the doctors said they saw no reason why, with care, his lifespan
need be anything like as short as he had previously been warned
it would be. Somehow, the unexpected had happened. A new illness
had brought in its wake the news that either the teams of army
doctors had, after all, been wrong or that he had somehow been
able to cure himself.

Predictably, Warner Brothers decided that the one thing they
were not going to do was to release information that their top-
money-making star was consumptive. "He is suffering from his old
respiratory and lung ailment," was all they would reveal. As for
Errol, the advice to take things carefully had about as much impact
on him as would an order to take off to a monastery.

He went to Acapulco to recover, which meant that he did what
he had always done, only a little less thoroughly. In Mexico he did
not have to bother to ask for a girl's birth certificate. Back from
his holiday, Errol told Buster Wiles: "Call Nora. It will make me
feel better."

Buster, as always, did as he was told. But now there was a problem. Nora's telephone number had been changed. She no longer
worked at the cigar stand and when he phoned the sheriff's office,
Buster was told that her father wasn't there either. While Errol had
been busy elsewhere, both father and daughter had changed jobs.
Assistant Sheriff Eddington was in the Navy and Nora had gone
to work at the Lockheed aircraft factory. But neither Buster nor
Errol knew this.

One night, however, Wiles was in a Los Angeles restaurant when
he saw Nora sitting at a table nearby.

"My God," he said. "I've been trying to get you for months."

Almost reluctantly she gave him her telephone number.

Nora was sharing an apartment with a twenty-year-old volup-
tuous redhead called Marie, whom she thought had everything that
she herself did not – sophistication, poise, and the most beautiful

bust upon which a man's eyes could gaze. Together they shared, too, the "graveyard" shift at Lockheed, from twelve thirty to seven in the morning.

She had barely got to sleep one morning soon after the meeting at the restaurant when Buster called. "I'm up at Flynn's," he said. "Come and have lunch."

"I can't," protested Nora. At which point her girlfriend butted in. "I'd love to meet Errol Flynn," she cooed. Nora still said no.

Every day after that, Buster called and every day Nora continued to say no – until finally she gave way. "Listen, Buster," she said. "I'd love you to meet my girlfriend." That, she was convinced, would do it. When Errol saw the redhead with the enticing bust he could not possibly be interested in anyone else. As for Nora herself, "I then weighed 105 pounds and was so flat that I was the type who never wore a sweater." And she was still in love with her fiancé, the marine.

Errol Flynn was never one to be put off by mere obstacles. He was courtesy personified as he met the two girls, one ready to be swept off her feet and into bed by the most handsome and glamorous man in Hollywood, the other hoping to be thought totally oblivious both to the man and the occasion.

He showed them to comfortable chairs, remarked on how charming they both looked, offered them drinks and then casually said to Buster: "Why don't you take Marie down to the farm?" It was like sending a child off to the movies, but Buster, at least, had no reason to complain. Her face and her breasts were everything Nora had said they were.

If Errol Flynn had a reputation as a fast worker, Nora had no reason to believe it at that meeting. He was kind, generous in his compliments, solicitous about her comfort. They talked about her marine. But it was part of a carefully laid plan. She told him that her fiancé had already been shipped out overseas. From that moment on it was just a matter of time, and all of it was on Errol's side. She was won over by his handsome tanned features and that reddish-blonde hair that made him look even younger than his thirty-four years.

On their second meeting Errol told her that he loved her and that he did not believe that a girl of eighteen like her, with such lovely legs, could still be a virgin. "I told him," Nora now recalls, "that if he had any thoughts of going to bed with me, he should forget them."

In the circumstances that was a very forward and intuitive remark for her to have made. She had lived a very sheltered life and as a good Catholic was saving herself for a good marriage, although at the time she may not have known precisely what it was that she *was* saving. She had never been told the facts of life and was not sure what men like Errol Flynn expected. She had warned him against bed without fully realizing that that was precisely what he had in mind.

For a time she agreed to go to work for him as a secretary. But it was clear he wanted more of their relationship than that.

Errol just as clearly wanted to impress Nora. On the first Christmas after their introduction he gave her a Russian sable coat. Her father suggested that she hand it back. "He's out of our league," the former sheriff's officer advised kindly. But when the two men met they shook hands on the agreement that the coat would stay in Nora's wardrobe.

"He could just charm the birds out of a tree," she recalls now.

Once he considered that his charm had had its effect, he popped the question: "Why don't you come and live with me?" To Nora the idea was inconceivable. If she had ever heard of men living with women without a marriage ceremony – and it seems unlikely – it was not something she would ever want to contemplate for herself.

Errol was amused at her naïvety. "Didn't you know, honey, you have been pimped?" he asked, and then, barely able to control the smile that creased his face, told her about Buster Wiles's role in the whole affair. "I was absolutely appalled," she recalls now.

But he had won over the naïve eighteen year old and before long she did go to bed with him. Soon after that she told him she was pregnant.

Everything about his reputation seemed to dictate the next step – a gallant apology to a good "sport" and off to pastures new. Instead, they talked. He suggested an abortion but she said that her Catholic background prevented her even considering the idea.

"Marry me," she pleaded, "just to give the baby a name. But I'll sign any papers you like promising to divorce you immediately after the child is born."

"We won't do that," he said; "let's get married. But don't tell anyone."

It was at that point, Nora told me, she realized he cared, "but also that he wanted to be able to have his cake and to eat it too."

Errol kept very little back from Nora at this time. He even told her about his increasing drug-taking.

"It all started," he told her, "when I first took opium and tried to find out its effects. It knocks hell out of me." But, he said, there was very little he could do about it. "But I'll beat it," he told her. "It won't get to me."

They agreed to go to Mexico for a short civil marriage ceremony which Errol felt sure he could keep out of the papers.

Nora wanted to be married in Acapulco, a town she loved. But Errol thought that was too close to her family for comfort and wanted no one to know about either the marriage or the coming arrival. Even so, it was in Acapulco in August 1943 that they were married. Errol left immediately afterwards for New York. Nora stayed behind, alone.

Her Mexican mother knew nothing of the wedding. Her father had given his blessing and had agreed to keep the secret. Nora neglected to mention that she was pregnant.

Others, however, did know. "Errol was such a stinker," she told me. "There were stories about Errol Flynn's girlfriend going to have a baby and all of his friends knew I was pregnant. Yet all the time, he was dating other girls in New York."

Flynn had not seen her for nearly six months, but he promised to come to Mexico in time for the baby's arrival. By some miracle, as far as Errol was concerned, no indication either of his marriage or of Nora's pregnancy reached the newspapers.

Nora was living in Mexico City. But Errol was as good as his usually inadequate word. He arrived there just before the baby's arrival and immediately panicked as he had never done on a film set, in the jungle, in a fight, or in bed.

"Errol, I'm going to have the child," she told him almost as soon as he ran into the house. "I'm late and I'm going to walk to the hospital."

"Don't do anything," he told her. "Wait there." He called an ambulance and in it she was taken to the American-British hospital.

Errol stayed in the house alone overnight. Next morning he took a cab to the hospital. As he walked through its spotless white corridors he could hear screams – Nora's. She was in labour and fighting with one breath both the pains of the final stages of delivery and the Mexican doctor who believed in natural childbirth. The doctor was delighted at her agonizing progress.

With every push, she shouted at the doctor in Spanish. It was not the sort of thing Errol Flynn liked to hear. As if he were Robin Hood about to rescue Maid Marian in distress, he pushed his way past a startled nurse and tried to burst into the labour room.

By then, the secret of the baby's arrival had percolated through to members of Nora's family. Her stepmother was in the anteroom just in time to pull Errol back. "Here, take these," she said, forcing two sleeping tablets into the expectant father's mouth. Whether he knew what he was taking or not, it did close his mouth.

On 19 January 1944 Nora gave birth to a daughter. They called her Deirdre. If Errol now gave the impression of the doting father, the mood was not to last. He still kept the birth a secret and pretended he was in Mexico on holiday.

His main concern was how to get to the nearest bar. And woman. It was in Mexico City that he met one of Nora's closest girlfriends. "Have you seen Nora?" she asked innocently. "No," he replied in the sort of noncommittal way that only an accomplished actor can really manage. "I've heard she's working as a secretary in New York." Nora got to hear of the meeting: "Of course, in the meantime he screwed her," she told me.

He and Nora decided to wait until they left Mexico City before making any kind of statement. But the matter was taken out of their hands. On 31 January the hospital made the happy announcement themselves: after all, it was very good publicity for them.

The Mexico Federal District Vital Statistics Bureau had recorded the birth of Deirdre, said the hospital, and had named the parents as "Nora Eddington and Leslie Flynn, cinema actor of Hollywood."

Their records showed the couple as having been married the previous August.

Errol was most uncooperative with reporters. "This makes the
third or fourth time I've been reported married in the last couple
of years," he told one of them. "At least, this ought to cop me the
bigamy award next year."

To another reporter who asked if he really was married, he replied: "I don't know. It seems I get married every time I go to
Mexico."

"Did you this time?" pressed the reporter.

"I don't know." He then went off with a pretty girl he called
Joan. "She's an old Hollywood friend," he explained, as much as
to say: "And I haven't married *her* either."

He had never worried before about not getting the girl of his
choice, but now he was concerned that news of marriage could spoil
everything with "Joan" and with all those other girls waiting in line.
As Nora had implied, he wanted to have his crumpet, that strange
kind of English muffin, and eat it too. The baby's arrival had provided an unnecessary complication and he was no more satisfied
by his additional foray into the world of parenthood than he had
been before. Once more a woman had brought him problems and
if the only way to avenge himself was to "use" some other female,
he was ready to do so.

Jack Eddington was contacted too. "My daughter and Mr Flynn
were married in Acapulco in August and I was asked not to reveal
the marriage," said the former sheriff at his naval station. "I didn't
know the baby was on the way," he added, "but I'm overjoyed by
the news of the birth."

Errol, meanwhile, was not exactly overjoyed by the news of
another birth. A twenty-one-year-old blonde called Shirley Evans
Hassan claimed Errol was the father of her two-year-old daughter.
Errol denied the charge, but Mrs Hassan said that she had met him
at a nightclub in February 1940 when she was eighteen – that in
itself was a relief – and had later gone to bed with him. She
demanded $1750 a month.

It was not the only case. Lucy Cassidy in the fan mail department
at Warner Brothers had earlier asked Flynn to look at a letter which

read: "Darling Errol, little Errol is getting to look more like you every wonderful day. He is two days off six months old, would you believe it?"

It was followed by another, much tougher letter. "Have you no heart?" it asked and then accused him of neglecting the child. More notes followed, sometimes six or seven pages long.

Worse was still to come. Alex opened the door of Mulholland House one morning when Errol was at the studio to see a woman standing under the portico. He thought she looked very suspicious, so suspicious that after showing her into the hall, he called the police. When the officers arrived, they found a loaded pistol in the woman's handbag. Later, she admitted that she had been writing the letters to Errol.

The Hassan case was settled more painfully. This girl was not new to Errol. Shirley had much earlier on sued him for assault and Errol had paid $2000 to her mother to settle. The sum had been agreed on condition that Flynn was relieved of all further claims. But this suit, a Los Angeles judge was told, was on behalf of the child, not her mother or grandmother.

The claims, followed by denials, grew menacingly. As far as Warner Brothers were concerned, the only loser was likely to be the studio. They persuaded Errol to put an end to the matter and settle for another $3000. After all, could he really be sure?

11
The Case of the Curious Bride

> *You have to believe that he could be a wonderful loyal friend to a woman and remain so even after so many years. He was always very important in my life.*
> Ida Lupino

It did not need an astrologer to predict that married life for Errol and Nora would be unconventional, to say the least. Neither did it take much knowledge of human behaviour to see that Nora was very much in love with him. How he felt about her was difficult at first to judge. For more than six months after their marriage they were living completely apart.

Three months after the announcement of Deirdre's birth, both of them were fending off reporters' questions about a possible divorce. They were quite reasonable questions, considering that Errol was happily back to his old way of life in Mulholland House while Nora stayed behind with her family in Mexico.

When Deirdre was two and a half months old, Errol did what he thought was his best to put his new wife's mind at rest. "It is highly improbable that we will get divorced," he said. Which really must have caused her heart to flutter. She did not yet know that such words from Errol Flynn were intended as a great compliment.

So far they had not seen each other – or Errol his baby – since the birth. Yet Flynn was now making as many statements denying divorce as he had previously made refuting stories of his marriage. The rumours multiplied when Sam Houston Allen, a Hollywood attorney, said that two men had phoned his secretary declaring they represented Nora Eddington and wanted Allen to handle the divorce.

As for Nora, all she would say was: "I won't say I'm contemplating divorce and I won't say I'm not. I don't know just yet." But she added: "I'm here to see my husband and my dentist." She also revealed which of the two errands she considered the more urgent. "I don't want to be abrupt – but Mexico is awfully hard on your teeth."

There was no question of her becoming a conventional housewife. In fact, she went straight to the home of her father and stepmother, and it looked as though there she would stay. But after a few days, she plainly could take no more. She hailed a taxi and asked to be driven to her husband's house.

Errol was ill in bed when Nora drove up to Mulholland House, and, with baby Deirdre in her arms, was welcomed at the front door by Alex. She was immediately shown into Errol's room. There father met and cuddled daughter. Two days later, Nora and Errol were seen together at the Brown Derby restaurant. It looked as though things were being straightened out between them.

As if to confirm their reconciliation, Errol and Nora announced they were "at home" and gave a luncheon at Mulholland House for the Hollywood set. The idea was specifically so that the guests could meet Nora. Among those who came were Gary Cooper, David O. Selznick, Ida Lupino, Helmut Dantine, Bruce Cabot and Louella Parsons.

The guests asked whether she still thought about divorce. "I don't know what I'll do," she replied. "I may now change my mind."

In his own way, Errol was as much in love with her as she was with him. But it was a strange kind of love indeed. He didn't want Nora and their baby in his house. That was for his own use and he wanted nothing to upset his lifestyle. They would have a home of their own which he intended to visit whenever the mood took him. She accepted the idea reluctantly, and a house was bought.

That state of affairs lasted only until Nora decided she had had enough. She marched into Mulholland House one day and presented Errol with an ultimatum to the effect of: "You either cease being just a casual caller and bedmate or there really will be a divorce this time." Nora won. By agreeing to sell her house and then by asking Nora to bring Deirdre and move into Mulholland with him, Errol seemed to be proving that his wife was, after all, someone special. He had an extra wing built on to the house, but only after one other condition was satisfactorily met.

Before choosing the furnishings for her new home, Nora told Errol: "I know the kind of life you like and I know what goes on at the studios. You can't pass up a pretty face. Just don't bring it to the dinner table. Don't humiliate me."

Errol kissed Nora and promised to be good. She was sure he meant it. The only trouble was that inside that seemingly superbly confident personality was a confused man. The Errol Flynn who had vowed to respect his marital home was the same man who could treat one woman as a princess and another as a doormat; who could make some men idols and others no more than the butt of his practical jokes.

It all fitted in with his decision to take for himself a crest – a strange logo that for ever after would be sewn into all his clothes, appear on his notepaper and fly from the mast of his boats: a square-shaped question mark.

The idea came to him after reading the caption of a Gauguin painting that he saw exhibited at New York's Metropolitan Museum of Art, a place which he made a point of visiting every time he went to the city. Underneath a picture of a group of Pacific Islanders were the words: 'Where did we come from? Where are we? Where are we going?'

He decided that the question mark fitted his philosophy precisely. Certainly it would always be a great conversation piece.

Raoul Walsh saw the uncertain, insecure side of Errol's personality. As he told me, "He was a Jekyll and Hyde character." At home with Nora, he would either be smothering her with love, affection and expensive presents – which he did not do easily, since he hated putting his hand in his pocket for other people – or be bad-tempered and irritable, finding solace in a bottle of champagne, a glass of vodka or a hypodermic needle.

The drinking – and she was content to know that in those days at home he didn't start before noon – did not really worry Nora as much as the drugs. When she realized how deeply they were biting into his body, she was horrified. Why, she begged him, why do it?

"I don't want to leave this world without trying everything," he told her. That indeed was the reason he moved from soft "pot" to the mainline drugs with which he could no longer stop poisoning himself. But he thought he could.

"I can shoot whatever I like into me. I won't let it get to me," he kept saying. But of course it did.

When he went on a self-imposed cure, life was unbearable for Nora and very often she was the victim. At one time she even believed he was trying to kill her. He hit her so badly that her arm had to be reset in a plaster cast. Yet afterwards and with the evidence in front of him, he could only ask: "What happened?"

If, as often was the case, Nora threatened to leave him over his drug-taking, he promised to make an extra special effort. "I'll go away and commit myself," he said. "I'll see that the studio publicity department issues a statement that I'm going away and nobody will know the real reason." But he never went.

It was not just Nora who worried over his narcotics intake. Suspicions about it were rife among the staff at Mulholland House, although probably only Alex knew for sure. Marie, the French cook, discovered the truth and left. She said that she could not live under the same roof as an addict.

Yet when he was not troubled by the guilt and anxiety that drugs brought on to him, Errol found reasons for justifying his addiction.

"You know, Ma," he told Nora, using a quaint middle-aged term for a girl still in her twenties. "Everything is so much clearer with them. I can see better, colours are clearer and more lifelike. I can hear better. I have a better sense of taste and smell and sex is so much more enjoyable, too."

It was not altogether more enjoyable for Nora. "When he *had* to have drugs," she told me, "it began to suffer."

But she added: "That was rare. When we were first married he was a marvellous lover. There was rarely anything inadequate about his love-making."

That appears to refute all the stories decrying his sexual performance that seem to have been circulating – and are circulating still

– ever since Errol had first become the talk of Hollywood. One girl claimed he had to sprinkle cocaine on to the end of his penis to prolong his love-making. Others said he was particularly deficient in size.

He knew about those stories and found strange ways of capitalizing on them. Once in the studio he invited director Vincent Sherman into his dressing room. Errol was completely naked apart from a towel draped around his middle. "Oh, Vince, about that scene ..." he called. And as he talked, he gently allowed the towel to slip – to reveal a gargantuan plastic penis which he had had built for him by Percy Westmore in the make-up workshop.

"Don't say anything, let's see what Alan Hale thinks of this," he suggested and asked Sherman to call in his tearaway buddy. "Alan," he said, "about that scene Vince and I were discussing ..." Again, the towel slipped to reveal the huge phallic object. Hale didn't turn a hair. "I'll take a pound and a half," he said and walked out chuckling.

This was, though, a brief interlude in what was proving to be a very difficult time for Errol, although he didn't seem to be worrying about his career. Nora has said: "He thought he was not too bad, but he knew he was not the greatest. He was not insecure about it though."

He was much more insecure about the personal side of his life which he always regarded as much more important than his career.

Errol was bad-tempered and difficult. Nora, for her part, was giving as much as she was able to take. Whenever she had evidence of his having an affair on the side – and for the first time he *was* keeping quiet about his activities in that respect – she would threaten to leave him, always followed by an emotional appeal to her not to go.

Marriage affected not at all his friendship with people like Hale, Raoul Walsh, John Decker and, more and more now, Bruce Cabot. But there were fewer men in their set. He would change his mind about people as often and as publicly as he used to change his girls. He would tell Raoul Walsh: "I rather like that fellow" and yet perhaps only hours later say: "I don't want to have anything to do with him. Let's go down to the boat."

By now Errol had a new yacht, the *Zaca*, the Samoan word for "peace". The boat had previously been used as a Navy schooner. It had two masts and could either go under sail or be powered by an engine. It was on the *Zaca* that Errol and Nora had their happiest moments. He taught her how to sail and she loved the feel of the ocean swell around them as much as he did. She was the one girl in his life whom he had not importuned on to a yacht's deck for a purpose that was either illegal or, in some people's eyes, immoral, and she accepted the boat as an extension of their home.

He used to love to teach her things. Once she had mastered sailing, he switched to teaching her tennis – a game at which he had become even more proficient as the years moved on. He played in a series of coast-to-coast matches to raise money for America's war effort. Every Sunday, too, Errol and Nora would play with Pancho Gonzales and Bobby Riggs and take bets between them as to who would win. Frequently Errol did.

Errol's home at Mulholland Drive, meanwhile, was gradually taking on the look of an art gallery. His experiences with the Olympiads had trained his eyes to know a valuable painting when he saw one and in the early years of the war his knowledge paid off. He acquired a Gauguin, *At the Beach*, and a Van Gogh, *The Man is at Sea*, both in somewhat suspicious circumstances. He paid a great deal of money for them; nobody disputed that. But there were rumours that the pictures had found their way to America after being looted by the Nazis in Occupied Europe and smuggled out via some neutral country.

In 1944 he took his art expertise a stage further. He and John Decker opened the Decker-Flynn Gallery at 1215 Alta Loma Road in Beverly Hills. It would be specializing in work by Impressionists and post-Impressionists. Errol put his Gauguin and Van Gogh on show there too. "I've gone into this business," he said at the celebrity-attended opening, "because I love paintings and want to make them available to the Hollywood folk." He also thought he could make a buck or two. Lili's alimony demands were growing more and more painful and he needed every potential money-maker he could get.

Errol with his daughter Rory.

Errol and Nora on board the *Zaca*. They loved sailing together and the boat was their favourite home – until Nora discovered that other women enjoyed going there too.

Errol the charmer – and the good friend. With Alexis Smith who "adored" him.

Errol and "the Geek", Princess Irene Ghila, who was his fiancée for some time. He had grown the beard for *Kim*.

Cutting the wedding cake with his third wife, Pat, in Monte Carlo in 1950. A few minutes later, Errol was served with yet another writ charging him with rape.

Errol certainly admired Decker's talent and showed that appreciation with a strange generosity not detected by other friends. He bought him a house. Decker, on the other hand, seemed to worship Errol. Nora to this day thinks that he was subconsciously in love with Flynn and resented any girl who entered his "lover's" life. "I wouldn't let him paint me," she says. "I was sure he would have snakes crawling all over my body."

The gallery, said one newspaper, was "within raw-egg throwing distance of the Mocambo". An apposite thought, since only days before Errol had got involved in yet another fight at the famous Hollywood night spot.

This one was mainly between two women, one a wealthy southern girl called Virginia Hall, the other a blonde singer named Toby Tuttle. Errol was at the club that night with Fred McEvoy, the second occasion when their relationship landed him in the midst of a squabble. It appeared this time that Toby had said something that Virginia did not like, and Errol just happened to be sitting nearby. But he had to agree he was enjoying their tiff immensely. "Why don't you do something about it?" yelled Toby and threw an egg at Errol's head. The yoke ran down his face while he protested that he wanted to stay out of any more public fights.

He should have known that any fracas in which he was involved was likely to become public property. If there were other celebrities present, it would be an assured fact, for not only were the gossip columnists around anxious to sniff out the slightest whiff of scandal, the stars themselves were fighting a running battle to keep their names in print.

The chandeliered home of David O. Selznick, the tycoon who had made history with *Gone with the Wind* and was currently riding high with successes like *Duel in the Sun*, was watched by the Hollywood press corps as though it were Fort Knox under siege.

Whenever he held a party, it was an event when something was likely to happen. With Errol Flynn there, it was simply a question of when.

On a hot summer's evening, with stiff-shirted waiters passing trays of champagne in crystal glasses from guest to guest and with canapés daintily served by waitresses in black dresses and little lace

aprons, a Selznick party was proceeding smoothly and entertain-
ingly. But because it was a hot night, one guest after the other sought
excuses to go out on to the terrace and then on to the manicured
lawn of the Selznick garden.

Errol was talking to John Huston, already a film director of note,
but still always referred to as the son of Walter Huston the veteran
actor. Both of them had had rather too much to drink and their
conversation was getting animated.

With olde-worlde courtesy, Errol suggested: "If you would be
kind enough, sir, to follow me, we'll step outside off this property
and into the nearest public thoroughfare."

It was on the spacious front lawn of the Selznick house that Huston laid the first blow on Flynn.

The ground shook as one strike followed the other, first knocking
down Huston and then Flynn. As one got up, the other went down.

Finally, Flynn called out: "John, John for the love of Mike, don't
get up again."

"That," said Huston afterwards, "was when I knew that I had
him."

They were both taken off to the Cedars of Lebanon Hospital with
assorted injuries and were detained overnight. Thereafter, they both
claimed to be the best of friends and not to know why they had
scrapped in the first place.

"I haven't the least damned idea," Huston told Flynn later. "I
thought you knew."

"Well," Errol returned, "maybe that's the best way to get into
a beef and I'm terribly sorry." Huston said he was sorry too. "We
must do it again, sometime. I sort of enjoyed it."

Errol was not necessarily enjoying his bouts with Nora. And they
were not always over his women. As Nora told me: "He was a man's
man. He would rather spend an evening with a group of drunken
buddies than go with a broad upstairs for a quickie."

Other people, of course, were now fighting a far more serious war,
one that in Europe was finally ebbing away but which looked like
going on for a generation in the Pacific. They no longer talked about
Errol's escaping from the battle. Any idea that he could pick up
arms on behalf of his country was plainly ridiculous: he was known

to be frequently ill and the drugs he took were exacting their toll. Warner Brothers, however, were conscious of his continuing status as a civilian. Finally in 1944, they persuaded him to "go north young man". For six weeks, accompanied by a motley band of magicians, acrobats and singers, Errol toured American bases in Alaska.

They covered 10,000 miles giving a series of impromptu shows. "The boys want nothing more than a shot at the Japs," said Flynn when he had comfortably returned to civilization. "If they get that, they'll settle for some more of the kind of shows we give them."

"The morale of the boys leaves you breathless," said Errol, who had made his usual good impression as a "man's man". As a mark of gratitude, the troops presented him with a blue fox which he named "Tundra Lil".

As far as a lot of people were concerned he was doing his fighting bit by playing the hero on the screen. Each role seemed as marvellous a propaganda ploy now as when he made *The Sea Hawk* in 1940. But "in like Flynn" began to be a disparaging term. On screen, however, he was always the brave one who wiped out the enemy single-handed.

The trail that began with *Dive Bomber* continued in late 1944 with *Uncertain Glory*, about a French criminal who finally does the brave thing and is executed in place of a resistance hero. It was another one of those pictures in which Raoul Walsh had to guide Errol, grabbing whatever he felt like delivering, and in this instance it was not much.

Objective Burma, however, was the last of the bunch. If an assortment of British ex-service organizations, newspaper columnists and one powerful cartoonist had had their way, it would have been the last of Errol Flynn, film star.

Warner Brothers, of course, had no inkling of that when they made the picture. The film, it was decided by the company's business office, should be given the big splash treatment, starting with a special press showing in New York in the presence of the star.

Jack Warner called in Walsh for consultation – not the only occasion when the director would be asked to act as an intermediary between the studio chief and the man who was proving ever more difficult. Warner couldn't talk to Flynn directly any more. Only days before, Errol had gone into his office carrying a bucket marked "tears". He said it was for use next time the studio cried poverty.

Now Warner was anxiously pacing the carpeted floor of his magnificent study, the kind of wood-panelled inner sanctum intended to both provide comfort for its owner and to inhibit his visitors.

When Walsh arrived, Warner was looking very worried indeed. "Irish," he told him, stabbing the air with his index finger. "I want you to take care of this guy. See that the SOB meets the press and that he doesn't spend his time just drinking." From a man like Warner who had a reputation for hating actors in general – the lifeblood of his organization – and Flynn in particular, it was a remarkably mild order.

The luxury train journey to New York, the accommodation on the forty-second floor of the Waldorf Tower Hotel and everything Flynn and Walsh could possibly need was charged to Warners. As soon as he arrived, Errol ordered twelve bottles of Johnny Walker whisky, ten of vodka and another ten of gin.

That night, a Wall Street broker phoned, inviting Errol to a party. "I've got a one-eyed bandit with me," Flynn told him. "Great," said the man, "bring him along." Raoul Walsh told me the rest of the story and it was plainly an evening to remember.

No sooner had Errol arrived at the party with Walsh than his eyes started wandering: sizing up the women, both those attached and the ones who were available. Finally, he selected one whom he was convinced was just right for him. She was not merely beautiful but also, as he could tell from the jewels shimmering on her magnificent bosom, very, very rich.

With two glasses of champagne in his hand, he walked over to the lady and, giving a slight bow, offered one of them to her. She smiled sweetly at him. It was obvious she was flattered by his attentions.

"You look so beautiful," he told her, kissing the hand not holding the champagne glass. "I just had to meet you." It was no more than the truth.

As the one-eyed bandit puts it now, "He fell for her hook, line and sinker."

"Have dinner with me tomorrow night," he asked. "Please."

It took no more than a glance at that handsome face for her to agree. When Errol heard that, he felt like a schoolboy allowed to carry home a girl's books. "Would you excuse me for a minute?" he asked, and when she gave her permission for him to leave, he found the nearest telephone and dialled the flower shop at his own hotel. He ordered three dozen red roses to be sent immediately to her home. And then he casually added: "Charge it to Mr Warner's account."

Day after day he plied her with presents: hundreds of dollars' worth of chocolates and bon-bons and then the *pièce de résistance*, two poodle pups. At $500 each, charged, of course, to Warners. Walsh asked him if he thought he ought to be quite so rash at the studio's expense. "The hell with them," he replied. "I work hard for them and they've got to pay me."

For a whole week he courted this girl like a (millionaire) teenager experiencing the first flush of romance. Then the blow came. "Uncle," Errol told Walsh, "it's all off. She won't have me." For the first time in years, Errol Flynn had been sent packing by a woman. The indignity of being overthrown was almost as tough as the pain of losing the girl with whom he really felt smitten. Forgetting all past conquests, he could only think that this was his old rejection problem. What was there about him that made the women he really wanted unavailable? His depression was real and deep.

He wrote her six letters and she replied to none of them. She wouldn't even answer the phone. "I don't know what to do, Uncle," he told Walsh, sitting on a leather chair in his hotel suite. "I'm going to jump out of that window." With that, he walked across the room and began to fiddle with the catch on the window, forty-two floors above Park Avenue. He had done it a dozen times before on film but never as convincingly as now. Even Walsh, who had had to guide him on the set of *They Died with their Boots on* like a Boy Scout taking an old lady across the road, was convinced by the way in which he was acting out this scene without direction.

"Wait," said Raoul, pulling him away from the window. "Don't do it. Leave this till tomorrow."

But Errol was pleading now, with real tears in his eyes. "Uncle," he said, "you're my greatest friend. Will you talk to her for me?" With that, Walsh put on his hat and went downstairs.

As he told me: "I went into the bar and thought, 'What the hell can I do? How can I bring them together again?' Then, downstairs, having a drink, it hit me."

He went back to Errol's room. "Did you see her, Uncle?" Flynn queried.

"Yes," Walsh lied. "I did."

"Did you tell her I was going to jump?"

"Yes."

"Well, what did she say?"

"She said: 'I'd like to know what time he's going to do it so that I can come up and watch.'"

That solved the problem. Flynn's expression changed from one of desolation to a look of sheer anger. "You can't trust these society bitches," he said and poured himself out a large glass of vodka.

Back in Hollywood, Jack Warner passed all the accounts except one. "What did the son of a bitch want the poodle pups for?" he demanded.

"Well," said Walsh without answering the question, "I stood on the corner and sold them."

The studio felt it had sold *Objective Burma* even more effectively. They did excellent business with the film in America. What they did not anticipate was the reaction it was to receive in Britain. Not only in this film did Errol Flynn appear to be the lone victor of a campaign that had for months constantly been in the newspaper headlines, but he did it in an American uniform leading a small band of Americans without any mention of British participation.

Now, when this had happened before, few people did much more than sneer derisively or giggle to themselves about the gullibility of Hollywood and the customers who paid to see its products. *Objective Burma*, however – and to make things worse, it first appeared in London under the title *Burma Victory* – was different. Both the film itself and Errol's subsequent reaction to the resultant uproar showed a marked insensitivity.

Britons could take films about Americans winning in the Philippines, because that was an essentially American "show". They didn't worry very much, either, about the films of the Normandy landings: the American participation there had been colossal and most people had the sense to realize that films were made with American markets in mind. But Burma was a whole different sort of war. It represented the courageous stand of the British to keep the Japanese out of India. The men of the 14th Army who took the brunt of the Burma campaign were often talked of as the Forgotten Army, cut off from the mass media until the dying months of the war. Then, they suddenly came into focus. Newsreel film showed emaciated, bare-chested troops up to their ribs in mud, carrying rifles above their heads while sweat poured remorselessly down their faces. The men who had come back from the campaign spoke of the living hell to which they had been subjected. And now they were being told that the battle had finally been won largely thanks to the help of Errol Flynn! It didn't bear thinking about.

The *Daily Mirror* in London spared a half page of its desperately precious newsprint – paper rationing meant that it printed only eight tabloid pages a day – for a cartoon by Philip Zec. In this, Errol in US battle uniform was sitting on a canvas chair bearing his name, surrounded by a sea of crosses and the figure of a lone ghostly soldier saying: "Excuse me, Mr Flynn. You're sitting on my grave." The London *Evening Standard* was kinder than most. Its critic wrote about the film: "This would have been a very good picture about something else."

Errol was totally unaware of the trouble until a flustered employee of Warner Brothers' publicity department came racing after him on the set of his next picture *San Antonio*, telling him the news. Errol replied in his usual laconic vein. "Son," he said, "why don't you just go home and lie down for a little while? Have a watercress sandwich and smoke a marijuana cigarette and I'll see you tomorrow." He was amazed that it had caused such a row. "I think it's a very good piece of picture making," he said more seriously a day or so later. "We weren't out to prove that the United States won Burma. We just wanted to tell a simple story about guts."

He was partly right, and so was the *Evening Standard*. It could have been one of the best war films of all those produced at the time, but the subject matter made it seem just callous. The film was withdrawn.

The American press could not understand the fuss. A New York *Herald Tribune* writer commented: "I think it is absurd to withdraw it. I am strictly against censorship in any form and at a time like this it is very dangerous to say a certain thing is or is not the proper propaganda angle."

The New York *World Telegram*'s Burton Rascoe thundered that the withdrawal

"is a pusillanimous act of the gravest consequences. There was no official ban by the Home Secretary or by any other British authority.... Some silly, petty-minded British movie critics objected to the film on narrow nationalistic grounds because the American film dealing with the accomplishment of an American unit in Burma did not include quite another story about the work of the 14th British Army."

As for Warner Brothers, they dismissed the whole film as "just movie hokum – typical Hollywood stuff". A spokesman said, "There was never any intention to make it a factual picture."

If Errol was worried at the time, he showed it no more than he demonstrated his concern over the numerous quarrels with Nora. She was still trying to make up her mind whether to go or stay. Countless times she assembled her things, and just as many times Errol begged her to remain. Once she even got as far as telling a newspaperman: "All the love that I have for Errol is gone – completely. What I want to do now is get a job. I'll file for divorce – probably here in Hollywood. I feel that Errol should make adequate provision for our child." But she decided to stay just the same.

Errol was coughing a lot, but he did not cut down on smoking from his attractive cigarette holder any more than he reduced his intake of drugs – which occasionally had the effect of making his eyes look as though they had parted company with the rest of his body.

Occasionally, he and Nora talked about the future – the distant future, Nora believed, but Errol thought he knew differently. "When my time comes, Mum," he told her, "don't bury me in

Forest Lawn with all those Jews." It was at emotional moments like these, as when he had his toughest rows with Warner, that his prejudices rose to the surface. They were the moments, too, when it became obvious his life was taking a different turn to the one he would have chosen. Time would prove he was going to be cheated even at his funeral.

12

The Sea Hawk

At times he could be really charming. But if he had a little drop too much champagne, he was terrible.
Raoul Walsh

To a film set, that unreal world of half rooms and plasterboard streets, Errol brought new tensions and yet new joys, too. Tempers could be fraught, the heat agonizing, and the boredom excruciating, yet the mere presence of Errol Flynn on the lot somehow made a number of people feel better.

With Alexis Smith as his co-star in *San Antonio*, his first Western since *They Died with their Boots on*, he was demonstrating both that he wanted to enjoy himself, and that he cared for Alexis's welfare. If he thought director David Butler was demanding too much of her, he made it very plain he was on her side. "Steady, old sport," he would tell Butler, "the lady's only human." She, for her part, did her best to cover up the excesses of his drinking, which was anything but easy.

Seeing him arrive on the studio lot was not a pretty sight. Staying up all night at parties drinking either his host or his guests under the table, he would get in the following morning red-eyed and with blotches disfiguring the otherwise still magnificent face. Yet even so, he was nearly always almost on time. I say almost, because any suggestion of Errol being completely punctual would have necessitated an immediate boardroom conference at Burbank to discuss such an earth-shattering development. But he was going through a conscientious patch now. That did not mean that he was not perpetually suffering from either a hangover or the remains of a drunken stupor, and the way Alexis tells it now for the first time, his condition involved the most unlikely people.

It was she who came to a deal with the service boys who hovered around film sets providing actors and technicians with whatever their whims dictated. She arranged for them to keep Errol supplied with a constant flow of hot black coffee, which they appeared to do. But no matter how many cups of coffee Errol drank, the worse he became.

No one knew at the time that Errol had made his own deal with the boys. For an agreed fee they had arranged to lace the coffee with brandy. David Butler was totally mystified by the whole affair. When he realized that Alexis had apparently taken the matter in hand, he was full of praise and support. But he just could not understand why Errol was behaving so strangely. Black coffee had been known to work slowly on occasions, but to make a man even more drunk?

Finally, Butler decided he needed medical advice. He called a halt to the filming and ordered the studio doctor to attend his star. "Do what you can, doc," he said and ushered the slightly worried physician into the Flynn dressing room, just down the corridor from the sound stage.

Outside, Butler waited patiently for the medical verdict. When producer Robert Buckner heard about the consultation, he, too, came along, with a parade of lesser executives in train. Half an hour went by, then an hour. But there was no sign of either the star or the doctor. Executives walked backwards and forwards outside the dressing room like fathers awaiting the first cries of their new-born babies. But still no Errol – and worse, still no doctor. Finally, the door opened to reveal the medical man swaying and staggering as he tried to push his way through the throng. Like his patient, he was blind drunk. Inside, a very happy Errol Flynn raised his glass in salute.

Another time, Errol announced he had given up drinking altogether – and to prove it had a crate of oranges delivered to his dressing room. No one knew that he also had a hypodermic syringe with which he had injected each orange with a shot of vodka.

Despite all this, *San Antonio* managed not to look as though its main star had spent much of his time in a state of intoxication. Said Bosley Crowther in the *New York Times*: "When a studio spends a couple of million dollars on a Western as the Warners spent on *San Antonio*, you might expect something more original than the picture now showing at the Strand." But, he added, there were just "a couple of gunfights fit to make your hair stand on end and some running chases on horseback which are good for a few minutes' sport. It is plain enough where the money spent on this picture went. It went into settings and mob scenes that are the fanciest we've ever seen – at least in a Warner Western.... Errol Flynn," he added, "plays the hero with his usual dash and aplomb."

After *San Antonio* the Flynns packed up and went to Mexico for a short holiday, where Errol drank even more than usual and experimented with a few new drugs. If he felt under the weather, he would go to a doctor and say: "I need a shot of vitamins. So mix it with something else." In Mexico it was easy to ask and, if you paid, just as easy to get done.

Nora, meanwhile, would threaten again to leave him and would begin to pack her bags. As she told me: "Then, he would look at me and I'd see his pupils dilate." It was not, she would decide, the moment to go, because his buddies or the crew of the *Zaca* certainly wouldn't be able to help him. The merry-go-round continued.

Nora talked of working in films herself and Errol mentioned the idea of featuring her in a major film. Warner Brothers were not, however, ready to sign another Flynn for a big production. So Errol decided to shoot one of his own on the *Zaca*. As things turned out, it was Nora who was almost shot, together with a cabin boy, and the whole thing in the end resembled a miniature mutiny on the *Bounty*.

In truth, it started because Errol was having yet another tussle with both the Department of Internal Revenue and Lili Damita's lawyers, who were making noises about the $1000 he was now supposed to pay into her bank account every Friday to make up for his arrears. With the help of his financial adviser Al Blum, Flynn figured that if he could find a way of using the *Zaca* for business, the whole floating palace would be written off as a tax loss.

He did not just say he was going to make films and look after his movie interests on board the yacht. No, he was much more subtle. "How about," he thought, "using it for a scientific expedition?" With that, he invited his father to come to California. An invitation that was enthusiastically accepted.

It was the first meeting between Errol and his parents since before the war. After even mother and son had embraced without any apparent discord and the two men had also warmly hugged each other, they set about announcing to all who would listen the purpose of the trip. With the professor dressed in his white coat to add a certain authenticity to the exercise, Errol called a press conference to reveal that his father and Professor Carl Hubbs of the La Jolla Scripps Institute of Oceanography were going to search the seabed between Los Angeles and Acapulco and would go on from there to the Caribbean. The destination of the cruise and the fact that John Decker was on board should have made the pressmen suspect the worst. But none did.

"I'm interested in the quality of the plankton," said the professor, after explaining his qualifications as a marine biologist. "According to the distribution of plankton, fishing is good or bad," he told them. Everyone believed him when he said he was going purely as a scientist.

Mrs Marelle Flynn decided to stay behind in Los Angeles, experiencing the novel delight of being a grandmother to Deirdre. On the voyage, the professor did, indeed, discover three new kinds of herring, which he called the Nori, after his daughter-in-law (nobody bothered to ask whether or not she considered it a compliment), the Erroli and the Zaci, but this all turned out to be by-the-by to more human discoveries, the most important of which was that Nora did not get on with either the crew or some of the passengers.

For Nora once more was pregnant and while other expectant mothers are merely sick and demand sardines and marmalade to eat, she took over the helm of the *Zaca*. This did not please the crew one bit. The captain, newly acquired for the voyage, had early on made clear his objection to taking orders even from Errol, but had finally come round to accepting Flynn's undoubted expertise.

Nora, on the other hand, was something else. She was on the cruise mainly to act as the star of the picture that Errol was shooting with a 16-mm camera. But the crew were not to be pacified. The *Zaca* might be only an 118-foot schooner, but the sailors were old salts, barnacled with all the superstitions of the sea, and having a woman on board spelt trouble. They were not wrong, although the trouble at first seemed to be all for Nora.

It was a choppy sailing, with rough high seas knocking even the most experienced sailor from one side of the cabin to the other. As one particularly huge wave tangled with the boat, Nora fell down a companionway and for a day or two feared she was going to lose her child. But she insisted on not being put ashore.

Then, the seventeen-year-old cabin boy, Wallace Berry, touched a harpoon a little too eagerly and shot the spear-like weapon into his foot. Now, you can't pull out a harpoon as though it were a pin in a cushion. It has to be cut away. The only kind of doctor on the trip was Professor Flynn, who was used to dissecting animals that were already dead.

Yet with Errol administering the prescribed amount of ether from the boat's first-aid cabinet, the professor performed the operation. He was assisted by Errol's archer friend, Howard Hill, the man who had taught him to use a bow and arrow in *Robin Hood*. They removed the harpoon and Berry was left sleeping peacefully.

Flynn decided to put into Acapulco ten days earlier than had originally been scheduled. There, a doctor looked at the foot of the young Mr Berry and congratulated his "surgeon". "You have undoubtedly done a very good job," he told the professor. "Had you not been so prompt, he would have lost more blood and developed gangrene." The fact that this had not been the only problem became clear when John Decker left the boat just as soon as a gangplank could be lowered, vowing never to return. Nora was the one who had been giving all the orders, he said, and he didn't like it any more than had the crew who disembarked with him. At once, the papers dubbed Mrs Flynn Captain Nora Bligh. The whole affair naturally enough was called *Mutiny on the Zaca*.

The professor was quick to come to Nora's aid. "She was no more of a Captain Bligh than any hostess would be with a troublesome guest," he declared. The "troublesome guest" in this instance was John Decker, who he declared had demanded more than his share of ice. "The man is an exhibitionist. He wouldn't be tolerated in England. The truth is that our supply of ice and water was limited. We had work to do. And I don't have to tell you what he wanted ice for." The suggestion, for those who did not immediately understand it, was that Decker was drinking more than was good for him, certainly more than was good for the professor.

Predictably, Decker was angry at the allegation. It fired his artistic temperament and insulted his integrity. "I'm diabetic," he raged, with a drink in one hand and a paintbrush in the other. "I take insulin shots. That's why I had to get to the ice box."

Meanwhile both Nora and the ship's cat Besnovitch were suffering from the effects of acute sea sickness. The yacht set off without them for a tour of the Mexican islands. On board were just Errol, the two professors and a couple of sailors who had decided that their sea biscuits were better secured with their ship's owner than with their captain.

Back at Acapulco, the scientists went ashore, while Errol – his next film now a dreadful prospect that would be made solely to keep Warner Brothers, their lawyers and his own bank manager happy – set sail again, this time through the Panama Canal and then on to waters unknown. He had planned to sail through the Caribbean watching the sun during the day and the stars at night. But for two days, Captain Flynn and his beloved *Zaca* were lost. When they finally spotted land, it was the coast of Jamaica, the beginning for him of yet another love affair, only this time with a piece of real estate.

It was his first visit to the island and everything about it seemed appealing: its landscape, its climate, its people. It reminded Errol of New Guinea. He doubtless again thought of nubile girls with black skins frolicking happily in the sun. But the one relationship he briefly built up while there was with a white woman.

He proposed marriage to her. "I'll divorce Nora," he said, not for the first or the last time. Both of them were to think better of it, however. Even if the lady and he had not consummated their relationship, from that moment on he and Jamaica were of one flesh.

Soon he had found a lawyer, had got the necessary documentation organized and bought himself an island – Navy Island, in the harbour of Port Antonio. He paid $80,000 for it.

As the *Zaca* lay at anchor off the shore, he set about surveying his new kingdom. Errol was now not merely in another country but in another world. There, he sat on the grassy slopes and thought about the future. He would build a house, and not just for himself. A letter went off to Los Angeles where his parents were settled and in it he suggested that they come and live on the island, too.

"Just the place for an oceanography lab," he wrote his father, whom he knew was shortly to retire from his Belfast Chair. "This is a dream spot where we can all live like kings."

Indeed, it seemed so. The island had a small village inhabited by forty natives, a boat shed, a large cottage. Hurricanes had taken their toll but there were still vestiges of the palm groves and of the banana and mango trees with which it had once been thick. Errol also became the owner of a huge document – the size of an open broadsheet newspaper – which stipulated he was not to build any forts on the island. He was determined that irrespective of whether, by and by, he and Nora would decide to settle down or to part, the island home would stay his for ever.

In March 1947 they both agreed to make a go of their marriage for as long as they could. At St Joseph's Hospital, a stone's throw from the Warner studio at Burbank, their second daughter was born. They called her Rory.

Errol was thrilled both about her and about the film he had shot on the *Zaca*. He had added his own soundtrack and had sold it to Warner Brothers. It was not to be released for another six years. *The Cruise of the Zaca*, as it became, was one of the good things about Errol's film career. There were not many others at that time.

It was plain that his life as a film star was in decline. For years he may have protested that he was no actor, but now it was becoming painfully obvious that he was bored by his work. He admitted that he "walked" through most of his pictures. Sometimes, watching him at this time, it seemed more like sleep walking.

His mental energies were being reserved for his writing, which he did now much more happily and more capably. He had just produced a novel called *Showdown*, a story, like *Beam Ends*, based on his time in the South Seas. Now he was planning a third book which he said would be "autobiographical around the edges". He was calling that *The Good Deserving Girls*. It would be mainly about Hollywood.

Errol set about being a good father, changing the babies' nappies and giving parties for them when they were old enough to appreciate the ballyhoo, for a Flynn children's party had to be more than the conventional assortment of ice cream and balloons for the guests to take home. The house was decorated like a film set and the entertainers who came to keep the children and their friends amused were from the cast list of Warner Brothers. There would be no mere out-of-work actors for *his* children. He had to have the best even if that were not usually the prescription for his pictures. *Never Say Goodbye* with Eleanor Parker made many a critic wish that that was exactly what Flynn would do. It was about a divorced couple who still loved each other almost as much as they adored their daughter.

Cry Wolf, Errol's first picture of 1947, had a title that was almost too inviting. If the studio had been pretending for years that Errol was just a handsome fellow with a lot of muscle, few wanted him to be anything else. This attempt at a serious role, playing the tough head of a family who melts only with the appearance of Barbara Stanwyck, was just asking for trouble.

The Errol Flynn story continued on what were more or less predictable lines, and for anyone who wanted the titles of his pictures to plot the progress of that story, the next one was made to measure: *Escape Me Never*.

It was made just as Nora had yet again decided to leave Errol, taking the two children with her, and when he had once more tried to persuade her not to do so. The film's story line was centered on the Swiss Alps and turned out to be the usual tug-of-love triangle, again featuring Eleanor Parker, but this time with the added advantage of having Ida Lupino around.

Ida was another of the Warner girls to come under the spell of Errol. Now she recalls with a deep love the memory of a man who was always more than just an actor or a companion for a night of fun, and who, as with Alexis Smith, showed her a respect that would have been tarnished by a mere affair. Other people think of Flynn affectionately. Ida Lupino still bitterly regrets turning down a proposal of marriage from him. The way she told me of their association, the sort of love he showed her was the kind he had for no other woman. She was, by her account of the relationship, the only female likely to qualify for membership of the Olympiads.

She was even given a nickname by the other members, and no finer sign of acceptance could there be. To "Uncle" Raoul Walsh and "the Baron" Errol, Ida was "Little Scout" or sometimes "Idsie". Even her mother was part of the scene. She was called the "Duchess".

Once, in the Warner commissary "the Baron" told Ida: "Little Scout, if you're ever in trouble, I'm the person to call in – and you know I would trust you with my life." It was a sincerely meant offer. Like all Flynn offers, it was a two-way affair. He knew that he might at any time need to call in the "Little Scout" to his own aid.

It was at three o'clock one cold morning when he decided he had to do so.

Errol was alone at Mulholland House because Nora and the children had finally gone, although for how long he didn't know. What he did know was that he thought he was dying. He had emptied a bottle of vodka, had pumped his arm full of one drug or another and could barely walk across the room. But he did, with considerable effort and agony, manage to get to a telephone and summon up just enough strength to dial Ida's number.

He had difficulty in forming his thoughts, but he could just stammer a sentence into the mouthpiece when she came on the line.

"Come quick, Little Scout," he said, almost whimpering. "I need you." The terminology had gone beyond a mere game. They now both used it as naturally in conversation as lovers use affectionate pet names and as children call their parents "Mummy" and "Daddy". On this occasion, he was employing it as a sign of sheer desperation.

In between gasps for breath, he gulped, "Little Scout, for God's sake help me. I don't think the Baron is going to make it through the night."

Ida promised to come immediately. She grabbed her coat and

called out to her mother: "Duchess, the Baron needs me. I must call 'Father'." "Father" was Dr Maurice Bernstein, a kindly physician whom she regarded as an adoptive parent. They agreed to meet at Flynn's home. The scenario which followed is one of those things that seem funny in retrospect, but which were nerve-rackingly real at the time. Ida arrived at Mulholland House in time to see Errol on his knees near the magnificent bar which just had to be the centerpoint of his home. Nearby was the glass tropical fish aquarium which spanned the length of a wall. Errol was between the two, fighting for breath.

She ran towards him, knelt down and cradled his head in her lap. "This is the Scout," she whispered softly and affectionately. "Little Scout," he replied. "Little Scout, I'm going to vomit. I can't do it in front of you." She told him to do it there and then "if I have to put my fingers down your throat." Which is exactly what she did.

Ida had been in the Medical Corps during the war and recognized this as a particularly unpleasant bout of malaria which, on top of everything else, he still had from time to time. "He was in an icy cold shake" was how she put it to me. Errol's malaria was another of the legacies of New Guinea that had remained with him and was impossible to shake off, although his recurrent bouts were now infrequent.

"I'm so hot," he said a moment later, "hurry, Lupee."

It was as though he had forgotten that she was right there next to him and thought he was talking to her still on the telephone. She walked over to the open front door and waited there for Dr Bernstein to come. Finally the doctor arrived. The first thing he did was to take Errol's temperature. It was 103. Both of them sat with him all night.

"The Little Scout is going to keep you warm, Baron," Bernstein said, joining in the spirit of the scene, while Ida sat and hugged her shivering friend.

Also her medical training came in useful. The doctor asked her to give him an intra-muscular injection. "Dockie," Flynn pleaded in a voice weak from his condition but showing a surprising demonstration of modesty, "she's not going to pull my pants down, is she?"

"She is," he said – and stood by watching the medical procedure put into practice.

Later, Errol pleaded for a shot of his more useful "medication". Ida obliged. She gave him a triple dose of vitamins and for a time he was none the wiser.

"He felt like a new human being," she maintains now. Later, however, he did grow suspicious. "Little Scout," he said, "never try to fool a friend like me."

"How do you feel?" she asked, ignoring his demand. "To tell the truth," he replied, "I never felt better in my life."

Nora in time returned to the house. Yet when she was away, Ida again had her uses; if always platonically. She was around when a man challenged Errol to a duel. He said that Flynn had taken a girl away from him at a party. "Took her away from *you?*" countered Errol not a little sneeringly, "Keep away from me. I'm having a wonderful evening. And keep away from my girl."

But the man, who spoke with a thick Teutonic accent, did not keep away and again in the middle of the night Errol called Ida to help. "Put on your raincoat," he said, "and bring the largest kitchen knife you can find. Do Act Two – now. And look mad."

The way Ida tells it, the curtain opened on "Act Two" just as soon as it took to drive to Flynn's place from her own house nearby. The front door at Mulholland House was ajar and she rushed into the main lounge where Errol was being faced by a strange-looking man wielding a saber.

"What's this Austrian doing here?" she asked menacingly, while the uninvited guest looked her way, not knowing whether he was dreaming or really was about to have a duel. Ida didn't bother with the stranger's thought processes. She charged at him with her kitchen knife while the man ran out through the nearest french window as fast as his little legs would carry him.

The following New Year's Eve, Errol phoned Ida to say: "You'd better stop off and get some blue jeans. We're going to a couple of parties." That was when he proposed – outside his house, as they looked down on the twinkling lights of the San Fernando Valley. He used to say he liked the way the house was situated because he could throw rocks at the Warner Studio from his back yard. This time, he was more somber. "That's the place," he said, "where Warner Brothers take everything from us." With barely a moment's further thought he added: "Don't you think the Scout and the Baron should get married?" She said kindly: "No. Not yet." He was not really surprised. "You know, Little Scout," he reflected not totally accurately, "you're the only one I've ever cried over."

As she told me: "He brought rays of sunshine to me. But I had the feeling that if we had got married, it wouldn't have lasted." Soon afterwards she married actor Howard Duff. "Now, I have the feeling that turning Errol down was the greatest mistake of my life."

If she were the only woman on whom he could at that time depend, he offered to her everything she seemed to need: a sincerity that always went beyond mere charm, and a sense of invariably being on the same wavelength, enjoying similar things and sympathizing with each other's problems. Even after she had rejected his proposal, they met frequently. On one occasion, he sent a message to her via a mutual friend, a newspaper writer. "The Baron says", he told her, "you should get your English fanny down to Nassau."

There, they talked about the book he was writing in longhand, the one that would be called *My Wicked, Wicked Ways*. She promised to back him when the cynics scorned his approach to life. "I'm going to tell them," she promised, "you never raped anyone. They tried to rape you." "I must admit, old girl," he replied, "I never had to rape anyone."

He and Ida were good for each other, even when they just did silly things. When they attempted to give a Viking's funeral to a sparrow that had died crashing into a window, they found themselves in trouble with the police department.

Errol prepared a coffin for the bird. It was a cigar box lined with one of his own silk scarves. Ida drove the "hearse" to the appointed burial ground – a vacant lot near Mulholland House – and Errol and Raoul Walsh were all set to be the pallbearers. They got as far as the open ground when they were joined by two officers in a black and white police car. They said there couldn't be a funeral of any kind there. But Errol had dug the grave with his own fingers and was not about to be put off. He was still kneeling when the officers got out their notebooks and prepared to warn him of the consequences.

He straightened up. "This little fellow creature, created by God," he said, "is to be buried. Are you going to put us behind bars for this?" The men looked at each other, shook their heads and drove away.

When Ida sailed with him on the *Zaca*, they demonstrated their defiance of convention by flying the skull and crossbones. Their relationship was equally strong on the set of *Escape Me Never*. It even extended to their dogs. Flynn had a shaggy terrier called Moody, and she had one named – despite her mother – Duchess. The animals used to sit and watch the pair performing in front of the cameras and then go with them to see the rushes. Looking back on those days now, Ida Lupino says: "We were spirits in another world."

As for the film they made, a rehash of an Elizabeth Bergner picture of a dozen years before, perhaps that should have been consigned to that other world from the beginning. By all accounts, the dogs were the only ones who seemed to appreciate *Escape Me Never*.

Certainly, Warner Brothers were worrying about him. Attendance figures were dropping off at his films and one only had to look at the ever more sozzled character who ambled into the Burbank lot to realize that the chances of Errol finishing his next picture at all were only minimal.

That he did, owed more to Raoul Walsh than to the patience or devotion of Warner Brothers. Walsh directed Flynn's new film, *Silver River*. It co-starred the beautiful-as-ever Ann Sheridan and the respected Thomas Mitchell, and would be the last time Flynn and Walsh worked together. It was again a Civil War story, with Errol playing a disguised Union Army officer who became a professional gambler.

Raoul made a deal with him: "Keep off the liquor until five o'clock and the studio will have to keep paying you." But after a few days, it was a discipline Flynn could maintain only if he spent every moment of the day in the company of the director. Preventing a man like Errol Flynn from hitting the bottle when he wanted to do so was as hard as stopping a cat from licking at a saucer of milk once he knew where it was. And Errol kept bottles of booze where no one else could have imagined them to be.

By the middle of the film's production schedule Warners were looking for ways to break his contract. He was staying up all night and crawling into the studio at ten every morning. Orders were issued to the gatemen to let Jack Warner know immediately Flynn drove up.

Walsh told me that it was then that he decided the time had come to warn Errol of the plight into which he seemed to be rushing. "Errol," he said, "you're getting low on funds. You've got to watch it. I'll pick you up at seven thirty every morning and we'll get to the studio by eight. Then you can have a nap in your dressing room and we'll get some coffee made and brought in to you." Flynn looked at his old "one-eyed bandit" friend, put his arms around him and kissed him warmly on the cheek.

To get his plan working properly, Walsh needed the support of Alex, the butler. He also needed the co-operation of Errol's girl-friends, as Nora was still not around. But he decided that there was no need to embarrass the young ladies. Every day, he drove up at seven thirty as planned. When Alex opened the door, he asked him "Is there anyone with Mr Flynn?" Alex either gave him the name of the young lady and then disappeared discreetly to knock on Flynn's door and announce the director's arrival, or said: "No, Mr Walsh. Miss X just left." As Raoul says: "There was quite a cast list." But the pair of soul brothers always managed to get to the studio on time.

Nora only occasionally went to the studio and she tried hard to ignore what went on in the moments that her husband was not actually before the cameras. Once when she did raise the matter, he told her quite seriously: "If I'm sitting in my dressing room and a pretty girl comes in and pulls my zipper down, takes it out and gives it a little kiss, I'm not screwing her. I'm not doing anything! I didn't touch her." Director Vincent Sherman tells of an invitation Errol made to him one day on the set of his next film, *The Adventures of Don Juan*. Two girls looking suspiciously like prostitutes were waiting behind the camera, making eyes at Errol, who had quite obviously brought them in for the afternoon. At the end of the shooting, Flynn pointed to one of the girls and told Sherman: "I thought maybe you'd like to come into the dressing room with us."

The director couldn't understand it. "How can you spend all day working and *then* perform with them?" he asked.

"Oh, it's nothing," said Flynn. "I just lie there reading the trade papers while they work on me."

When he and Nora discussed this sort of thing, he would always deny that he was courting notoriety. "My private life is my own," he insisted.

That does not mean that he didn't care what Nora thought of his female companions. The Flynns would spend weekends together on the *Zaca* and on occasions with friends like Rita Hayworth and her then husband Orson Welles (they used the boat for their film *The Lady from Shanghai*). But Errol would still occasionally find excuses to go alone, for what purpose he was loath to reveal.

Nora told me about the weekend he phoned her with the news: "Hey, Ma. I'm having the boat painted. You don't have to come with me."

Errol went down to the *Zaca* and then telephoned Mulholland House again: "There's a lot to be done and I'm going to stay over."

Stay over he did and Nora happily spent the weekend at home without him. Seven days later, they were together on the newly-painted craft.

She loved those weekends. They dressed in sports shirts and slacks and, over dinner, they talked about their sailing plans for the hours ahead. This particular Friday night was as idyllic as ever. Just before she was ready to serve the meal, Errol casually suggested to Nora in his usual warm, affectionate voice: "Ma. Go and get some wine." He really should have known better, for the wine "cellar" was in the chartroom, the bottles stored next to the captain's log.

When Nora saw it, she could not resist the temptation to read the pages chronicling the activities of the previous weekend: "Mr Flynn and Miss ... (her name written in easily readable script) boarded at 18 hours and Mr Flynn and Miss ... left at ..."

Downstairs, Errol was happily contemplating the meal to come when he realized that Nora had been away too long for simply fetching a bottle of wine. He froze in his seat. "My God," he thought. "She's got hold of the log."

He ran up into the chartroom, at one end of which stood Nora, venom apparently bursting through her lips, holding the bottle that she had gone to collect in the first place. As he came towards her, she threw it and missed.

"How," she screamed as the sticky wine trickled down the wall behind Errol, "could you screw her in *our* bed?"

"I didn't screw her in our bed," he replied nonchalantly, a look of innocence enveloping his whole face. "I took her into the state-room." But he insisted – just as she was preparing another bottle for target – "I didn't make it with her at all. She had body odour."

That argument was in private. In public, Errol's name was still being linked with curvaceous women who quite plainly would have attracted him. When the husband of nightclub singer Lee Marquis filed for divorce, Errol was named, together with George Raft.

Even though he was now drinking such a lot that no one gave him very much of a future, it was easy to see what girls saw in Errol Flynn, and the story of girls going into his dressing room and unzipping his trousers was by no means apocryphal.

Girls would approach him now as often as they had done ten years earlier and seemed to get as much of a thrill in brushing up close to him as he did himself. Their hands would stray as they brought him cups of coffee. When they introduced themselves off the sound-stage, a handshake would become the mere preliminary to guiding his fingers either down the cleavage of their dresses or under their short skirts.

If he did little to discourage these blatant advances, he was still aware of some of his responsibilities. He was conscious of not being a good enough father and tried to spend more time with his three children, bringing Sean to Mulholland House as often as he could. Somehow Errol was stricter than Nora, but Deirdre says that at times she felt closer to him than she did to her mother. When she was four he bought her a Shetland pony which she called Brownie. It was an introduction to a life in the saddle, although ten years later the saddle on which she could mostly be found was that of a motor cycle. She was to become a stunt girl. It was years before she realized her father was a star and Sunday afternoon in the company of Alan Hale, Bruce Cabot, Guinn "Big Boy" Williams and sometimes Gary Cooper too, were just times with Daddy's pals.

By now, Sean's mother, Tiger Lil, was presenting Errol with further problems. He had asked a judge to order Lili to pay her own taxes, instead of adding them to his already hefty alimony settlement. When Errol failed to turn up in time for the hearing, Judge C. M. Sheldon declared: "This court does not wait for late-comers and I shall make no exception in this case." Errol lost.

In November 1947, Warner Brothers signed a new contract with Flynn, a move they would soon regret. He would, it was agreed, make one film for the studio every year until 1961 and from 1950 would have the right to make one other picture a year away from Warner Brothers.

The first to be made under the new contract was *The Adventures of Don Juan*, a send-up of every swashbuckling role Errol had ever played and, indeed, of his whole reputation.

The film had been a long time in the planning: Raoul Walsh was to have made it more than two years earlier, but a set-builder's strike had put paid to that idea. By the time it was ready for the cameras, Vincent Sherman had taken over as the director.

The first thing Errol told Sherman was: "I want you to know that despite all the stories you may have heard about me, I'm not going to drink – I'm going to behave myself."

And for the first six days of shooting, the impossible seemed to have happened. Errol Flynn, as far as anyone could see, was as good as his word and firmly on the wagon. Shooting began at nine and until the end of the camera work at six o'clock each evening he was sober. But then on the seventh day, he called Sherman into his dressing room and showed him the reviews of the newly-opened *Escape Me Never*. Reviews like Bosley Crowther's *New York Times* comment that:

"*Escape Me Never* was no great shakes the first time round, being a trifling bit of flim-flam about a small lady's loyalty to a cad. As now performed by Miss Lupino as the lady and by Errol Flynn as the cad, it becomes something harsh and unbelievable, like a terrible *faux-pas* in a grade school café. Mr Flynn ... throws himself into his performance with the enthusiasm of a singing waiter in a Hoboken café."

"Pretty funny, aren't they?" asked Errol, who always seemed to laugh off bad reviews as though he knew all the time what to expect and that he thought the notion of his earning a fabulous salary in spite of them to be very funny indeed. But this time he *was* hurt. The next day, he started drinking heavily again. However, it did not show on celluloid.

Camera angles were arranged so as not to catch too much of the growing puffiness of Errol's face and scenes were shot in almost miniscule takes because he could not stand the pressure of having to learn too many lines or actions in one go.

He still managed to jump from balconies, ride horses and sweep beautiful women off their feet as though he were in perfect health. For one brief moment, one of the women he "conquered" was Nora. She appeared in a scene, sitting in a coach.

In a way it was a family affair – if you included in the term family Errol's gang of hangers-on. For years, his own "in" crowd had consisted not just of people like John Decker and Alan Hale but also a group of extras whom he would arrange to have appearing with him in every film he made.

While making *Don Juan*, Vincent Sherman needed the extras. "We'll be shooting in the corridor," he called out to an assistant director. "Let's have Don here and Sol there...."

His request was met with complete silence. "Vince," asked one of his assistants. "Can you do anything else?"

"Why?" he replied. "Aren't they on call today? They're all on salary."

"Yes," he was told. "But they're not here. They're up at Errol's – cleaning his tennis court."

But you couldn't complain about Errol's behaviour when next he showed up – not if you wanted him to complete the picture, and in the end it did seem worth completing. Bosley Crowther was kinder about *Don Juan* than he had been with *Escape Me Never*.

It was, he said, "a great big adventure thriller quite as innocent as *The Adventures of Robin Hood*".

The film was really one of the best Flynn vehicles of the period, but it brought in no great fortune at the box office. It did, however, serve to confirm Errol's image as a Don Juan, which the magazine *Movie Stars Parade* thought meant they could say what they liked about him. He sued for libel because the magazine published an article they claimed he wrote himself called "My First Kiss".

"After I met Olivia," he was supposed to have written about Miss de Havilland, "I looked forward to the tender passages with the same placid appraisal as a wolf lavishes on a herd of spring lambs. Yee-ow! I had kissed a beautiful girl without remembering one single thing about the taste or feel of her lips."

The matter was settled out of court. Inside a courtroom, however, Errol was fined $50 for kicking a policeman in the shins. It had started when the taxi in which he was travelling with Warner Brothers' publicity man Robert Wahn was stopped by a patrolman who wanted to see the driver's license.

Errol plainly didn't like the cop looking into the back seat and saying: "Say, you're Errol Flynn the movie star. Well, don't cause any trouble." The policeman claimed he was then rabbit-punched in the neck and kicked, although Errol denied any knowledge of such dreadful happenings. Flynn was booked at the East 67th Street police station and put into the bullpen there.

Four hours later, he was released on $500 bail – to turn up for a hearing before magistrate Doris I. Byrne the next day. The trouble was, Errol did not turn up. Later that day, with Miss Byrne having ordered the $500 to be forfeited, Errol was arrested as he sipped something strong in the bar of the Savoy Plaza Hotel. In court he explained he had overslept.

"Hearing adjourned until tomorrow," said Miss Byrne, restoring his bail. "Be here."

He was. Accompanied by John Perona, the nightclub proprietor who had posted the bail in the first place, Errol pushed his way through a crowd of two hundred people, mostly squealing bobby-soxers, and called out to them: "It's a frame-up." More quietly, he told Mr Perona: "This is the worst public appearance I have ever made." He said he had failed to turn up on time because he had lain awake all night worrying about the impending hearing.

Later he told reporters: "The whole thing is a gross misunderstanding. I was grabbed by the lapels and pulled out of the cab. I thought I was being charged with stealing a taxicab. Who am I to steal a taxicab? And I'm the last fellow in the world to argue with a policeman."

In court, Patrolmen Joseph Bergeles and Joseph Gardner said they had asked for the twenty-two-year-old taxi-driver's license because they thought he looked too young.

In court again Errol apologized. "I'm sorry about the whole incident," he said as he shook hands with the injured officer and then tried to pay his fine with a $500 bill. He was told to find the right money, which he promptly did.

Meanwhile, his past was catching up with him. In Malaya, *Objective Burma* was withdrawn "in deference to the opinion of the Government and Army authorities" and in London *Cry Wolf* was being reviewed for the first time, and dismissed by the *Evening Standard* as "pretty desperate for a story" with Errol working hard but getting nowhere. *Silver River* opened there at the same time and *The Times* said it needed "a little thought and a hint of imagination". Which was precisely what Errol was putting into his little corner of Jamaica.

13

Escape Me Never

I couldn't get rid of him for seven years.
That's the irony of things.
Nora Flynn Black

If Errol and Nora thought Jamaica would heal the ever-widening cracks in their marriage, they were wrong. Minor rows developed into serious rifts. Practical jokes began to take on the look of grounds for divorce. None more so than when in May 1948 they were due to fly from California to New York and Errol took off with a magazine photographer instead of Nora. She was left behind at the airport. Errol tried to brush away any thoughts of discord. "There were troubles with plane reservations, sport," he said, "none with the wife."

But when the plane landed at Columbia, Missouri, Errol had an attack of remorse. He found his way to a telephone booth, dialled the Mulholland Drive number and when Nora came on the line, sang the opening verse of "Meet Me in St Louis". He followed it with a sufficiently strong battery of kisses over the wire for her to agree to meet him later at the city in the song. When Errol and Nora were finally seen together, it was still not in the full bloom of matrimonial love. There was a distinct coldness about them. Would they return together to Hollywood? Errol said he was certain they would, but the way he said it left most people with the impression that they were tied together not so much by affection as by legal chains. "If Nora comes back to Hollywood without me," he said, "it'll be with her arm in a sling. She promised to come with me and if she tries to turn back, I'll twist her arm."

Friends noted that the rows were over the good times that Nora seemed to like. She wanted to go out to parties while Errol preferred staying at home, if with new female company whenever his wife was not around. They remarked, too, that the little girl to whom Errol had become attracted while she sold cigars at the court-house had grown up. She had both cut her hair and dropped her neckline.

Eventually Errol went home and Nora went to Palm Springs. "Just a short visit," said Errol. "This is it," said Nora. "Things have become intolerable."

She said she didn't want a screen career of her own.

"I just want our life to be better. I thought if I lived alone with the children for a while, it might help my confused state. For the last year and a half I've been so busy with the children and everything I haven't had time to better myself. There are lots of things I like to do. If I lived alone, maybe I could accomplish certain things. I'm just trying to find a way to make our lives happier. After all, I'm twenty-four."

In November, six months after the first public bust-up, they were together again. Errol broke open a champagne bottle to celebrate the occasion. Warner Brothers doubtless drank a toast, too. Divorce was still a sticky subject in 1948 and there was nothing like public domestic bliss to ensure the box-office takings rising. They certainly continued to do so in France, for its film-going citizens voted Flynn the most popular male star in their country. The vote was announced by the magazine *Cinémonde*, which also gave Ingrid Bergman the most popular actress label and announced that both stars would get an award.

Errol let slip he would like to go to France to pick it up – if nothing else it would give him a chance to gripe at the studio: "Warner Brothers wardrobe department will have to provide me with a new suit. I haven't had one since 1925." He seems to have forgotten he was in New Guinea at that time.

For the moment, Warner Brothers had other ideas, before arrang-ing for Mr Flynn's European trip to be paid for by another studio. Early in 1949, they took advantage of the studio payroll to bring as many artists as possible into one picture called *It's a Great Feeling* which, in fact, didn't really feel great for anyone connected with it.

To impress the movie fans, Warners announced a cast that would include Errol Flynn, Gary Cooper, Joan Crawford, Sydney Greenstreet, Danny Kaye, Patricia Neal, Eleanor Parker, Ronald Reagan – then hardly beginning to think about a career in politics – Edward G. Robinson, Jane Wyman, Doris Day, Jack Carson and Dennis Morgan.

Errol's part was tiny. But his impact on the other Warner Brothers' personnel at this time was anything but small. For Errol had found a new way of making his presence felt. He installed a public-address system in his convertible. Without warning anyone, he had fitted a loudspeaker underneath the big white open car and a microphone by the wheel. As he drove past a pretty girl, he called out to her the sort of thing he usually kept for those quiet minutes on the way to his dressing room. "This is Errol," he said in between whistles, and promptly invited the young lady to sample some of the pleasures of meeting with him later on. It caused a tremendous stir when news of the electronic dating system got about; after all, this was the age when a conventional car radio was status symbol enough.

It was while making the picture that Errol revealed to one of the technicians on the set why he so much enjoyed going to bed with his still adoring young girl fans. "It's the excitement, you see – *their* excitement. When someone is your equal and has been chased after by someone else it isn't the same. They get too blasé."

Which was also the way Warner Brothers considered Dennis Morgan had behaved when he turned down a film script – something that had only rarely happened with Hollywood contract players. The result was that Melville Shavelson and Jack Rose were called in to write a new script for him in three weeks. They had to produce results that would neither need new sets nor new stars, but could take advantage of people who were ready, willing and able to oblige the studio simply because they had contracts that said that they would.

As an additional convenience, Warners had a young girl still fairly inexperienced after two films but very enthusiastic to show

With Anna Neagle in *Lilacs in the Spring*. Anna and her husband Herbert Wilcox gave Errol work when no one else would.

In *Too Much, Too Soon* Errol played his idol, John Barrymore, with Dorothy Malone as the star's daughter.

The three wives of Errol Flynn. (Top) with Lili Damita in 1937, (center) with Nora Eddington in 1948 and (bottom) with Patrice Wymore in 1957.

In *The Roots of Heaven* with Trevor Howard and Juliette Greco. Eddie Albert is behind Errol's shoulder.

Errol and "Woodsie", Beverly Aadland, shortly before his death in 1959. They joked they were going to make a film of *Lolita*.

Pat and Errol's son Sean driving to the funeral in Los Angeles.

what she could do to provide the female interest. Her name: Doris Kapelhoff, professionally known more simply as Doris Day.

The picture had to be made because it had been booked into the theaters months before a frame was exposed. These were still the days when exhibitors were treated by studio sales staff to extravagant promises of what they were going to deliver and so had to come up with something. The "something" in this case was a wild piece of fiction in which Dennis Morgan and Jack Carson try to produce a screenplay for Doris Day, who has been working as a studio waitress. Their film within a film turns out to be so bad that even the screen-struck waitress gives up and goes back to her little town in Wisconsin to marry her childhood sweetheart, Jeffrey Bushdinkel. Doris is seen in the final minutes of the picture standing at the altar with her bridegroom, both with their backs to the camera. As the couple turn to kiss, the man turns to reveal his identity – Errol Flynn. Carson says: "Oh that poor girl", and the film ends. It was Errol's shortest role since lying on the mortuary slab in *The Case of the Curious Bride*.

Errol's first picture for another studio, *The Forsyte Saga* – called in the United States *That Forsyte Woman* – was produced at MGM. In this, he played Soames and looked more handsome than he had for years, aided no doubt both by his own Victorian business suits and by the magnificent bare shoulders of Greer Garson as the fabled Irene. It was his best role since *Objective Burma* and far less troublesome.

Basically, the film was of the first book of the saga, otherwise known as *The Man of Property*, and if the restrained American accents of Robert Young as the architect Philip Bosinney and of Walter Pidgeon as Young Jolyon could be forgiven, it was not a bad movie at all. Indeed, in addition to the change of studios, there were two things that set it apart from previous Flynn movies. It was chosen as the royal film to be shown before King George VI and Queen Elizabeth – now the Queen Mother – and Errol was remarkably well behaved.

"He couldn't have been more charming," Walter Pidgeon told me. "If he was ready for a shot and was a little slippery with his dialogue ... well, with some guys you'd say: 'Goddam it, why doesn't he get on with the job?' But not with Errol. He was like a French poodle. You couldn't get mad with him. He was too professional to allow anything to interfere with his 'work. Sometimes, he was darn good."

Giving the movie the royal honours provided Errol with an excuse to come to Britain at just the minute when he could not have got out of America quickly enough. His marriage to Nora had finally fractured beyond repair.

Nora left, saying that she had no intention of going back to Mulholland House – ever. Her decision was made easier by the divorce earlier in 1949 of Joanne Dru and singer Dick Haymes. Nora had been seen with Haymes on a number of previous occasions.

They had gone to the Hollywood Racquet Club together after which Flynn had had Haymes followed by a private detective. Errol told Nora: "You'll have the money *and* the boy singer!" He was bitter about the end of their marriage. "I'm going to Europe," he said, "and it's an open port there." He meant that in Europe he could get away with all the drinking, drug-taking and womanizing he wanted without having the finger of Hollywood moralists pointing at him.

The divorce finally came through on 7 July 1949, after Hollywood columnists had been trying to find all sorts of reasons for the marriage to continue. Louella Parsons, who had been anything but kind to Nora in recent months, had quoted her only days before as saying: "I'll never leave him. No matter what he does. I just hope that one day he will realize how much I love him."

Errol waited to clear up the details of the settlement before going off to Europe. At first Deirdre would spend a lot of time with him, but soon she moved in with her mother. Rory, too, lived with Errol for a short period after the divorce and the day that his lawyer, Bob Ford, came in to discuss the alimony and other arrangements, he had to wait until after his client had finished reading Rory the comic pages of the evening paper.

Ford had come to sort out two alimony problems: what Errol was going to pay Nora and the money still owed to Lili Damita. Flynn was still fighting Tiger Lil over the tax question. Originally the courts had awarded her $12,000 a year, tax free, which meant that Errol had to pay another $6000 to the Internal Revenue Department. Now she was demanding $18,000 tax free, which would mean Flynn having to pay a total of $30,000 because the tax would by then have reached $12,000. What Nora would get had yet to be talked about.

Soon afterwards she married Dick Haymes, but Rory remained with Errol, looked after by Nora's stepmother Marge, who saw the divorce as no reason to sever her own relationship with Errol. She stayed on as his secretary and housekeeper. Mulholland House became the venue for the most uproarious parties in Hollywood – always with Marge dancing attendance, even when the women guests were call-girls imported specially for the evening. When Errol went to Europe, she remained behind with the little girl.

Flynn said he was going to Europe to see the art galleries in Venice and stay at the Savoy in London. Did he think he would ever marry again? He told Hedda Hopper, who was always his favourite columnist (although he had recently slapped her behind for writing something about him he didn't like), "That is like asking a man who has just recovered from a near-fatal surgical operation whether he thinks he'd like another."

While in Europe, Errol did his best to look serious. Now he had plans to produce his own pictures and for once pretended to be more interested in finding new films than new women. His first independent production would be called *The Buccaneer* which he said he had written himself, and arrangements had already been made for it to be released by Twentieth Century-Fox. Playing a part in it as well as producing, he would have had a chance to recapture his image of old but, like many things at the time, it fizzled out. Errol found difficulty in retaining enthusiasm for anything.

He did, however, continue to play the part of the devoted father, receiving from Marge a new picture of Rory every week and buying a trunkload of dresses for her at every stop.

In Paris, he proved that the French still adored him. He answered every question the local reporters put and posed happily for each shot the photographers wanted to take. On the Left Bank, girls in the existentialist crowd forgot their principles and tore practically every shred of clothing from his back.

Then, quite suddenly, it seemed he had made the Big Conquest
– in the form of a nineteen-year-old Romanian princess who arrived
on the scene in a cloud of perfume and garlic. Her name was Irene
Chika, whom he called in his usual irreverential way, "the Geek".

Errol was smitten, promising the aristocratic lady everything she
desired, including marriage and a part in pictures. She was independently wealthy and very beautiful with blue eyes and dark brown
hair. But what sort of princess was she? "I'm very vague about her
lineage." said Errol who plainly didn't think it mattered a bauble.
"Irene has all the qualities I most adore in a woman – honesty, sincerity, a sense of humour and an outlook which is rare – a willingness
to do anything to help the man." Quite plainly this was before the
age of women's lib.

She came with him to London where he proclaimed: "I'm
through with hell raising. No one can bust up this romance." And
with that he announced their engagement. His present to his new
fiancée: a package of iced French snails, laced with garlic sauce.
Louella Parsons commented when she heard that: "She is the first
girl I've seen to lead Errol Flynn by the nose."

King George appeared to lead him equally indelicately. When
the King was introduced to Errol standing in the line-up at the
Odeon Cinema, Marble Arch, he remembered the actor's bust-up
with the British Press. "How's Burma?" he asked. "I think she's
pregnant, sir," Errol replied. The King laughed appreciatively.

The newspapers in London were still not quite so grateful for
his dramatic talents. The *Daily Herald*'s Paul Holt said: "Mr Flynn
as Soames Forsyte wears his *pince-nez* with a foolish air, not believ-
ing a word of what he says (nor expecting us to, either)." The *Daily
Mail* was kinder. "As Soames," wrote Fred Majdalaney, "Errol
Flynn gives a good superficial sketch, but misses the essential tra-
gedy of the man, for which the otherwise sound script and direction
must share the blame."

While in London, Errol set about seeing the sights he had last
known as a youngster who had just shown a bunch of provincials
what he could do in Northampton repertory.

One of the first calls he made was at the Dover Street shop
of Alan McAfee, bespoke shoemakers – the rather dowdy windows

and the wood panelling inside having changed little from the days when he bought there his pair of riding boots together with two pairs of black and white shoes and another in brown and white.

"It's about those shoes you made me last time, sport," said Errol to the man in the smart conservative black suit.

"Yes, sir," the man replied, "we'd be *very* pleased to make you some more."

"Oh, no," countered Errol. "I don't want any more. I was just wondering if you'd let me return these and give me my money back. You see they were ordered by the wardrobe department at the studio and they've never been worn. I thought it would be a shame to waste them and it *would* be nice to get some cash."

The shoes had cost £5 a pair at the time that Errol was flying on a dizzy cloud about to take him to Hollywood. Now, an international star with alimony trouble, he was trying to get back £20. The shop, ever the soul of courtesy and discretion, persuaded him that it was not really the sort of thing that they did.

Errol was in London on other business too: making the film *Kim* at Elstree Studios. Frank Westmore, the make-up artist, was responsible for turning Errol into an Afghan horse dealer who looked like a maharajah. In his book *The Westmores of Hollywood* he describes Flynn being accompanied by a "slave" who served him with a continuous supply of whisky from two bottles which he had brought into the make-up room at six forty-five in the morning. Before leaving the chair, Errol had drained the entire contents of the first bottle – and stayed cold sober.

The princess was on hand for most of the time at the studio, too. She clutched Errol's arm as they paraded through the studio grounds, sat on the set waiting for shooting to begin and walked through the local streets. But what about the wedding? "Eet has not yet been settled," she said. "There will be talks with my mother." She denied that the family still owned a chateau near Bucharest. "Poof, gone," she said. Errol smiled contentedly.

From Britain, Flynn and his princess went on to India, to do some location scenes for a film that was quickly gaining for itself a reputation for being shot in more places than Joseph Dillinger.

Kim was based on the Kipling story of the boy from a British family who dresses up as an Indian native beggar. Dean Stockwell was to play the boy and have the lion's – or perhaps it should be the tiger's – share of the movie, but nobody thought it important to film him other than in California.

The second biggest role was that of the lama who virtually adopts the boy. Paul Lukas had this part, making the Eastern priest look and sound as though he had just stepped off the train from Budapest. As for Errol, he played well enough the horse dealer who got involved in a story that never seemed to know where it was going next. His own was one of the smallest roles but he still got the top billing.

Errol had not liked India all that much, mainly because he found vodka hard to come by and the curry was always that much too hot and too strong for him. But it was as good a place as any to play practical jokes: like the time he arranged for two Indian uniformed officials to arrest Paul Lukas on a trumped-up forged passport charge.

Lukas was near a fatal heart attack by the time the policemen told him how serious they regarded his "offense". He was a few strokes away from foaming at the mouth when he finally realized that the nearby native in a turban and khaki greatcoat was Errol Flynn, who found it difficult not to fall down pounding the floor in hysterics. Flynn later said that it was a young lady with big breasts and a low neckline who persuaded Mr Lukas not to take the incident too badly.

Errol spent much of the time in India – his first visit there since the trip westwards from New Guinea – hunting wild animals and threatening to bring back to Hollywood with him a creature called a mouse deer, which he said had been given to him by the Maharajah of Mysore.

The maharajah was a generous man who admired Errol's sporting outlook and enjoyed seeing him walk off with the girl in all his films. He also loved the ribald stories of Flynn's real-life conquests.

"Flynn," he said, "what do you want?"

"How about an elephant?" Errol replied.

The prince gave an order and a boy came back with two baby

elephants in tow. "Take your pick," said the maharajah. "The boy goes, too."

Errol thought about that one. "No. I don't think I could manage the excess baggage."

"Right," said the prince. "How about a mouse deer?"

Errol looked over the animal (natural habitat, Central India) and said: "Thanks, sport. Would love it."

A padded cage was built for the deer, which had a bobbed tail and two long fangs and, once having been put on a plane and got into the air, promptly dropped dead. The poor creature couldn't take the altitude.

Some of Errol's friends wondered how he could stand the aristocratic altitude of life with a princess whom he still called "the Geek". But he kept on saying that they loved each other. The way she had nestled her head in his lap and looked up into his eyes as they sat on the deck of the *Zaca* during a short French Riviera holiday, it certainly seemed that way. He had sent word to Mulholland Drive about her, and Marge, as he still liked to call his ex-mother-in-law, said she would be happy to keep house for them both.

Kim was to be completed in Hollywood but Errol and the princess stepped off first at New Orleans, where they occupied adjoining suites at the Roosevelt Hotel. "I have no acting ambitions," she said. "Errol will do all the acting in the family."

Errol was keeping everyone guessing, mostly hinting that marriage was just around the corner. Irene, he said, was a "nice dame who can't cook and doesn't know any lawyers. But she's loaded with charm. She likes hamburgers and banana splits better than anything else. It'll be cheap to keep her." As soon as the dame learned to cook there would be a wedding. First, however, Errol had two other movie assignments.

Both of them were Westerns for Warner Brothers and both of them made the company wish they had had nothing to do with Mr Errol Flynn.

In the first of these, *Montana*, Errol portrayed an Australian, which was only the second time since *Desperate Journey* that he had played his own true original nationality, although his accent sounded distinctly American. The fact that he had a part at all was due more to his ingenuity than to anything else.

Warners were almost paranoid now in trying to find new ways of ending the contract they had signed with him just two years before. His behaviour in *Montana*, they were convinced, would guarantee them their chance. On the set, he was late, drunk and unable to remember lines: all sufficient grounds to break the agreement.

But before it was too late, Errol got wind of the studio's thirsting for revenge. To Arizona where the remainder of the picture was being shot, he brought with him a representative of the Screen Actors Guild to look after his interests.

Jack Warner, meanwhile, had hired a private eye to watch out for him, and especially for any give-away signs that could lead to a dissolution. The detective himself was a man of initiative. He noticed a loft above Errol's dressing room and decided to use it to his best advantage. All he had to do was climb the ladder which conveniently had been in place there all the time. But Errol was cleverer. When he heard movement above, he suspected he knew the cause, waited till everyone had gone home, and then pulled away the ladder. He left behind him that night a very angry, frustrated and slightly frightened private eye, literally aloft.

That little local difficulty solved, Errol's plans for marrying "the Geek" went ahead while the court decided on new arrangements for his children. Now, Nora would get "physical custody" and legal guardianship of Rory as well as of Deirdre. But Errol would be allowed to see the children on alternate weekends and at Christmas – at least until nine o'clock on Christmas Eve or from eight until five on Christmas Day. It was a painful settlement, and he didn't want to accept it.

The day he heard the news, Errol was totally distraught. He decided he had to fight it and now that the court had made up its mind, only Nora could save the situation. Perhaps, he thought, if he went to see her she would see reason.

He got into his car and while driving away felt a harsh bump. He also heard a squeal. The car stopped, Errol jumped out, and saw beneath one of the front wheels the squashed form of his dog. He decided he could not go on – with the journey or with the fight. He spent the rest of the night burying the dog and crying over its grave. He felt and he looked completely broken. He no more looked thirty-nine than some of his early girlfriends had looked eighteen. Although there was still much that was handsome and distinguished about his features, his face was lined and his jowls were flabbier than ever.

Every now and again he would feel so ill he could not leave his bed. More than once he collapsed, but chose never to tell anyone about it. He wanted people to think he was still the kid who could outdistance anyone in the boxing ring, the tennis court or the bedroom. As if to bolster that image, his practical jokes got bigger and less funny.

Once, when he heard that his friend Lou Costello was going to show films at his children's Christmas party, he arranged for a "blue" stag movie to be smuggled in among the Disney cartoons and comedy shorts. As the film played on to the screen, letting the children view one sex antic after the other, poor Costello stood transfixed to his projector like a man who has just become impaled on a high-tension wire. Later, Flynn "swore on the Koran" that he was not the cause, and lest the full truth of that "oath" be misunderstood, added that, of course, he was not a religious man. The next vow he would take, he was telling people, would be before a justice of the peace.

Meanwhile, he had decided that his fiancée needed a new name before she became Mrs Flynn. "I'm calling her Miss Irene. With the name she had before, she sounded like a burlesque queen," he explained. "She's a good egg and she's got some brains, too. It's about time I picked one with brains."

She certainly looked loving and intelligent, asking all the right questions on the film sets to which she would go with Errol with great avidity. Yet perhaps not *quite* all the right questions.

In his next Western, *Rocky Mountain*, Errol played a Confederate officer who goes to war with the Indians as well as with the Union, and makes love to the girl whom he had saved from certain death and worse at the hands of the Navajos. The girl, a beautiful redhead called Patrice Wymore, had first been introduced to Errol by Marge Eddington. She certainly made a big impression.

In August 1950, without warning to anyone or with even the faintest dribble of a press leak, he announced that he would not be marrying "the Geek" after all. Instead, he was engaged to Patrice Wymore.

14

Rocky Mountain

I liked him immensely. He had a great joie
de vivre, *and he was a very bright man.*
God knows, he was attractive. Errol was
always very, very nice to me.
Alexis Smith

She was, as he later put it, a square. Thick glasses perched on her
nose. No make-up. And when he first wandered into her dressing
room, all he wanted to do – or so he said – was to get out again
quickly.

But then the glasses came off, the make-up went on, and Errol
Flynn decided that Miss Patrice Wymore, twenty-one-year-old
stage actress, daughter of an oil man from Salina, Kansas, and much
prettier than those first unguarded moments seemed to indicate, was
different from all the other women with whom he had ever been
associated. The weakness of that decision was that he always seemed
to say something of the kind when he built up more than a fleeting
relationship with a woman. This time, however, he felt he had a
case.

Pat was not running after him as other girls – Nora excepted –
had always seemed to do. Neither was she playing hard to get. Indeed, he said at the time that he was struck that she did not seem
to bring any female wiles to bear on him at all.

He was even more impressed by those glasses. She may have taken
them off on the set, but she wore them when she reluctantly went
to dinner with him the first time. The perfect woman. "All I have
to do is hide her glasses and she'll never be able to find me," he
joked.

It was not difficult to see Errol and Pat were going to try to make a go of it. At a party at Mulholland House Flynn turned to the ex-mother-in-law who was still looking after his domestic needs. "You know, Marge," he said, "doesn't she remind you of Nora?"

The idea of their marrying was not as straightforward as might be supposed. First, Errol had to tell the princess that he had other plans, and Pat, too, had not been without her matrimonial intentions. Indeed, forty-year-old Sammy Lambert, a Broadway producer, had been quoted as saying that he expected to marry her just as soon as she returned East from California.

But in a cross-country telephone call at four in the morning she told him that she was going to marry Errol instead. "People said I was a fool to let her go to Hollywood," he said after getting the news. "I've heard those things happened there. I never believed it until now. Marrying Flynn isn't the best thing in the world for Pat. Maybe he can advance her career. But once he drops her, she's through.... I guess the glitter and glamour of Hollywood changed her."

In August 1950 Errol flew into Salina with Pat to meet her parents. "When you come right down to it," he said on arrival at the Kansas airport, "you can't beat an American girl. American girls are best."

The Wymores seemed overwhelmed when they met their prospective son-in-law. "I liked him when I first met him," said her father. It was difficult for him not to do so. Errol had told Mr Wymore how much he loved his daughter, how well she had spoken of her father and how he envied a man who had been able to cultivate such adoration from his offspring. They were already making plans for a local wedding within three months. Errol gave his fiancée a diamond and sapphire engagement ring. In return, she presented him with something she considered would be useful in Jamaica – a tractor. "A tractor, by golly," said Flynn when he heard. "It will come in real handy when we settle down on our farm in Jamaica."

Meanwhile, Pat set out introducing her "catch" to her friends. A round of parties and "showers" was organized for the younger female set of Salina while the Wymores drove a hundred miles for a dinner party with Errol at Wichita.

But Errol now had business to attend to. He was going to Paris to make a film he was producing himself called *Bloodline*. It would basically be about the early days of New Orleans, but Paris looked more like nineteenth-century New Orleans than New Orleans did. Plans were made for Pat to join him in Paris, later on.

Errol arrived in the French capital about a month after everyone else involved in the picture – including Vincent Price, Agnes Moorhead and Micheline Presle – had got there. They had all been in Paris for four weeks with the intention of getting their costumes arranged and their lines learned. Instead they had had a month's holiday. Without him they could do nothing. Still, they didn't worry: Errol would be paying.

When he finally did drive up in a sleek black Cadillac, he told them he didn't yet have the cash in hand, but not to concern themselves because he would find it. They went to work, but they did not get their money. William Marshall, the director, and Flynn had got into a fight almost immediately, but Errol was plainly not worried. He was much more concerned with catching up with Pat, who promised to join him at any moment.

In one scene, Errol and Vincent Price had to have a fight on top of a wharf. As they got to the edge of the parapet, they both lost their balance and fell into the sea. "It was like a Mack Sennett comedy," Price told me.

Off set in those anxious weeks, Flynn proved to be the same lovable charming rogue his reputation had always said he was. He and Vincent Price seemed to get on well enough, although Price later sued him for lost income. For the moment, however, they discussed their mutual love of art and the old days when Errol and Lili Damita had been, as Price put it, "the most stunning couple you could imagine".

But a lot of people connected with the film hated Errol's dependence on booze. They also tried to get their own back for all the disruption they claimed his drinking had brought to the film. When he gave a party in Paris, most of the women in the company as well as the wives of the other actors and technicians decided not to attend. But he persuaded them to come. "When they saw him they just melted," Vincent says. "It was that charm again."

In Paris Errol attended to the details of searching for locations and of casting. He wanted two "character actresses" for a bar room scene, but more than a hundred girls flaunted their charms at the Ballancourt Studios, leaving him bemoaning the fact "that nobody in France wants to be a character actress. They all want to be pretty." He was feeling quite at home in France. For a year the *Zaca* had been moored on the Riviera. Now he had plans for using her for a honeymoon in the same location.

At the end of September Patrice flew into Paris and Errol was at the airport to greet her. "Honey, I'm so happy to see you," he said, and it really looked as though he meant it. "Golly I've missed you." He repeated the phrase over and over again. When would the wedding be? "Just as soon as we have the church and the minister organized," he replied. "I want this to be Pat's first and only marriage. That sort of thing is very important to a girl."

Pat said that she was not going into the marriage blindly. She had known about his past, had heard all the stories, but when he said she was different, she believed him and that went for her folks, too.

"I respect this girl," said Errol, looking into her eyes now with what would have passed very well for devotion. "You have to respect girls who wear glasses."

He was trying to be serious and frank at the same time. He told her: "I can't promise to reform, but maybe I shall conform a bit more. I love you."

To the *Los Angeles Times* he emphasized that for him this was going to be the third and final time. "We hope to raise a big family. I want enough boys to make a crew for my boat. Pat is even going to learn to cook – and if she can't cook, I might make her first mate on my yacht."

In October the couple moved south to Monaco and set about arranging what they neatly described as a "double-feature" wedding – a civil ceremony, as was the local requirement, followed by a church service. The civil marriage at Monaco's Town Hall was easy enough to organize, but the church ceremony was different. They just could not find a clergyman willing to marry them.

It wasn't simply because of Errol's past reputation that the local clergy were averse to solemnizing the match. Many priests had seen men at the altar whom they knew to be sexual athletes almost if not quite of Flynn's prowess. The trouble was that he had had two marriages before, even though neither of them had been in church.

Errol knew he would never get to bless the marriage either a Catholic priest or even an Anglican clergyman – nominally his last religious affiliation had been as a member of the Church of Ireland, which was part of the Anglican communion – but he thought that a Lutheran, or perhaps Presbyterian, church would be easier. Neither was. Finally the Rev. Frank Guenthal agreed to come from Paris to perform the ceremony at the tiny Lutheran church at Nice. He could speak enough English to conduct the ceremony in that language and both Errol and Pat wanted to be able to understand what was going on. It was going to be the biggest wedding on the Riviera since Rita Hayworth married Prince Ali Khan. The Monaco police got their dress uniforms out of mothballs and mobilized an extra guard of honour for the occasion. A mob scene was expected, and indeed one took place as Errol, in cutaway black coat, and Patrice, wearing a floor-length gown of white *point-de-Lyon* lace over ivory satin, said "*oui*" at the Town Hall. The ceremony was performed by the dapper little mayor of Monte Carlo wearing a red sash across his breast.

Errol looked down at his blue suede shoes a couple of times, but apart from that was wreathed in smiles throughout the mere ninety seconds it took to make him and Patrice man and wife in the eyes of the Monagasque Government. That is, apart from the ten documents they were each required to sign.

After the ceremony the couple drove to Nice, where four thousand people surged around the tiny chapel, climbing trees and lampposts if they couldn't find suitable positions in the street or on nearby rooftops. No photographers were admitted and one who was able to slide in was speedily ejected.

The bride was attended by four girls who had managed to get into the cast of *Bloodline*, now renamed *The Towers of New Orleans*, on the grounds of their beauty rather than their character. Members of the all-Jamaican crew of the *Zaca* had places of honour in the chapel. Appropriately when Pat walked down the aisle, the organ played "Drink to me only with thine eyes".

The grey-haired pastor, a man who had worked in New York in the early years of the century, was determined to tell the bridegroom that although he was performing a ceremony others had declined, he hoped that Flynn was taking it all sufficiently seriously. "This is not a contract that can be cancelled at will," he said solemnly.

The ceremony over, the couple drove back to Monaco for a wedding reception and what they anticipated would be a happier life than Errol was reputed to give his wives. But it didn't happen like that. At the reception, instead of speeches and telegrams of good wishes, Errol was handed a writ. Once more he was being charged with rape.

15

Too Much, Too Soon

I liked him very much. He had a tremen-
dous personality and was a great fellow. He
had real star quality.
Vincent Price

The charge was read to Errol just after he and Patrice had cut a
massive wedding cake in the ballroom of Nice's Hôtel de Paris. He
had, the paper declared, "lustfully, lasciviously and carnally had
intercourse" with one Denise Duvivier, aged seventeen.

The offense, it was said, had taken place a year before and on
the *Zaca*. Now, other men, even when their minds were not clouded
by a mere detail like a wedding reception, would have instantly
denied that any such thing could have been true. Errol, however,
felt that on the very day that he had sworn his undying love to his
beautiful red-haired wife he had to be honest. He frankly could not
remember.

He could not truthfully say there had been no young girls, perhaps even seventeen year olds, who had come on to the deck of the
Zaca and who after a drink or two had removed their clothes and
allowed him to have intercourse with them. He had told Pat about
his past and was hiding nothing. But Mlle Duvivier? Her name conjured up no images for him – no beautiful face, no alluring breasts,
no exciting legs.

Once Errol had realized that the charge was not a practical joke
on the part of some misguided publicist, he decided he had to send
for a lawyer. But he did get some legal advice before one could be
found. A reporter friend told him there was no such thing as bail
in Monaco. Once he answered the charge, he would have to go to

jail. On the other hand, if he stayed in Nice, nothing could possibly happen to him.

All Errol could say to Patrice was: "Listen, honey, I don't know the details of this yet, or what the hell it's all about, but I've some bad news for you on your wedding day. There's a summons out there for me for rape."

She looked understandably shocked, her face taking on the shade of her wedding dress. But she pressed his hand as if to say that she had faith in him. "Well," she replied with what was to become a customary matter-of-factness, "we'll take care of *that*." They hurried out of the building together and drove to the *Zaca*'s moorings. The next morning the United States Navy, in Nice on a goodwill visit, fired a sixteen-gun salute. The guns were officially for the French city, but Errol heard coming from the speakers of the ship nearest to him: "Now hear this, now hear this: Errol Flynn just got married. Leave him alone."

Fortunately for Errol, they did not leave him completely alone. A couple of days later, Flynn fell on the slippery wet deck and sprained his back. Thanks to the nearby Navy, he was hauled, unconscious, by breeches-buoy aboard an accompanying battleship. He stayed dead to the world for a week and spent the next month on his back suffering from fractures of several vertebrae. Not the sort of first month of marriage to Errol Flynn that Pat had anticipated.

Pat, or "Wymore" as he persisted in calling her now, nursed him for all the time he was ill. When he was able to get up, he decided to sail into Monaco and answer the rape charge. He said later it was the only brave thing he did in his life.

The charges were officially read to him by a white-haired judge in the very room where so few weeks before he and Pat had had their civil wedding ceremony. Flynn heard that Danielle's parents were demanding $2800 in damages in lieu of their daughter's honour: a sum which they said they would give to charity. They added that the offense had taken place on the *Zaca*, but not on one of its beds. It was in a shower compartment. There, they alleged, the naked girl had been pushed against a wall while Errol pressed an electric button. This had swung shut a door behind them and so given him the go-ahead for raping her without interruption.

All this Errol denied. He had to admit he thought the idea of a switch at the back of the shower compartment was "marvellous". He'd have to remember it. But, so far, no such implement had yet been fitted on the *Zaca* or anywhere else to his knowledge.

A picture showing the girl with a man looking very much like Flynn was being passed now from one court official to the other. When it reached Errol, he had to agree that it did look as though it had been shot on the *Zaca*. Or had it? A closer look at the snap made him less sure. And then he remembered. The boat in the picture was not his but the yacht of a friend on which he had been a guest for a party. A succession of girls, as was their wont, had asked to pose with him for photographs. Errol, never wishing to turn down the chance of such close proximity to young ladies – many of whom would arrange on such occasions to have his hand pressing down on to the more intimate parts of their anatomy – usually obliged. All he could think now was that Danielle was one of those girls, but by looking at the picture he still could not be sure.

Then he was brought face to face with the young lady, a perfume sales girl at a local store. At that moment he knew she could not possibly be one with whom he had ever had sex. There was no make-up on a very ordinary face, she had an unimpressive figure and worse. Never, said Errol, not bothering now to swear on the Koran because this time he meant what he said, would he dream of dating, let alone having sex with, a girl with hair on her legs. While Patrice waited at a café outside the Town Hall, Errol denied emphatically any connection with the charge.

Danielle persisted. She told the magistrate: "I went aboard the yacht with a photographer. The following day, I was bathing not far from Mr Flynn's yacht. He saw me and invited me aboard."

The hearing was entirely in secret. Errol was defended by a former mayor of Nice, Maître Cotta. Neither he nor the prosecution lawyer was allowed inside as the two sides told their different stories. Ten policemen barred the doors of the courtroom to be sure no strangers squeezed in.

This made Errol worry for the first time. What if he were given some incredibly barbaric sentence and no one knew about it? What if they refused the most simple and reasonable request? He solved the problem by insisting that he did not understand French, and demanded an interpreter. At least that way there would be one witness to the whole sorry proceedings. His request was instantly met.

Meanwhile, all of France was being regaled with pictures of Errol Flynn and the poor innocent girl he was said to have seduced, most of the newspapers making it very plain that it was not the first time he had been in that situation, but always stating equally clearly that on the previous occasion he had been acquitted of all charges.

Outside the court, Danielle gave her version of the proceedings. Errol, she reported, had been asked: "Do you know this girl?" and had replied: "Yes."

"Where have you seen her?" she said he was asked.

"On the quays of the port."

"Did she ever go aboard your yacht?"

"No."

Then she said that she herself had made a detailed drawing of the shower room and had described exactly what had happened. All Errol would say when he joined Pat at the café was: "It's attempted blackmail."

The magistrate, André Biasset, whose powers extended only over some 370 acres, was plainly frustrated at just how little he really could do. What was to stop Errol sailing away on the *Zaca*? At one stage he said he was thinking about throwing out the case and sending it off to America for hearing, since the boat was registered as an American vessel.

The Flynns just pretended that nothing at all had happened and spent the night at the Casino. Next morning they announced that Errol would not be going back to court. "It's supposed to be secret, but people are talking about it, sport," he said in obvious reference to Danielle.

By this time there were other people who shared with Errol the view that he was being "got at". A group in Berlin formed a club for the defense of Errol Flynn, similar to the one formed by William Buckley in 1943, to protect him from the "insulting rumours". In Hollywood a party of women went to church to recite special prayers. "That," he said when he heard, "is no laughing matter."

The magistrate asked at least to be allowed to have a look at the

Zaca. Errol obliged, and pointed out that there was no electric switch. He also added that he – and indeed any other man who was sound in wind, limb and sexual organs – would find it very difficult indeed to perform in such cramped circumstances. M. Biasset, a man of the world if not of the sea, was forced to agree that it would not be easy, and dismissed the whole affair.

By now Errol had considerable respect for the workings of Western justice, especially when a few months later an American judge finally dismissed all claims made against him in the 1944 paternity case.

With the rape affair over, he and Pat made the Riviera their home, inviting friends on to the *Zaca* as though it were Mulholland House. Errol even invited Jack Warner along, which as things turned out might have been a less charitable gesture than it first appeared.

"Use the *Zaca* as much as you like, J.L.," he told him. "I've got to stay on shore for a bit."

Out into the Mediterranean the *Zaca* sailed – and ran out of fuel. A police patrol boat went alongside and from it came the shouts of a customs man bellowing: "Unless you pay all the wharfage fees you owe, Mr Flynn, you will have to stay where you are."

He would not hear that the man on board was anyone but Flynn, but neither did he demand that the money be paid there and then. How could he? The yacht was out of French territorial waters. He could, however, refrain from assisting the boat back to shore. In the end, Jack Warner, movie tycoon, had to get one of the *Zaca*'s seamen – at some vastly inflated rate of pay – to row him back to the beach as though he were a victim of the Titanic disaster.

Eventually, Errol had to pay up, if not make up with J.L. The *Zaca* was worth more to him than any wife had ever been. With the bills finally settled, he and Patrice sailed back to America.

16

The Cruise of the Zaca

I liked him very much. Everyone was smitten with him. He was a marvellous man to be with.
Lewis Milestone

Errol gave every impression of trying to improve both his behaviour and his image. He even seemed to be drinking less. Certainly there was no evidence of his spending a great deal of his time in the company of other women. And he was busy absorbing the heavy-going pages of Plato's *Republic*.

"I am just sick and tired of being known as a very nice sort of guy," he confessed at this time, attempting to crush his reputation for ever. But he had to add: "It shook me rigid one day when I worked out that I had twenty-five bad habits, ten medium-sized ones and a whole string of lesser bad habits. I decided to really get round to pruning them down."

Well, of course, he never did. But for two years or so everything in the private Flynn garden appeared to be lovely. Professionally, though, things were anything but good. It was quite clear that Hollywood had had enough of the Flynn approach to life and work and wanted no more of him.

For the moment he satisfied himself with his loving wife who, he maintained, had a built-in radar which told her when things were going wrong. When they quarrelled, he would try to settle it with a bouquet from the most expensive florists he could find.

Errol proceeded to introduce Pat to all his old cronies, including Nora. They seemed to get on remarkably well together – to the extent that Pat invited her predecessor to Mulholland House.

"I didn't want to go back to our old home," Nora told me. "But Pat wanted me to do so."

The night that she went had all the hallmarks of an embarrassing encounter, but Pat tried hard not to make it so.

"Would you like to see our wedding pictures?" the new Mrs Flynn asked the old. "I'd love to see them," Nora replied and together they went into what had been and once more was the matrimonial bedroom. In these surroundings, Pat took out their wedding album and watched happily as Nora thumbed through the pages.

"If I hadn't known differently," says Nora now, "I would have sworn those pictures were of Errol and me."

Later on, the bedroom would be changed. A friend told me he saw a grand piano there, although Errol was never known by anyone to be in the least bit musical and there was indeed to be little harmony in his life. As before, much of the discord was caused by financial problems.

He constantly worried about money, and from the start of his marriage to Pat the economic state of Errol Flynn had begun to look very precarious indeed.

He was spending almost $500,000 a year, much of it on alimony to Lili and Nora. To bring in more cash in the early fifties, he rented the *Zaca* to Ali Khan, but that still did not produce anything like enough. When he charged Lili with "living extravagantly", the judge threw out the complaint and asked him to look to his own affairs, since he was not paying his bills. A firm of business lawyers had had to go to court before it could get $25,000 Flynn owed them.

A lot of his money had also gone into making films which he later tried to stop. Two of them were for William Marshall. *Bloodline*, which after first turning itself into *The Towers of New Orleans* had become *New Orleans Adventure*, and was now *The Bargain*. It was, most people agreed, no bargain at all.

He had arranged for it to be distributed by the Republic studio, but Warner Brothers, whose contract with Errol allowed him to make outside pictures for a "major" company, said that Republic was not that in anyone's estimation. It was the smallest member of the Motion Picture Producers Association. So Errol, anxious to preserve his $2 million contract, asked the court to prevent Republic from releasing the film. He said he had worked for Marshall for ten days at the rate of $2700 a day, but he had been paid nothing. As a result of the hearing, the picture was temporarily shelved. That gave Flynn a chance to try to stop the other Marshall film.

This was *Hello God*, which had been made in Italy just before Errol moved to France. It was a sixty-four minute black-and-white disaster that showed a completely different uniformed Errol Flynn from the one who usually appeared in war films. No longer was he winning the battle by himself. Instead, he played the most unbelievable Flynn characterization which an audience might have the misfortune to see – a pacifist. Putting it kindly, it was a fantasy picture in which Errol waits at the gates of heaven to greet four soldiers killed at the Anzio Beachhead.

It was poor enough for Errol to realize it would do his reputation no good at all. What was more, he also knew it wouldn't help to keep going that precarious contract with Warner Brothers. Something had to be done and he chose to do it in a manner more fitting to the Flynn style than was his part in the film. He arranged for a friend to steal the negative. The task was completed and a grateful Flynn expected that that, short of a minor financial adjustment, would be the end of the matter. It wasn't. What he did not know was that Marshall had enough rejected footage to piece the thing together again, using stock film and additional sea-shore sequences which he had shot at Santa Barbara.

"Flynn doesn't look his best in some of the rejected shots," admitted Marshall. "But we'll have to use them. I like Flynn as well as anybody, but in business he is pretty difficult. Somebody must be giving him bad advice."

The man from whom that advice came, Flynn's business manager Al Blum, reported a different story. Marshall, he said, had told Errol merely that he had a feature picture requiring a sound commentary and possibly a few brief appearances. "But what he really has is a hodgepodge of junk – old newsreels, clips from other pictures, bad photography – no quality. It's just terrible. And also, I'm afraid of its political aspects."

This was, after all, the time when Senator Joe McCarthy was seeing a Red underneath every Hollywood bed. So what if he actually went looking *into* Errol's bed? Blum didn't dare to contemplate the answer.

Errol did not fancy it either. As if to prove how much of an all-American boy he was, Flynn repeated his contribution to World War Two. He went out to a battlefront, entertaining troops in Korea with Jack Benny and other Hollywood personalities.

Back home, the court ruled that *Hello God* could not be released, and apart from a few sporadic showings in Europe, it never has been. That did not, however, serve to halt the ever-mounting money problems. While on board the *Zaca* at Kingston, Jamaica, Errol heard that Los Angeles county court was now suing him for $3230 in back local taxes, while at the Superior Court, Judge Clarence L. Kineald had awarded Lili Damita yet more alimony – $105,712 worth of it. This included $40,000 in back payments, $61,000 for tax and nearly $4000 he was said to have owed towards the education of Sean, now eleven years old and almost a stranger to his father. Meanwhile, Nora claimed she was owed $7000.

Errol tried to joke about his financial plight. It wouldn't get him down, he said, "so long as I can reconcile my net income with my gross habits".

Errol tried to find a way of getting some money for himself. In March 1952, he thought he might be able to do so by suing a Canadian millionaire, Duncan McMartin, for $20,000. He said the man had struck him a "vicious blow" to the side of his face in a hotel. McMartin replied that he had merely given Flynn "a friendly tap on the cheek in a goodbye gesture". When, at another nightclub, McMartin struck him again, Errol added a further $10,000 to the suit.

Errol won the case, but not as well as he might have done. Had McMartin not accused him of a smart piece of business tactics, he probably would have been awarded more than the $14,000 the judge allowed. McMartin told the court that Flynn had sold a twenty per cent share in his claim. Errol said afterwards that he went into the suit solely for novelty's sake. After being a defendant so many times, he wanted to see what it felt like to be on the other side.

It would be nearer the truth to say that Errol was just lucky that McMartin struck the first blow. At this time Flynn was building up as many feuds as he had once had friendships. A visit to a night-club could indeed be a dangerous occupation since there was usually someone like McMartin ready to flex his muscles. His old image would not lie down. People remembered the times when Errol's fisticuffs had got him into trouble before and were excited by the possibility of being involved themselves in any new scrapes. They were prepared to create the opportunity if it did not present iself automatically.

"If you get up to whack somebody," said Errol, "you're called a brawler. If you don't, you're yellow. So Pat and I are just going to stay home and pull the shades."

Of course, they didn't. But Flynn did keep away from clubs where Humphrey Bogart was likely to be drinking. Many places banned them from being under the same roof together. They were just too much alike and had the gift of upsetting each other without any particular reason. It had become common knowledge they now dis-liked each other so much that an evening sharing a table – or even a floor – was likely to end in a fight. "I love Bogey really," said Flynn in 1952. "You might say our friendship is based on complete disloyalty."

With Bogart he knew how things stood. They just avoided each other. It was much harder with complete strangers. At a nightclub at Nassau a man struck him and "caused intense pain". His opponent had alleged that Errol had been dishonest when claiming to have landed a 150-lb marlin in Jamaica.

"Dishonest?" thundered Errol in mock disbelief and affront. "What, me? Sure I did it for a publicity stunt. Certainly it had been prearranged. But it wasn't dishonest. Just calculated to deceive." It was just another example of Errol's gift for making facts and the English language fit his own needs.

But Errol was deceiving no one by his own extravagance, which continued as the debts piled up and as he continued to worry about them.

He even tried to buy the San Francisco cable car railroad "because I hate to see old monuments go". Fortunately for his bank balance, it went elsewhere. Errol, however, carried on spending money on his homes and on extending the farm and the house at Jamaica, to which he paid three-month-long visits as though he were the custodian of the Bank of America.

Just occasionally, his luck really seemed to change. He won $10,000 on a TV quiz program for correctly answering a five-point sailing question on the right way of approaching other vessels.

If he had a reputation for thinking of Errol Flynn before anyone else, there were times when that reputation seemed undeserved, notably when his friend Freddie McEvoy – the man in whose house the stories of Errol's alleged rapist activities had occurred – drowned while the sportsman's yacht, the *Kangaroo*, sank in a storm. Flynn was more disturbed then than after almost any other loss in his life. To him, McEvoy was a good sport. Praise came no higher. When his friend's affairs were being looked into, Errol offered to adopt McEvoy's stepdaughter, but the idea was never taken up.

To the children of Los Angeles, he presented a seven-year-old gibbon brought over from Borneo to be housed at the Griffith Park Zoo. He said it reminded him of his days in the jungle, days for which he still occasionally yearned. He even talked about going back to New Guinea and to some of the old haunts. The one thing he did not want was to pay his own fare. Once more – and not for the last time – he thought Raoul Walsh might be able to help.

He knew Walsh was a friend of newspaper magnate William Randolph Hearst.

"Uncle," he said, "see if you can get the old man to find me a correspondent's job."

Walsh was talked out of any such idea by Doug Martin, husband of Louella Parsons. "If he goes, Raoul, they'll kill him. They still haven't forgiven Errol there for what he did with those coins that were supposed to turn to silver." The curse of the full moon was threatening to catch up with Flynn nearly twenty years after it had been laid. Errol wisely thought better of the whole adventure.

In some ways he was thinking afresh about a lot of things. There were stories that he and Pat were near breaking point.

Most people had higher hopes of their marriage than of their joint film career. When *Rocky Mountain* was released, Bosley Crowther said in the *New York Times*: "Errol Flynn is an ever gallant fellow but he seems to carry gallantry too far in Warner Brothers' *Rocky*

Mountain." The critic was not enamoured, either, of *Kim*. He wrote of the "brazen brashness of Errol Flynn in the gaudy role of the red-bearded horse thief", but thought little enough of the whole thing. The story was "dragged . . . to a somewhat tedious length".

But Flynn pictures always had their devotees. One of them was Errol's near neighbour, songwriter Sammy Cahn. Cahn ran a 16-mm film club in Beverly Hills and Flynn was the only star known to have 16-mm prints of his movies. He gladly lent them to the club. At the end of their Flynn film season, the club members gave Errol a standing ovation in his absence. Although he had promised to come, he had to back out at the last minute.

No one was going to give an ovation of any kind to *The Bargain* when it was finally cleared ready for release, although audiences were by that time so confused it is doubtful if any of them realized what they were seeing. The picture which had also been called *Bloodline*, *The Towers of New Orleans* and most recently *New Orleans Adventure* was now *The Adventures of Captain Fabian*, distributed after all by Republic as a "Silver Films Production".

It was about a sea captain, played by Flynn, seeking revenge as part of a family feud. As was now usual, the feuds on the screen only echoed rows of another kind. Errol had claimed that he had personally adapted the screenplay but a judge found otherwise and he had to pay his former friend Charles Gross for doing the work. Three years later, Vincent Price launched his case and was awarded $15,000 against Errol. He said he had been promised $35,000 by "Errol Flynn Productions" but had received only $20,000.

All in all, it was a film that everyone should have been spared both the expense and the trouble of seeing. "H.H.T." described it in the *New York Times* as an "absurd, yawn-provoking hodge-podge of romance, intrigue and swashbuckling capers". As for what were then believed to be Errol's writing capabilities, the near-anonymous critic said: "Mr Flynn, apparently after a thorough perusing of *Saratoga Trunk*, wrote the screenplay himself, keeping his role down to a few suave walk-ons. . . . Mr Flynn . . . seems itching to close one eye at the camera."

Which was precisely what Errol was trying to do – and to all of the film town, too. In 1952 he told Louella Parsons that he considered Hollywood to have lost all its colour. The price he had to pay to be at the top was too high.

"This place was made for fun," he told her, sitting on her most comfortable couch, "but there is no joy here. It's getting so that you're afraid to say 'hello' to a friend lest he report it as a misdeed. A man's home is supposed to be his castle, but he's no longer safe even there. Somebody's always prying or snooping about."

Even his literary endeavours were giving him problems. In 1952, the Irish Government banned his book *Showdown*. They said it was "obscene and indecent".

Some things were improving, however. In London, audiences were finally able to see *Objective Burma*. One reason could possibly be that he was about to make a film at Elstree. In any case, Warner Brothers were playing it fairly safe. They included in the Burma picture a prologue which explained that the 14th Army and the Chindits did, after all, have something to do with the victory in that theater of war. Even so, Richard Winnington in the London *News Chronicle* was unimpressed: "Seven years afterwards, the film still looks ridiculous, ill-made and insulting," he said. "Not just because by omission and inference it mocks the British campaign in Burma, but because it mocks all men who fought on any front."

His last two pictures had been painful to watch: *Mara Maru*, about a deep-sea diver looking for a sunken PT boat loaded with diamonds; and *Against All Flags*, a swashbuckling feature for Universal co-starring Anthony Quinn and Maureen O'Hara. That movie was about as invigorating as the tropical fish swimming in Errol's aquarium.

In *Against All Flags*, Errol had one opportunity never presented to him before: instead of salary, he took half the picture's profits. He would have been better off with a regular check, but he seemed to like playing the big stockholder. He ordered work on the film to finish at four every day, because people would work harder if they knew they were going to get away early. And apparently work harder they did. Everything jumped well ahead of schedule ... until Flynn broke his left ankle in a fight scene because he still insisted on not using a double. Shooting was held up for five months until he recovered. The "pirates" in the picture and the ship built on the backlot specially for the movie were meanwhile used for another film.

In between movies, Errol and Pat spent most of their time in Jamaica, living on the *Zaca*, a choice Errol would even have made had the house he was building at Port Antonio been more advanced than it was. From the yacht, he could still easily get to the 3000 acres on which he was developing a good herd of cattle and was also growing coconuts.

Errol was keener than ever to persuade his father – and, of necessity, his mother, too – to join him in Jamaica permanently. He even built a church there for them, not because the senior Flynns were any more religious than he was himself but so as to make it more like the Ireland they had come to love. Before long, they agreed to come. It was useful for Errol because he had just bought the Tichfield Hotel at Port Antonio as the latest part of his expansionist program for the island. With his parents on hand, they could keep an eye on the place for him.

The only trouble was that it became yet another excuse for rows between mother and son. Mrs Flynn appointed herself manageress of the hotel, and took exception to every man booking in with a lady who might not be his wife. When Errol went nude bathing, it was in her eyes an offense quite as bad as statutory rape. Errol and his mother had never got on; now every argument became part of a war of attrition. Before long, the hotel and his mother would become just too much.

The very presence of Errol Flynn on any movie lot was being regarded by studio bosses in much the same way. To keep his name before the public he had managed to get Warners to release *The Cruise of the Zaca*. To that he added a ten-minute documentary called *Deep Sea Fishing* which mainly showed Errol and Howard Hill catching marlin with bow and arrow.

The Master of Ballantrae, which was released by the company, seemed at the time to be Errol's last link with his old studio. It was about an episode in the story of the fight between the Stuarts and the Hanoverians, with Flynn as a Stuart supporter and Anthony Steel playing his younger brother, a king's man. The picture was better than most of the films that had gone before it. The fact that it succeeded, however, had little to do with any attempt at sobriety on Errol's part. Jack Cardiff, who was the director of photography, has said that Flynn on his arrival at Elstree on the first day, went straight to the bar and ordered six neat scotches. According to Cardiff's own book, they were introduced to each other at lunch that day. Flynn said to Cardiff: "Hey, Jackson. I'm glad you're gonna photograph me. Don't worry about this fat. I'll fuck it off in three days."

Errol appeared to be enjoying making the film. After all, Stevenson had described the "Master" as "an unco' man with the lassies and ever in the front of broils". Flynn was once more getting to know the local scenery, including, by all accounts, a young film starlet apparently on the threshold of a long career. June Thorburn, then twenty-one and about to star in *Pickwick Papers*, was reported to have met Errol at a party given by Noël Coward, after which she received a message asking her to phone him. A few years later she was killed in an air crash.

While working at Elstree, Flynn stayed at a blue-painted Georgian house at Church Row, Hampstead. A year later his landlady sued him for unpaid gas and electricity bills amounting to less than £30, not at all the kind of sums he was used to fighting over.

From Hampstead he moved into the Savoy, where he was fetched out of his bath by the arrival of a certain Mr Fred Colley. Errol, in a mustard-coloured dressing gown and smoking a cigarette from an amber holder, was told: "I have a writ for you, Mr Flynn." It was a claim for £195 owed for a radio transmitter for the *Zaca*. "It's all right, old boy," said Flynn, who closed the door on the visitor as if he were the postman bringing his fan mail.

Errol went to Italy and then on to Sicily to add the finishing touches to the Stevenson film. When it was released, *The Times* said the picture was "more likely to please an audience which either does not know Stevenson's work or sets no great store by it. Action, of course, there is in abundance, the presence of Mr Errol Flynn in the cast is enough to suggest that. ..."

After *Ballantrae*, Errol settled down to the life of an Italian film producer, with all the prospect that appeared to offer of "*la dolce vita*". With an Italian company he co-produced a film hailed as a sequel to *Don Juan*, indeed in Italy it was called *Il Maestro di Don Giovanni*. In America it was to be known briefly – for that was exactly how long it ran – as *Crossed Swords*.

Apart from Flynn playing his usual role, the picture had an entirely Italian cast, led by the imposing Gina Lollobrigida. He related to her very well. Not so easy were the extras: men who seemed to enjoy swinging cutlasses at each other long after filming had finished and girls who were either scratching out each other's eyes or weeping uncontrollably at the crimes committed against them by their hairdressers.

He found great difficulty in understanding the words of a song with which the girls, in between their tears and their violence, serenaded him in English. Eventually he had the lyric written down for him: "Let down your nighties, don't lock yourselves in. It's just that virgin, Errol Flynn." A dialogue coach had been having fun and the girls hadn't a clue what they were singing.

He also sampled the Italian nightlife. At a Venice club, a jitterbug dancer – it took a long time in those days for American fads to reach Italy – asked him to "dance" with the result he was thrown around so much that he injured his back. He tried to persuade other people as well as himself that he was perfectly fit. Yet he was anything but. When he came down with an attack of jaundice at about this time, Pat was told by his doctor: "He's a very sick man, you know."

There was still a fighting spirit in him, though. The newly-named Errol Flynn Enterprises company had more plans. One of them was for a film he wanted to make called *The King Farouk Story*, based on the life of the man with whom Errol could sometimes be found drinking on the Via Veneto and for which he wanted to star Orson Welles. Another idea was to produce *The Adventures of William Tell*.

17

The Adventures of William Tell

There was a sensitivity about him.
Vincent Price

Perhaps things would have been simpler for Errol had he made the
Farouk film. After all, people were still very interested in, if appalled
by, the activities of the Egyptian monarch whom Errol had met at
a party and called "Big Jim". They were never part of each other's
set, but on more than one evening, with bottles of champagne and
vodka in front of them, they had sat together and compared an
idyllic past with a depressing present and ended up taking a couple
of girls to an address in Rome that Farouk kept for such a purpose.

Yet Errol decided that the story was too close a subject for comfort. So irrevocably, he turned to the tale of the Swiss archer forced
to shoot an apple from his son's head. Once settled on that, he determined to put everything he could into it. He had finally tired of
his reputation – a justifiable one, he knew – for being a playboy
who had once been lucky enough to be a star. Suddenly, he now
wanted to become an actor.

With a team of Italian backers, he worked out that the picture
would cost $860,000 after being shot in the then entirely new
medium of Cinemascope. Up to then, only one film had been made
in this wide-screen process – *The Robe* – and that had not yet been
released.

After a series of meetings a deal was struck with the Italians. They
would put up $430,000 if Errol would do the same. He agreed, and
was set to make *the* film of his life. He wanted that now as he had
wanted little else before. So far there was not enough to show Pat
that he could still be exciting and magnetic on the screen. He needed

to prove it to her. What was more, there would soon be another Flynn to impress. Pat was pregnant. His new child would have to have a father to be proud of and there was a contract in Errol's hands to show that it was all going to happen soon. So work began at Courmayeur, a beauty spot in the Alps, immediately his legal advisers gave him the go-ahead.

Meanwhile, Pat patiently awaited the birth of their baby, staying in a fashionable Rome apartment near Errol's friend and business associate, Barry Mahon. The Flynns liked to talk about the impending arrival. Errol was sure it would bring real success to their marriage. "If it's a boy," he declared, "I'm going to call him Seventeen. That's my lucky number."

The baby arrived on Christmas Day – when Errol had to leave thirty guests to get their own drinks so that he could drive the mother-to-be to the hospital. The friends were still in the apartment when he returned with the news that he had another daughter, to be named Arnella – "after William the Conqueror's mother," he explained incorrectly – William's mother was Arletta.

So he abandoned ideas about a child being called after his lucky number. That really should have been an augury of things to come. Had Errol had the foresight to recognize it as such, he might have saved himself a fortune as well as a great deal of trouble.

For one thing, he could not start shooting before a costly labour problem was sorted out. The American Federation of Labor discovered that the film was to be made with a work force largely supplied by the Italian Communist-dominated General Confederation and threatened to "black" the whole project, which would have meant it could never be shown in the States. Only some gentle persuasion from Flynn, using techniques similar to the ones he had previously reserved for getting young girls to his bedroom, managed to solve that matter. But he had worse problems to think about, problems that did not become apparent until after half an hour's usable film had been shot and a great deal of money spent.

Early on, he had sent a telegram to his old friend Bruce Cabot. This said simply: COME OVER AND PLAY A PART STOP THREE MONTHS FUN AND THE ITALIANS WILL PAY THE EQUIVALENT OF FIVE GRAND.

Cabot ran – and then for weeks proceeded to run out on Errol, returning to work only when the money got tight. But members of Flynn's set were never discarded for mere misbehaviour. After he had gone back to work, Errol was happy to invite Cabot home to dinner with Pat, and Cabot equally happily went.

Being nice to Cabot was just one mistake Errol made. Another was to reject a bosomy young Italian actress whom he had tested for a role in the film. He decided she had no future in movies that weren't intended purely for an Italian market. Her name – Sophia Loren.

Just about the only sensible thing Errol did do at this time was to hire as his director Jack Cardiff, the man who had impressed him so much with his camera work in *Ballantrae*. It would be Cardiff's first job as a director, although he would be doubling up with his usual work, too.

He could do nothing to help Errol, apart from making any film that he could get into the cameras to look good, and there were all too many things combining to stop *William Tell*'s progress. Quite suddenly, the Italian backers told Errol they had run out of cash. The man who had promised to provide $250,000 towards the cost of production had, it transpired, only given $50,000. The effect on Flynn was shattering. Errol had invested all his resources and neither he nor Mahon could get any more. The day he found that out, Flynn walked through the streets of Rome like a zombie. The world seemed unreal. He had not really been broke for twenty years and the feeling it gave him to be back in that position now was frightening.

To make things worse, he had just heard that the American Board of Internal Revenue was yet again cracking down on him – with the claim that this time he owed them $820,000. He did not even bother to pretend to himself that he could borrow the rest of the money that he needed either to complete the picture or to pay his tax. At forty-three, Errol Flynn looked and felt like an old man.

Even money which he assumed would be there for the asking had gone. From Los Angeles he received news that Al Blum, his business adviser, who patently had not done his job for years, was dying of cancer and had spent all Errol's remaining cash on a private plane and a new Cadillac for himself.

But the real blow was struck by Bruce Cabot. The man who, despite everything, Errol considered to be his best friend consulted lawyers immediately he heard about the crash and sued for unpaid salary. While he waited, he sequestered both the cars of Flynn and Mahon and all of their wives' clothes.

Errol would have been angry about anyone doing that to him. But Cabot! He claimed that for fifteen years he had been "stuffing him down Jack Warner's neck" – to say nothing of offering Cabot the Italian job in the first place, suffering from his failures to turn up for work and entertaining him to dinner only the night before – when Cabot both knew of the collapse and said nothing about the action he was going to take.

With everything falling around him, Errol's health took more punishment still. He was felled by another attack of jaundice, this time worse than the one months before. A doctor told Pat: "Your husband is a very sick man. His liver is exhausted and we don't think he'll pull through." Errol overheard that conversation and crawled out of bed. As he said in his own book, he was determined not to die before Jack Warner did.

Slightly recovered, he spent four days in London in November 1953 to try to get some kind of financial backing. Instead of going into the City to talk to stockbrokers, Errol dined at the smart restaurants and sat in the leather armchairs of the clubs of people he thought were friends. He was a great believer in the adage that the best way to get money was to pretend that he didn't need it.

On the BBC's radio chat show, *In Town Tonight*, he kept nothing back, but made it all seem like a big joke.

The interviewer, John Ellison, asked him how he was feeling. "Never better in my life," he replied.

"When did you finish the film?"

"Finish it? John, you shouldn't talk about it. I'm bogged down at the moment. That's why I'm in London. I came here to *pretend* I had nothing on my mind at all – I just came to borrow £50,000."

"Fifty thousand? That's a lot of money."

"What do you mean, £50,000 is a lot of money? It's nothing."

Was there nothing that could be done, Ellison asked. Well, Errol said, all he had was thirty minutes of film. "They don't make silent pictures any more, do they?"

He returned to Rome saying he had promises for all of the £50,000 he needed, but practically none of that materialized. Asked if this made any difference to future Flynn production participations in Italy, he replied: "You may have said a mouthful there."

More than anything, Errol was angry with the United States Embassy in Rome and its Ambassador, the famed Clare Booth Luce, whom he tried to see five times, but always without success. He said he would rather not ask for help from Warner Brothers. Almost immediately after that statement an announcement was made that the contract he had had with the studio for more than twenty years had been ended by "mutual agreement".

Meanwhile, the Italian courts were getting tough. Errol's creditors included hotel keepers, a lumber company which had built an entire Swiss village for the venture, and local furniture stores. The bailiffs now took all his cameras, film stock and other equipment. The only prop that could not be taken by them was a crossbow. It had already been stolen by a sneak thief.

Finally, a stream of near-penniless actors, technicians and extras began drifting away from Courmayeur in a dawn caravan of old cars, trailers and buses. They looked like refugees from a different kind of débâcle, and left behind them hotel bills unpaid to the tune of $14,000.

Errol's maid Layo was smuggled out overnight from her hotel room by his chauffeur. But there was no escape for Errol himself who, once the first shock had passed, had been showing an amazing facility for looking totally sanguine. Perhaps it was the knowledge that for the first time in his life he was entirely the innocent party.

Not that that made life any easier for him at the Rome penthouse which now was beginning to resemble Stalingrad during the Siege. The maid was the front-line army defending the bastion both from a horde of creditors and a group of pressmen anxious to get their hands on the once more bloodshot-eyed figure of Errol Flynn. As usual, his own principal refuge was in his drink and his drugs.

In the Brown Derby restaurant at Beverly Hills, Errol repeated the things he had done in London. He bought drinks for everyone around and treated a friend to the most expensive dish on the menu. When you were in hock for almost half a million dollars, what did another hundred or so matter? It was at the restaurant that he reluctantly agreed to part with his Gauguin for $50,000. When the time came to remove the picture from Mulholland House, Errol felt as though he were on the way to the cemetery with the body of a beloved relative.

Other money came to him less painfully. He got wind that an Italian vermouth company was using his picture in their advertising. He sued for $5000 and collected. He also went back into television quiz games with *The Big Surprise*. Once more, he answered questions on sailing, listing this time the different kinds of navigation used, identifying pictures of boats and stating when national colours were flown. He collected a total of $30,000. His financial situation was also helped by renting out the *Zaca* again, this time to Mary Pickford and her husband.

For a time he still talked about finishing *William Tell*, but the dream sank like the money he had put into the venture. When word got out just how broke he was, the creditors started homing in on him like vultures after a safari. Eventually, in the Rome courts, he sued, and got custody of the film's negative. As he said, it was not easy to find anyone willing to shell out half a million dollars for a few miles of exposed celluloid.

Some friends were kind. Without his knowing, a man living in Cuba put $10,000 into his bank account. Errol complained that it smacked of charity but gratefully accepted it just the same.

There was no suggestion of charity in another offer made to him while he was in Rome. It came from Herbert Wilcox, husband of the British screen darling, Anna Neagle. The Wilcoxes had heard about Errol's trouble at the same time as they were looking for a male lead to play opposite Anna in a screen version of her successful stage show, *The Glorious Days*. They offered him the part.

Flynn talked to Barry Mahon about it. They agreed on his getting £25,000 for the picture – chickenfeed compared to what he had been used to receiving. "I'd have never got him had he not needed the money," Wilcox told me. But the producer knew Errol really hoped he would be taking over *William Tell* from him and, of course, Wilcox had no intention of doing that. Nevertheless, Flynn did not bother too much about the fripperies of the deal as he sat in his office. Wilcox asked him: "What about the contract, Errol?"

"What about it?" he replied.

"When do we sign it?"

"You sign it for me," said Flynn.

Needless to say, Errol did sign before work on the picture began. On the first day of filming, Wilcox asked him: "Won't it be pleasant to play a nice guy for a change?"

"I'm not very fond of nice guys," Errol answered, unsmiling. As if to demonstrate the fact, he took the Wilcoxes on to the *Zaca* for dinner and treated them to the spectacle of a fight between himself and the captain. Tempers were frayed on both sides, but Errol was determined to show that he was the one who was going to win. Like a child fed up with a broken toy, he picked up the captain and threw him overboard.

In the studio, Errol was a lot more conventional. He even kept girls off the set, although he was heard to suggest to more than one young lady that a visit to his hotel room in the evening could prove more rewarding.

As Wilcox told me: "He could turn on the charm like North Sea Gas." News of this impeccable behaviour had some surprising repercussions. Errol was even invited to attend the annual Burma reunion of the 14th Army at the Royal Albert Hall, just to show that *Objective Burma* had been forgiven. Flynn said he had a previous engagement and could not go, although he joked that the real reason for his absence was: "I haven't won the war yet."

In *Lilacs in the Spring*, as the film became known, Errol appeared once more in the uniform of a British Army captain weighed down this time both by a chestful of medals and the thought of having to do a song and dance act. He sang and tapped to the tune of *Lily of Laguna* as part of his role as Dame Anna's music-hall partner and also as her husband. According to her, he was a delight to work with when he was sober. She said on a television program that he learned his dance steps "like lightning". But "on his bad days, I can't remember anyone so terrible". He'd arrive for work no earlier than noon, unchanged and unshaved, just in time for the picnic lunch that had been provided for the cast.

When the film was released, Leonard Mosley, the critic of the London *Daily Express*, declared that Errol "now looks and acts like an understudy for Michael Wilding".

Herbert Wilcox had to admit that Errol worked well on the dance floor, although "he was no Fred Astaire". He liked him well enough to sign him for another £25,000 role in *King's Rhapsody*, which to the theater coach trade in Britain was an act of devotion indeed. It had been the last stage show by that idol of the mass audiences, Ivor Novello.

In the meantime Errol had another British film to make. This was *The Warriors*, also known as *The Dark Avenger*, although the darkest avenger of all to Flynn still seemed to be one Bruce Cabot. Not content with the cars and the clothes he had impounded, Cabot now sued for £17,000 in the British courts, because with his Jamaican home Flynn was a colonial resident. Lord Justice Morris dismissed the suit.

Flynn's ex-wives were another problem. Both charged he was behind with his payments. By this time Nora had divorced Dick Haymes, although her picture often appeared in the movie papers. Errol and Pat were sitting reading at home one day when she passed him a copy of a movie magazine. Errol saw it, grew red in the face and phoned his bank ordering them to stop Nora's next alimony check.

"Why did you stop that money?" Nora asked when she saw Errol soon afterwards. He pulled no punches in telling her. "I got so pissed off seeing you wearing that new fur coat in the picture that I decided I needed the money more than you did," he said.

With no chance of the big break on his own, Errol tried to find a way of getting back into favour with the big studios. "One day, Wymore," he told Pat, using her surname with the same kind of affectionate deprecation he had adopted to call Nora "Ma", "one day, I'll win an Academy Award."

There had been talk of his teaming up with "The King", Clark Gable. Flynn loved the idea, but Gable wasn't nearly so keen. "I'm not going to appear in a picture with that son of a bitch," he said.

"He'd make me look terrible." He had obviously not seen Errol recently. The ravages of time, drink and drugs were now making *him* look terrible.

For the moment, he had to content himself with *The Dark Avenger*.

Had the film been shot a few years earlier, *The Dark Avenger* – or *The Warrior* or *The Black Prince* as it was originally to have been called – might also have done permanent injury to Errol's career. As it was, without anyone expecting anything more from him, it was allowed to slide painlessly to oblivion. The only notable thing about it was Flynn's co-starring with Joanne Dru, who was the first wife of Dick Haymes who had in turn of course been married to Nora.

Once more Errol was surprising people with his conscientious application to the role of being a father. Back on the American continent after the Elstree film, the Flynns flew to Rio for both the carnival and a film festival. On the plane, Fred MacMurray called out to his fellow passenger Walter Pidgeon: "Hey, look at this."

"This" was Errol Flynn with baby Arnella on his lap, feeding her from her bottle.

Lest this excursion into domesticity give him a bad name, Errol made up for it in Rio by successfully chasing a curvaceous young Japanese girl up the branches of a tree. The girl was a starlet chosen to represent her country's film industry, which Errol automatically took to be an indication of her availability. He got as far as a hand under her skirt when the girl jumped to safety. Yet Errol could still try to protest: "Women mean nothing to me any more. I'm a respectably happy married man."

This time he was saying it in the company of Sean, now a strapping fifteen-year-old who joined his father when he returned to Britain to make his first TV series, *The Errol Flynn Theatre*, at Bray Studios. These were still the early days of black and white TV drama and the idea was that Errol would repeat what Dick Powell was already doing very successfully: playing the role of compère as well as acting in six of the films himself. The first, *The Mirror*, starred Pat with Philip Friend.

As usual, there were problems. Making the series, Errol fell and slipped a disc. Filming was halted while he was confined to bed in his hotel room.

But he was certainly doing his best to show how he had completely reformed. When filming of *King's Rhapsody* switched to Spain, the Flynns took a $125-a-month villa in Majorca and Errol promised there would be no booze, "just a glass of champagne for breakfast". Later on he was seen to succumb to the temptation of cheap Spanish wine which seemed to be flowing like the water on which the *Zaca* and so many Flynn dreams floated.

If *King's Rhapsody* had been one of those dreams, it was one that he had to forget quickly. In every conceivable way it was a nightmare. Only Anna Neagle and Pat who co-starred with them came out of it with a modicum of pride intact. The two women had the musical numbers between them. But the cinema-going public had by then discovered television and this outdated Ruritanian romp was not the sort of thing to make them forsake the small screen. Errol's showing in *King's Rhapsody* was nominated by Milton Shulman in the London *Sunday Express* as "the year's most forgettable performance".

Yet things were to get better. Quite unexpectedly, he had a call from Universal, asking simply: "Would you like to come back to Hollywood?"

At this stage in Errol's career, the call seemed to offer all the magic that a few years earlier could have come only from a young lady unbuttoning her blouse and saying: "Would you like to come to bed with me?"

He ran. The film, *Istanbul*, turned out to be no better than *King's Rhapsody*, but it invigorated him. One of the supporting actors, Martin Benson, remembers a scene in which he and Flynn had a fight. Benson's suit, which he had to provide for himself, was badly torn in the skirmish. When he realized that, Errol stopped shooting instantly and demanded that the wardrobe department provide his "opponent" with a new suit. "That was Errol's famous charm," Benson says today.

One of the clauses in Flynn's contract was that he laid off the hard stuff for the duration of the picture. And certainly, you couldn't smell a drop on his breath or see a bottle in his dressing room. An observant visitor, however, might have noted an extra-ordinary number of flower vases about – all minus the flowers. Every one of them was well stocked with vodka.

The film's proceeds only smoothed the edges of his financial worries. Now he was down to only one car – a converted yellow cab. His financial advisers suggested one sure course of events: he must go bankrupt. Errol refused. "All my life I've been very proud of my credit and I still intend to pay off 100 cents on the dollar," he told them.

The hardest part of that decision came in October 1955. A court ordered him to forfeit Mulholland House, scene of so frequent a marital row and so many extra-marital assignations. The place where girls dropped their panties as easily as others dropped writs through his mail box, the house where Barrymore sat and where other members of the Olympiads boozed their way through their amoral history of primitive art was to go to some new owner.

This seemed likely to be a firm of publicists in the process of suing Flynn and William Marshall for $1988.62 cents the sum that still remained unpaid for their work on *The Adventures of Captain Fabian*. The judge ordered that the PR men should get the house in lieu of money because no takers had been found for it. It had been advertised, but the only applicant was a San Diego man who sent a telegram and then didn't show up to look over the property. At the last minute it went elsewhere and to the one person – Bruce Cabot excepted – to whom Errol least wanted it to go. Lili Damita took it in exchange for unpaid alimony and so also settled her ex-husband's debt. Flynn's wicked, wicked ways were having disastrous repercussions.

His financial situation was now so desperate that he was continually thinking about the only thing of which he could be certain. To Raoul Walsh, the man he constantly repeated was the only person he could trust, he said: "Uncle, when I kick off, I want to be buried in the Swiss Colony vineyards."

Before that could happen, he called in that friend to help save his sanity – for just as he was about to move from the house for the last time, narcotics investigators came and took away a number of prescriptions. It seemed likely there would be a prosecution. In the end, there wasn't; but Errol would not have dared hope for that at the time. What he knew was that the world was crashing in around him from all directions and he wanted Walsh to provide the sort of comfort which at that moment he believed only another man could give.

Walsh arrived at the scene of the "resurrection" of John Barrymore to find the house in a state of complete neglect. Newspapers lined the floor and there was dust everywhere. Alex the butler had gone. "My lungs have had it," Errol told him. "The quacks say my liver is shot to hell. So what does it matter where I go?" With that, he drove away to the boat. Mulholland House would never see him again.

Now, with nowhere of his own in Hollywood to live, Errol went back to his first American home: the Garden of Allah. There, a constant stream of girls called at his bungalow to keep him company. They only left, according to Sheila Graham's book *The Garden of Allah*, when Pat was around. One evening when she was there, the couple had such a violent row that the verbal pyrotechnics could be heard all over the estate.

The Garden was Arnella's first American home, too. At the time she spoke perfect French and Italian, but no English. Her one concession to the habits of the Anglo-Saxons was to agree to be called Mike.

This was the first time she had got to know her half sisters Deirdre and Rory, who gave their father a "Welcome Home" party soon after his return to the States. It was quite the strangest party ever to have Errol as the center of attraction. All the other guests were schoolgirls and Errol was careful not to let his attention stray, lest someone, somewhere, get a wrong idea.

There was quite clearly a great bond between Deirdre, Rory and the man they now called "the Baron", never Daddy, and for his part, he worked very hard at cultivating it.

It was as though he knew he had failed at most things and was determined to be a success in the one role for which he thought he could not be replaced. But he had bided his time. When the children were very young, he had not thought he could contribute much. But when he was able to communicate with them, he was ready to do what he saw as his duty.

He told them he insisted on their having good table manners and he demanded that the youngsters were courteous when they were approached by adults. "Speak only when you are spoken to," he ordered Deirdre, and neither she nor her sister ever had the temerity to argue. He could lose his temper very easily. But he could also be equally conscientious in sharing the fun with them.

They went to amusement parks, sneaking in through the gates without paying, and when they went to eat at Chinese restaurants, they would try to find ways of taking the crockery away with them.

To Sean, Errol saw his responsibilities differently. He didn't think the boy was sufficiently strongly chipped from the old block, so in response to a request for money he wrote: "You needed $100. I added an extra $25 for condoms and/or flowers."

They all knew by now something of Errol's reputation, certainly of his fame in the film world. But he didn't tell them. Friends would ring them up with news they had picked out of the papers.

Errol carried pictures of his children with him everywhere: in his wallet and in a tiny gold book he wore on the end of a gold chain.

This domestic happiness was also an escape from everything else. A court was told he still owed his agents, MCA Artists Ltd, $13,560. Flynn was discharged only after two hours of questioning and by promising not to dispose of any of his property for thirty days. During that time, MCA could assess and then draw what they needed.

In truth, money by now had become little more for him than figures on a sheet of paper. Somehow it would be found. Somehow it had to be found. There was always his past to consider, like the sum he had just agreed to pay Lili in the future: $23,000 a year alimony as well as $50,000 into a trust fund for Sean.

On the positive side, there were several people owing him at least $1000. He also still owned fifty-one per cent of his Jamaican cattle and coconut ranch (which was losing money) and two acres of land at Apple Valley in California.

But almost every mail brought news of more demands. Nora

resorted to a subpoena in January 1956 to get him to answer charges
of failing to support her two girls. He was $4325 in arrears, she main-
tained. He paid up to the tune of $7000 by the end of April.

Clearly, he had constantly to be on the look-out for more ways
of raising funds. The magazine *Confidential* seemed to offer one of
these. He sued it for a million dollars, as had Clark Gable, Robert
Mitchum and Doris Duke.

For years the magazine had been earning a reputation as the
scandal sheet of America, specializing in the Hollywood set. What
made Errol furious was a statement that after their "marriage in
Hollywood" (the magazine forgot about the high jinks in Monte
Carlo) Errol had said to Pat: "See you later, darling. I've got a date
with a call-girl." It would take two years for the case to be settled.

Meanwhile, he was getting up to some strange tricks of his own
choosing, like asking Hedda Hopper to sign a document when she
came to interview him. This read: "I, Hedda Hopper, do hereby
agree that while Errol Flynn is my guest he shall be protected from
lawyers, process servers, former friends other than well-meaning
ones and that this conversation with me shall not become a part
or parcel of any future legal proceedings whatsoever."

Certainly it was all very jokey. But if many a true word were
spoken in jest, that gave some indication of the way the Flynn mind
worked at this time. Nothing was allowed to escape his cynicism.

When he landed in jail on a charge of drunkenness, it was no
more than he would have expected to happen to him, even though
he swore not a drop had passed his lips.

It happened when he was a guest at the Publicists Association's
annual Ballyhoo Ball. He had gone there with his friend Cedric
Kehoe and a twenty-one-year-old actress called Maura Fitz-
Gibbons. The trouble was that Errol started a game of "Hunt
the Badge" with an off-duty policeman who didn't appreciate the
sport.

To people like the club's hat-check girl Simone Friedman, Errol
Flynn still represented glamour and romance, the sort of things that
her husband William believed should be left behind whenever he
stepped out of a cinema. At the Los Angeles station house where
William worked they had other things on their minds. When

Simone asked Errol for his autograph, William didn't like it at all. He took one look at the star and said: "You're drunk."

"Who are you?" asked Flynn with a broad smile.

"I'm a policeman," replied Friedman, who then got out his badge to prove it.

To Errol that was as good an excuse for a lark as any. He snatched the badge from the officer, looked directly into his eyes and said: "I'll give you $5 for it." Friedman snarled and that should have been the signal for the game to stop. But it did not. Errol handed the badge to Kehoe, he gave it to Maura and she put it in her glove. The policeman watched incredulously as Maura then said she had "lost" both glove and badge.

Flynn and Kehoe both laughed raucously. But not for long. More than a thousand people, mostly in fancy dress and nearly all of them from the film colony, saw Errol being carted off by Officer Friedman. The indignity of it all was enormous. Later, he was released on bail. Then, after the publicists had issued a statement apologizing to Errol for the affair, the judge dismissed the whole thing for lack of evidence. Errol sued for $40,000 but never collected.

All he was saying now was how much he wanted to get back to Pat, who was waiting for him at Majorca. When he did return there in the company of Sean, he gave a party aboard the *Zaca* to show how happy they were together – a party in the old Hollywood tradition with everyone, including Errol, diving fully clothed into the water. He said he had a lot to celebrate. He had finally paid off his debts – thanks, he said, to Pat.

"She saved my life," he told friends. "I'd have run when the going was so tough, but Pat without a word of complaint helped me straighten out my affairs, stuck with me and gave me encouragement. I never thought I'd ever say I'd be lonely for a woman, but do you know something? I can't bear to be separated from her. She gave me a confidence I had all but lost."

Even on the *Zaca* they did not always share the same bed. The yacht was anchored off the Spanish coast one night when they did. Both were sleeping in the nude when they were awoken by the sound of voices in their stateroom. Four complete strangers – two men and two women, two of them Spanish, the others French and

American – had swum to the boat, climbed aboard and burst into the cabin saying words to the effect of: "Hi, Errol, where's the party?"

Flynn ordered them off and, displaying his body in the full glory that no film audience had ever seen, proceeded to fight them, if necessary to their death. By the time that the last Spanish invader had left, a sizeable quantity of the man's front teeth were embedded in Errol's fist.

Errol was ill for four days after that, caused by a virus picked up with the unwanted teeth.

Of course, he always had another kind of virus in his system. The one that never allowed him to settle down. A few months after this episode, even the idyll of his marriage was of the past. Errol was roving again. Without Pat.

18

The Big Boodle

*I had not seen Errol for years, but there he
was. I could have smelt that liquor half a
block away. Totally drunk, he fell over
when he embraced and hugged me. Very sad
because he had started to assume the
stature of an actor.*
Irving Rapper

Suddenly, Errol was being seen without Pat at all the places where
they had formerly seemed so inseparable. Now, apparently free of
his money problems – and it was a very temporary state of affairs
– he was once more at clubs and restaurants with other pretty girls,
mostly younger than Pat.

With friends, he would appear to be happier than ever, but it
was a front. Alone, he was morose, worrying about almost everything, particularly about his looks. The hard body of the boxing
champion and tennis wizard had turned, as had his jowls, to fat.
His hair was grey and getting very thin, which concerned him a
great deal. In a move born out of sheer desperation he took to washing it in a shampoo of pure vodka. For a time he was convinced
it worked miracles, but before long he rediscovered a better use for
the spirit.

"You know, old boy," he told one of his drinking companions,
"one of the biggest fallacies is that life begins at forty. Don't you
believe it. At forty your hair begins to fall out, your teeth loosen,
your bones begin to ache and you wake up feeling lousy. I know.
I've been forty too long." He was now forty-eight.

To her closest friends, Pat would say that Errol seemed to
be losing interest in all the things that used to fascinate him. "A

brilliant man following the line of least resistance," she told one
girl. To Errol himself she said bitterly: "I don't think you should
ever have got married." They had not talked about divorce. Indeed,
they had not talked very much at all. One day, Errol left Pat in
Jamaica and appeared not to want to go back to her. Occasionally he
phoned.

Nora was also worried about his disappearance. When Deirdre,
then thirteen, had to have an appendicitis operation, Flynn refused
to pay the $325 bill. Unfortunately, the girl picked up the extension
and heard "the Baron" say no.

Had he known that, he would doubtless have been more careful.
Upsetting the children was one thing he would never have permitted
himself in what he liked to consider his saner moments. He knew
that he was not always responsible for all the things he did when
he was under the influence of too much drink or too many drugs,
but this evening was not one of those times. Now he was saddled
with the fact that he had not only been mean – but had been heard
to be so.

It took a hearing at Santa Monica Supreme Court to finally re-
solve the matter. Flynn was ordered to set up yet another trust fund,
this time in support of Deirdre and Rory. He had to deposit $6500
in their names on the first day of each year. The fund would be administered by their maternal grandfather, Sheriff Jack Eddington.

He agreed that it was probably a wise move for him not to take
charge of that responsibility himself. "I have a great talent for
spending money," he admitted. "And a decent chap never lets his
public down."

Neither did he want to let down the people who were expecting
so much of his battle with *Confidential*. When it finally came to
court, he decided to fight it as though he were fencing with a villain
on the screen and rescuing a maiden in distress all at the same time.
This time, the maiden in question was the purity of Hollywood.
He was riding a charger into the castle of evil on behalf of all the
movie colony.

At the same time, the State of California was bringing its
own case of criminal libel against the magazine at a jury trial. Also
being mentioned were Clark Gable, Desi Arnez, Maureen

O'Hara, Dorothy Dandridge, June Allyson, Forrest Tucker, Robert Mitchum, Corinne Calvet, Mae West and Joan Crawford.

Flynn became the articulate spokesman for them all: "All of us have done things of which we aren't proud, but it is a craven and cowardly thing not to hit back," he said. And he went on: "I think it is about time someone stepped forward to unsully the fair name of we thespians. I think it is about time the actors and actresses came forward and said: 'I did this thing or didn't do it as related in the magazine'."

As for Errol's own case, Justice Irving Saypol ordered the magazine to name names, such as that of the call-girl with whom Flynn was supposed to have spent his wedding night, and those of drug addicts alleged to have taken part in a "lewd and obscene performance" at that time. In the end, Errol settled for $15,000 – an offer made on the steps of the courthouse by the editor.

When the jury hearing the State's case against the magazine failed to agree, the judge ordered *Confidential* to pay just $5000 in fines. Another magazine called *Whisper* had to pay a similar amount.

By now, Errol had other interests. In 1957, he went to Cuba and found the early campaigns against the corrupt rule of President Batista to be stirring his own spirit of adventure. He was there to make a film for United Artists called *The Big Boodle*, which had all the marks of a second-rate second feature. He played a croupier at the Havana Casino. It was done just for the money and it showed.

Had he not already signed a contract with Twentieth Century-Fox, it is doubtful if he would ever have received any more film offers. But by then work had already begun on a new picture. Errol's was a very unusual role indeed: for the first time since *Don't Bet on Blondes*, he was not the star. But he wouldn't regret his "demotion". *The Sun Also Rises* showed an Errol Flynn his public had all but forgotten.

The real male star was the studio's own hero in the Flynn mould, Tyrone Power. Ava Gardner and Mel Ferrer also had bigger billing than Errol did, but it was his performance as the playboy Mike Campbell which made this version of the Hemingway story *Fiesta* memorable.

"Errol Flynn of all people steals the acting honours in the film in a rollicking caricature of a drunken Briton," reported the *Daily Express*'s Leonard Mosley.

With every desperate sip at the bottle and each ploy to get into bed with a girl, Errol showed that he could, after all, call himself an actor.

"I don't know why everybody is praising me so much for this," he said when the tributes began to multiply like law suits. "I was only playing myself."

There was talk of his playing a *reformed* drunk in a film with Debbie Reynolds. "Now that really will test my reputation as an actor," he only partly joked. At last, the sun had definitely started rising for Errol Flynn.

It was not so much that the old Flynn was back again, more that a newer, more confident Errol was drinking both in the bars of Beverly Hills and on board the *Zaca*. "You can't get rid of Flynn that easily, sport," he told a bartender, pouring his tenth glass of vodka at a single sitting. But was he happy? To the extent that at last, after all those years, he seemed to be in demand from the studios, he was. If he never considered work important in the old days, he did now. It had given him a new self-respect.

About this time, Irving Rapper was asked by Jack Warner to consider filming the recently-published autobiography of Diana Barrymore. A few days later, he said he wanted to make the picture very much indeed, but that it should be even more the story of Diana's father, John Barrymore. And, he said: "There is only one man to play Barrymore – Errol Flynn."

Warner's comments were lost in a flood of obscenities, but after a time even he had to agree that Flynn would be an inspired – and once he had thought about it – obvious choice.

Strange things happen in Hollywood and before long Rapper was transferred to another project, but in *Too Much, Too Soon*, Errol Flynn was more brilliant than he had been even in *The Sun Also Rises*. This time, he was not so much playing himself, although there was a lot about Barrymore that was also Flynn, but laying a wreath on the grave of his "illegitimate father". Had he been portraying Theodore Thomson Flynn he couldn't have done it with more love.

He did, though, continue to see the funny side of his type-casting.

"When I open a film script," he said at the time, "and it explains there's a man who's a shadow of his former self, once handsome now decadent, then I know that's my part. Oddly enough, I make more money today being a shadow of my former self than when I *was* my former self."

Some people took the apparent change in Errol a little too seriously. A rumour got around that he had stopped drinking.

"Malicious gossip," he countered, particularly now that he was making the Barrymore film. In that, he was actually being paid for swigging from a hip flask.

When the time came for this demanding piece of acting, he was unable to perform: he had emptied the flask while waiting for the cameras to be loaded.

If it were a traumatic experience returning to Burbank, Errol didn't show it. That would have meant nailing all his colours to the mast and the man whose yacht ensign was still a question mark would never have done that. But he was a sicker, older man than the one who had whistled at girls through the public address system of his car.

Not that he kept away from the women any more now than he used to do. He might be forty-eight, but he still liked them young and on the adjoining lot where they were filming *Marjorie Morningstar* – about a young girl who fell for an older man – there was one blonde lithe youngster who stirred the juices inside him.

19

Cuban Rebel Girls

*As a sexual athlete, Errol may in truth
have attained Olympic standards.*
Mr Justice McGarry

They told him she was only sixteen which really should have indicated the need for Errol to keep his hands off. But he didn't. The fact that Beverly Aadland had been born just before he faced the jury at the Los Angeles Hall of Justice on three charges of statutory rape did not affect the desire he now felt to take her to bed.

At that stage, there was little to indicate anything special about his relationship with Beverly. There were stories of Flynn being up to his old tricks, although not much more. Yet in her he had found both a bed companion and a soul mate. He dated her once and could not wait to see her again. He and Beverly grew closer to each other every day and night. The casual meeting at the studio had developed into a strong attachment.

They booked into separate hotel suites, one in his name, the other in her mother's. Mrs Florence Aadland acted as chaperone by taking one of the suites for herself. Agreeing to this arrangement was the first signal that Flynn regarded this girl as someone special. The seal of his approval was the nickname he gave her, "Woodsie" – short, he told her, for "Little Wood Nymph".

She was a girl made to the Flynn requirements: a good head – an IQ of 140, close to genius level – on top of slender shoulders, surmounting a slim body. She had practically no bust, but her legs were long and shapely enough to model for nylon stockings.

Beverly was the kind of girl Errol wanted to take over as his own private property. He didn't yet think of marriage, but she seemed in some strange way to be both innocent and worldly. She met his sexual requirements perfectly, but when they were not making love they could actually talk the night away.

Errol of course was not going to broadcast the news of his new attachment. He had no intention of spoiling things for himself just when his career had taken such a dramatic turn for the better. *Too Much Too Soon* had been nothing less than a triumph and not even his "Woodsie" could deflect his attention from that phenomenon.

After all those years as the laughing stock of Hollywood and with Errol laughing louder than most, he was now being taken seriously. There was even talk of his getting that coveted Oscar for *The Sun Also Rises*. For the first time he could see for himself the satisfaction that came from just doing his best. Perhaps, he wondered, just perhaps, it would do for him what *From Here to Eternity* had so recently done for Frank Sinatra.

The man whom Raoul Walsh had told to forget about impersonating Barrymore and to remember he was Errol Flynn now had the opportunity that he had wanted for so long. But in his latest film he did not impersonate his idol. "I tried to take him before he became the buffoon, before he started to burlesque himself," he said when the film was finished. "It was a period in his life when he was lost and trying to get hold of himself."

At that moment, Flynn did indeed think he had found his own self, especially when critics' comments varied from compliments on his "curiously compelling performance" to tributes to his "hitherto unnoticed richness of voice".

The part of Diana Barrymore, who was still the central character, was played by Dorothy Malone. But it was Errol's film. Darryl Zanuck thought so. After seeing *Too Much Too Soon*, he invited him to make another picture for Twentieth Century-Fox – *The Roots of Heaven* – to be filmed both in Paris and Africa.

The invitation was accepted, although first Errol had other plans, and not just for Beverly. He wanted to show that the man who all those years before had excited the girls and matrons of Northampton could still do "his thing" on the stage. When he received an offer to play the lead in a stage version of *Jane Eyre*, it was positively too good to turn down.

He should, however, have resisted the temptation. In Cincinnati, after six weeks on the road with *The Master of Thornfield*, and just before its scheduled opening at Broadway's Belasco Theater, he walked out.

"The play is a disaster," he declared, "No better than *Jack and the Beanstalk*." Errol claimed that Peter Ashmore, the director, had told him that "not even a combination of Sir John Gielgud and Sir Laurence Olivier could deliver those lines without getting a laugh". So rather than risk laughs he didn't want – there was never any difficulty in getting them when he did – he decided to stick to filming.

What Errol did not say was that at forty-nine he found the job of memorizing long speeches to be totally beyond his powers. Sometimes at rehearsals there were tears in his puffy bloodshot eyes as he wrestled with his lines. After a brief interlude, it looked as though his career were on the skids again. But there was still *The Roots of Heaven* to come. And he did have Beverly. With Pat back in the States, Errol took Beverly to stay with him in Jamaica. When the time came to fly off to Africa to make the film, she went with him to the airport at Kingston. On the plane he wrote her the first of a long series of love letters in which he would bare his innermost thoughts.

"Woodsie, I'm already sad. This bit of airport adieus are a bit too much – a bit too emotional for me – tears and fast goodbyes. Thanks for your sweetness today. Salute. Errol." The letters continued throughout the time he was away.

One of them showed Errol the father figure:

"I want you to be the fine and intrinsically honourable, decent young 'un you are. Tonight there are tears in my eyes – and yes my heart, too, is full of deep, abysmal emotions to explain what I feel about you. Words – mere words, written or even spoken – cannot convey what I feel for you in this all too crusty heart of mine. I know and so do you that you have to face some facts, some situations when you get back to Los Angeles that are going to be far from easy for you. It's going to be tough."

He was warning her that a prosecution for corrupting a minor seemed likely and this time he could not truthfully plead not guilty to what was, inevitably, going to be regarded as another case of statutory rape. He tried to put the thought out of his mind and the trip to Africa was helpful in that regard.

With him he took a small suitcase: his portable bar. It contained a supply of vodka, a good stock of drugs which he kept hidden, a cocktail shaker and tins of "broiled sparrow" and quail eggs. "Quail eggs," he told Beverly with the experience of once having already done the world tour the hard way, "are an absolute must in central Africa, the cradle of civilization. Be sure, I do not go unequipped."

As always, he was being philosophical and, as always too, not hiding the truth about himself: "I always felt like an imposter," he wrote to her, "and I didn't deserve all the fame and acclaim and money I got.... I'm feeling so good now, if I felt any better I'd be sick."

He didn't feel that good when he came down with a temperature of 103 in Africa. And he missed not just Beverly but female company of any kind. He and his co-star Juliette Greco hit it off well enough, but she was not going to sleep with him and the supply of local girls was limited to the kind who had plates in their mouths.

He had to look for other amusements. In Africa, his old disregard for anyone who was not white and Anglo-Saxon showed itself again, just as it had in that other jungle in the Pacific. When he came across a group of Africans performing an assegai dance, he generously provided them with a bottle of pep pills to make them do even better.

Perhaps he thought the experience would be rather like watching for the result of giving a portion of fatty pork to the ducks. Only this time he didn't stick around for the consequences. Working in consistent temperatures of up to 140 degrees meant that he needed all the diversions he could get.

In the film, he played a British deserter who after going over to the Nazis devotes the rest of his life to saving Africa's elephants. In that he was helped by a fanatic, originally to have been played by William Holden but who in the end was portrayed by Trevor Howard. The two of them seemed to have got on like a straw hut on fire (fuelled by vodka fumes of course).

While on location, Errol announced he was forming a club, with himself as president and Howard as his deputy. He was calling it The Roisterers. The president's duties, he informed the assembled company, were to lecture on John Barrymore and W. C. Fields.

Because he was Errol Flynn, he was constantly on the look-out for something new. He found the gallery of the operating theatre at the local hospital particularly fascinating, and spent hours there. On one occasion, the director John Huston asked a member of the crew: "Where is he?" "Dr Flynn," the technician replied, "is in surgery."

Errol was noticeably taking things slightly more slowly now, but still performing whatever practical jokes he could get away with. Just before leaving for the French Cameroons, he sent a note to the movie's writer, Romain Gary. He asked: "What the devil is the film all about?" The letter was signed "Trevor Howard".

There were no tricks, however, in the notes he sent to Beverly from Box 99, Fort Archambault, French Equatorial Africa. One of them read:

"Hi Little Girl Woodsie, I write this by the light of a hurricane lamp. An electric fan is throwing warm, hot air air at me as I sit on my camp stretcher and is blowing the paper up my nose. But – in my throat there is a sort of lump – a hard sort of core that doesn't let you swallow too well. Nothing physical, just pure emotion I guess when I think of you, but very deep and profound so much so that I find my eyes befogged and glazed and my pen trembles a bit. Of course, it's only sweat that comes from my eyes – perhaps tears of true feeling – feeling for an odd, strange and different little girl I hold in high regard. Yes, very much so."

At times he worried about her keeping faith with him: "Oh well, go to sleep little one. Remember that this heart has for you a strong fierce beat which you can really wreck if you treat it lightly – Errol."

He felt he was guardian of more than simply her bed. "Presumably," he wrote, "you have never delved into anything more profound in the literary sense than reading the funnies on a Sunday morning. Why don't you try reading a book?"

The letters proved that the man who had dedicated a lifetime to acting the playboy was still amazingly articulate. "Your almost hedonistic delight in any pretense to the rudiments of culture or acquisition of the basic ladylike behaviourism (I think we shall have to avoid this subject. If ever I find you being ladylike I'll clip you over the side of the ear) is deplorable," he wrote. Another letter began: "Woodsie – what a funny adorable little idiot you are. Do you just think I can pick up a phone here and call you? But I do know one sure thing – that my heart, my rebel heart, goes out to you as I write this.... Woodsie, you are hooked."

She didn't always reply to him, but when she did the effect was like that of two swigs of vodka and a shot of whatever drug he was currently trying out:

"Both your letters gave me the very strange, very strong vibrant feeling that you really care for me and I can hardly credit this but hope and long with this tormented empty calloused heart that it is true. Is it? True, I mean that what you write, you mean? That you really love me? It seems incredible. I don't think I'm by any means gullible to the degree that one is overwhelmed by a mere expression of something deep between two older people – one so much older than the other and a hell of a lot of other things. No, your letters sound real. God alone knows I want to believe in you. So much. This letter is evidently stupid but comes from the heart and that's quite a lot, don't you think?"

There was so much about her that he liked. "You know, she reminds me of when I was young," he told Nora when they met up again in 1959. About her was the simplicity of a youth that for Errol Flynn seemed to be a part of distant history. She read comics and she giggled a lot. She made few demands on him. To her, a good meal was a hamburger. When Nora asked him if he had ever given Beverly a present, he said: "No." Then he thought about it. "Yes, I have," he said. "I've given her a bracelet." Nora told him: "That's not jewellery. That's costume jewellery."

The second Mrs Flynn found it easier to talk about Beverly than did the third. Pat was furious that she had neither seen nor heard from her husband. Rumours had flown around that she was going to Mexico for a quickie divorce. "I was expecting that sort of thing," she said. "But I'm afraid I'm just an old-fashioned girl. To me, marriage is for keeps."

She could not hide the fact that Errol had not been in touch, although she tried to brush it off as unimportant. "Well, you know Daddyo," she said. "If he sends a telegram, he gets writers' cramp. I haven't even had a card from him for months."

If he were getting writers' cramp, it was in producing his memoirs. He had received an advance of $9000 from Putnams for an autobiography to be written with the help of a "ghost" if he needed one. In fact, the commission to write a book meant much more to him than the vast sums the publishers were convinced the project would make.

At first, it seemed as though he were coping very well indeed. The idea of a book that would "tell all" excited him almost as much as an offer from Warner Brothers would have done. It was, after all, a chance to gain prestige from what had always been a useful skill. He was able to put thoughts down on paper quite as easily as he had ever been able to relate them into the ears of a pretty girl.

Even at the lowest point in his life, he had kept a diary into which he had poured random emotions rather than mere accounts of the day's happenings. In one recent entry, he had questioned the part that religious faith could have played in his life:

"Still can't find peace of mind. Why does it elude me?" And then he added in Latin: "*Quos deus vult perdere, prius dementat.*" (Whom the gods wish to destroy, they first make mad.) He never would say publicly that he feared insanity, but it is conceivably a thought that ran through his mind as he tried to make some sense of the pathetic existence into which he had plunged himself. Now those thoughts would get a much wider audience than ever before – but his book wouldn't allow the truth to interfere with a good story.

Some of his most soothing moments had come when he had done his earlier writing. He had always enjoyed making good use of his intellectual gifts and since most of his work had been autobiographical, he was able to draw richly on the previously opened veins.

For a few weeks, he went off to Mexico to work on the book –

away from Woodsie, from Pat and from all the other problems. Naturally, his drink and his drugs were not to be left behind. But on a good day, he could produce up to fifteen handwritten pages of the manuscript which he handed to his editor, Howard Cady, in a condition that was practically good enough to send straight off to the printers. The book – as yet untitled – became more and more important to him.

It was fortunate that it was. For the first time in living memory, his reputation as a stud was in danger of being questioned – if any of the nymphets he had selected for a night's pleasure in Woodsie's absence had felt disposed to reveal the secrets of his bedroom accomplishments.

To his close friends, he confessed he was experiencing "some trouble", which they construed to be the first signs of impotence, but he certainly didn't halt the chase. That would have meant a proclamation that he was no longer interested, and he would never do that, lest the word got around.

Yet he was admitting to himself that he was more insecure than ever before. The square question mark now protruded from the handkerchief in the breast pocket of his jackets, but the query as to his sexual prowess was a different thing. And as if to prove it, when he got back to the States, Beverly was made aware that she was his main concern again. Work on the book slowed down.

When people started talking none too kindly about their relationship, Errol said his real aim was to gain experience for the film the pair were going to make of the novel *Lolita*, which had just begun to shock the American public and dealt with an arrangement so like their own.

He was very plainly even more captivated by his Wood Nymph now than he had been before the trip abroad. And although he worried about the California law there was little pretense that they were doing anything but sleeping together.

When Errol went to London, Beverly went with him. Certainly, she seemed to be good for him. In her presence, he appeared to shake off the years. Perhaps it was the consummate actor putting on a show: this time pretending that he was not quite old enough to be her father. He did not even mind when she swooned in company to the sound of a Frank Sinatra record and added: "What would I give for a date with Frankie!" Together they went to a ball, to nightclubs and to the races. At Ascot, Errol forked out £5000 for a tip but it was worth it: the horse won.

The final proof of Beverly's acceptance as his woman came when she was asked to participate in still more extensions to the property in Jamaica. Together, they planned the swimming pool in which the now heavy, paunchy figure of Errol Flynn would soak when there were no strangers around. He wanted the pool built in the sun, she wanted it in the shade. In the end, they compromised. It was half in the sun, half in the shade. Another room that Errol wanted built of glass she wanted to be of stone. That, too, resulted in a compromise. One of the walls was just a massive window.

If "Woodsie" represented an innocent earlier life, she did have a sense of maturity about her. She said of Flynn: "He is a combination of a two-year-old, mother, father and mad lover."

Meanwhile, Pat was complaining of being "humiliated" by him. "I'm still trying to make our marriage a working affair," she said. "I want to see him as soon as possible. We are either going to make it work or we will have to make another decision. He never writes to me and I can never get him on the telephone. You'd think he'd take time out to write to me and to Arnella but I haven't heard from him for a long time." Arnella was now five.

She said that she had not consulted a lawyer but Errol was saying privately that when he asked her for a divorce she had demanded a $500,000 settlement. At Phoenix, Arizona, Pat declared that she was shocked by Errol's talk. "I can only assume that an Irishman with a couple of drinks under his belt is liable to say anything." Finally she asked her agent Marilyn Hinton to speak on her behalf: "Pat's only motive is not to say rashly 'right, go ahead [let's get a divorce], if that's what you want.' It is concern for her daughter."

Pat was now resuming her professional career and singing in nightclubs. Finally, she filed a claim for separate maintenance.

Needless to say, hers was not the only claim running around at this time. The Internal Revenue Service were still on Errol's tail. In March 1959, they claimed he owed them $219,469. Then there was the little matter of the *Jane Eyre* play. Huntington Hartford the Third, the supermarket tycoon, threatened to sue him for $500,000 – the amount he had personally invested and then lost in the exercise. Actors' Equity were equally disturbed. They suspended Flynn for "unbecoming conduct" which meant that until he was reinstated, he would not be able to act on an American stage again.

Visitors still wanted to know what he was going to do professionally. He told them that the book was his main preoccupation. But Putnams were getting anxious. They deputed a writer named Earl Conrad to help Errol along.

With Pat away, Errol – with Woodsie at his side most of the time – agreed to go back to work, using the Jamaica hotel as his base. He and Conrad agreed that the "ghost" would act as interviewer, with a shorthand-typist taking down every printable detail (and when the vodka flowed, few of the details were printable) of their conversation. But there were many times when his attention wandered to other things.

Woodsie wasn't exactly delighted with the amount of time that the book was consuming – time that she was convinced would be better spent with her. He for his part was not entirely gracious when she protested. Those were the moments when it seemed to him that his little Wood Nymph was less than his equal. Not that he allowed it to concern him that much.

Once he had drunk enough and injected sufficient narcotic substances into his blood stream, he didn't worry about anything. Any conscience he may have had about lying took flight with his concern about religion. Errol instinctively knew the ingredients that would help him along the fine line that separated a good laugh from history – his Sunday evening sessions with the boys had honed his art of story-telling. Earl Conrad had no real way of knowing whether he was telling the truth or not.

The vodka did wonders for Errol's imagination. Perhaps he was reliving, and dealing with, his earlier regrets at not coming through the hazards of his love life and career quite as well as he always said he had – much like the way a politician finds the perfect riposte to a heckler twenty-four hours after he could have used it.

To help him with his task, Conrad wrote to both Errol's parents.

There were no problems with the professor. Mrs Flynn, however, said she didn't believe her son wanted her to say very much – an incredibly muted reply from the woman whom Errol still believed was his number-one enemy. The hate he felt for his mother welled up in him as he recalled the way she had, in his view, mistreated him during his childhood. It was one of the angry times when he allowed his language to reach depths of obscenity that few people had ever heard from him.

He used similar terminology whenever he recalled – and now he had reason to do so once more – the rape trials.

Neither was he any more polite about his legal and business advisers. When he had cause to write to one of these gentlemen, he pointedly addressed himself in his letters to "Dear Jew".

As if to prove he were still superior to any desk-bound mortal, he devoted his afternoons to exercise – mostly swimming and deep-sea fishing and diving. It didn't do much to improve his physique. His pallid complexion was becoming more yellow than ever – plainly his liver was still trying to beat the rest of his body in the race to the kill and looked like winning. He seemed bloated and you didn't have to be with him long to note that his hands were shaking uncontrollably.

Once more, he talked about death incessantly and those were the times when any useful work on his book was reduced to a mere trickle.

He still tried to give the impression that he was the Casanova of Jamaica – but with Woodsie as his only "client" – when she was around.

He also continued to act out the role of estate owner, talking to his employees in his best pidgin English. It was his concession to meeting what was still in his mind their inferior social status.

With a dozen black servants in constant attention – and with Woodsie hovering around him as he sipped his vodka – he also fell into other habits of the neighbourhood, like going horse racing at a makeshift track he had built in the middle of his land, and singing with the natives their songs like "Zombie Jamboree".

But he was no more content now than he had ever been. He still yearned to get away and do something notable. Quite suddenly, he made up his mind to start writing for the newspapers again – and if his book would suffer for the time being, so be it. There was one place that interested him more now than any other: Cuba.

Dr Fidel Castro was leading his rebels towards a successful conclusion of the revolution and the thought spiked Errol's blood to action again. If he missed the real fighting in the Civil War in Spain more than twenty years before, he was now going to prove how he and revolution went hand in gun. In Cuba, he not only saw shooting but felt it. He was hit in the leg by a ricocheting bullet that squeaked his way as he hid behind a pillar.

What perturbed him most was that the women soldiers looked so much like the men. He described them as being "armed with bras, low-heeled shoes and guns". But they had much in their favour, he thought. Of course, he was speaking as an expert. "They may not be 'chorus girl' beauties but they had something that was wonderful, a camaraderie and fine faces." When he got near the women, he said he had not been surrounded by so much virtue since last he was in church, all of forty years before.

He also met Castro, and told the bearded leader that he should call his army "patriots" instead of "rebels" – which, he added, "has the touch of Jesse James about it."

"Who's he?" asked Castro.

With the help of Earl Conrad, a number of stories were published in the United States and in Europe and even in the local *Havana Post*, now in the hands of Castro's friends.

He wormed his way into situations that most foreign visitors never got near. When one Batista colonel surrendered, he watched enthralled. He had told the troops that he was a newspaperman, so was given a ringside seat at the ceremony.

But he didn't take too kindly to watching a team of Castro's men form themselves into a firing squad. He said it seemed like the worst death imaginable – and he would have much preferred the chance to take an overdose of drugs. Since he put himself into that potentially fatal position every day, it was plain that he saw no horror in that way of going. Perhaps, too, a man who always wanted to take an active role in whatever he did – whether it was going to bed with a girl or pumping noxious substances into his veins – couldn't take to the idea of having no control over his last moments. The notion of facing an array of guns with his eyes blindfolded was just too horrific to think about.

But a lot of Errol's time was spent on less serious matters. He tried in vain to get Castro's men to appreciate his sense of humour, although, he said, the best joke of all was right there in front of him – the food. All that Castro himself ate when he was with him was tinned tuna or *arroz con pollo* – chicken with rice, with a distinct emphasis on the rice. Castro didn't like Flynn's jokes either. Flynn explained this by saying that the bearded leader did not have time to "see ironies, paradoxes or amusement in what he was doing".

He said he was going to write a book about Castro and was busy scribbling notes during his talk.

For much of the time, Errol carried a walking stick and wore a black kerchief bearing Castro's insignia. He knew people were trying to debunk him. One of Castro's men had said: "We're always pleased to meet people from the newspapers, but Mr Flynn is not a real journalist." Yet to them all, Errol offered a toast and said: "I think it is envy and animosity." In truth, it usually was.

He was far more upset by another Cuban who did think he had a sense of humour. "How come," he asked Errol, "that you look so young in the movies and are so old now?"

Errol continued to write to Beverly but he had not been in contact with Pat for weeks. Yet as usual he sent her a live present from Cuba: a small, local animal called an olinga. She was not impressed. "How appropriate," she said drily. "An olinga is nocturnal. A night prowler. Nothing could more remind me of Errol."

He reflected sadly on his broken marriage. "Patrice is a wonderful girl," he said in Cuba. "No one better. A good wife. For someone else. She can cook and she is pretty and she is not for me. When we married I reformed her. It didn't work. How could it? You know me, sport."

The truth was she bored him.

Castro did not. Soon the rebel would become the dictator and would align himself with the Soviet bloc. But in 1959, fifty-year-old Errol Flynn felt invigorated. "Castro," he said, "is one of those men who come along occasionally in human history. . . . I think he has lizard blood. I never saw a man jump around with such energy." Castro himself said he remembered meeting Flynn but not much else.

For once Errol was not so concerned with his usual predilections. He told one girl who appeared to have the hots for him: "Sorry, dear, I can't find ducking bullets conducive to sex."

20

Hello God

*I never thought he would be ill or die. But
he did both.*
Herbert Wilcox

The Cuban visit was not entirely a search for adventure for
adventure's sake. Whenever Errol did anything there was usually
another motive lurking in the background. This time there were
two: if he were to make a film of his own there, it would not only
help him out of his current tax problems, it would also provide
Beverly with a chance to break into films. He had been hinting about
making her a star for months.

The result was that he shot some location footage for a picture
he called *Cuban Rebel Girls*. It was an entirely appropriate title, for
after experiencing a ricocheting bullet, meeting Castro and seeing
the undeniably brave bearded troops, nothing made a bigger impression on him than did the girls. Nothing *ever* did.

He never intended to make a masterpiece, which is fortunate
because if he had, he would have been sorely disappointed. *Cuban
Rebel Girls* was without a shadow of a doubt the worst picture he
ever made. It was also his last.

The idea was that he would provide sound commentary and play
himself, Errol Flynn – but Errol Flynn war correspondent in the
battle zone. That much was partly legitimate. He had now had a
couple of commissions to turn in newspaper pieces about the Cuban
débâcle and was indeed to do so. He shot the rest of the movie in
New York with Beverly playing one of the rebel girls.

Manhattan was now a more useful center to him than Jamaica.
It was where his publishers were and, in any case, the Caribbean
island had left a bad taste in his mouth. He sold the hotel. "I'm

fed up with hearing about people complaining that the soup is cold," he tried to joke.

By this time, his principal worry was that the *Zaca* would fall into the hands of the Internal Revenue Service. He arranged for it to sail northwards up the coast from Los Angeles and thence into Canadian waters off Vancouver.

Another concern was still the possibility of a prosecution over Beverly. Morals officers had been sniffing around and asking awkward questions. He decided that they should both leave the United States as quickly as possible.

He was also feeling far from well. "Just a touch of the old malaria, Woodsie," he told Beverly. "I usually feel this way after being in the tropics." Which, of course, was true. This time, however, he felt very much worse. In a more morose moment he told her: "Bury me in Jamaica – where the Hollywood people can't trample on my grave."

He coughed so much it was painful to listen to him. There was a gnawing pain in his chest and he generally felt so weak that had anyone waved a Robin Hood bow and arrow in his direction he might have collapsed from the fatigue of having to watch it move.

Without telling anyone, he saw a doctor who immediately passed him on to a specialist. Both men gave the same verdict: he would be lucky to survive another twelve months. His heart was weak, his lungs perforated like postage stamps and the yellow tint to his eyes showed that his liver could not go on doing its work for long. Of course, he was not making its task any easier by appearing to be personally financing the American vodka industry. In addition, he was swallowing so many assorted pills and plunging so many hypodermic needles into his veins that he could no longer be sure what he was trying to achieve.

Yet his heart poured out a love he had not felt for years. When they were apart, he wrote Beverly a stream of letters and sent her telegrams. One read: VERY LONELY VERY LONELY WHY NOT LETTERS HUG HUG. Once, he telegraphed her in New York from Jamaica: DARLING SMALL COMPANION. LEAVING FOR NEW YORK THIS WEEK CAN'T WAIT. When he arrived in the city, he dashed off another wire: DO NOT HAVE YOUR TELEPHONE NUMBER STOP

TRIED ALL NIGHT STOP TELEPHONE ME HOTEL WARWICK IMME-
DIATELY.

He and his Woodsie took an appartment at the Shoreham Hotel. Here, he supervised the final stages of the production of his book. It now had a title: *My Wicked, Wicked Ways*. The name was chosen by Howard Cady, after reading the early adventures of the boy who suddenly discovered the differences between himself and little girls. The admonition of the mother for the "wicked, wicked" behaviour of her son, as Errol recalled it, was too good not to use on the spine of the book.

Errol read and reread the galleys of the book. They gave him more pleasure than he had known outside a girl's bed in years. But there were even more pressing needs for a man who was clever enough to know that now not just his years but also his months and perhaps even his weeks or days were numbered.

He was sufficiently aware of the situation to know that what he really wanted now was to see his children again. He decided to return to Los Angeles and telephoned Nora:

"Please bring Deirdre and Rory to meet me at the airport."

Nora was surprised. "But ... you'll have Beverly?"

He said: "No. I won't."

The girls were excited at meeting the Baron again and in her way so was Nora, who had remained strangely fond of the exasperating Peter Pan who had once been her husband.

When she saw him being helped down the aircraft gangplank at Los Angeles Airport, Nora could only weep. He was supporting himself with a cane. When he was close enough to kiss her, she was struck with the way his nose – "that beautiful nose" – had widened monstrously. His skin was veined and purple, his eyes bloated. Suddenly he was a very old man. The magnificent physique had become a refuse sack. In the car, he told her: "Don't worry about me. I have lived twice." He was quiet for a minute but then he turned to her: "You know, if you had stuck it out, maybe I'd have been all right."

It was too late for that now. But he kidded both himself and television director Arthur Hiller that he could still work. With Hiller he made a thirty-minute film at Columbia Pictures for the Alcoa-

Goodyear Theater. He appeared as a Wild West peddler in *The Golden Shanty*. He found it difficult not only to remember his lines, but also to get on and off the wagon which was his principal prop. The gruelling schedule – in earlier days he would have regarded it as an amusing interlude between nips of vodka – showed on the screen.

At a Hollywood party, he spied the girl who had fallen in love with him so many years before. He went up to Olivia de Havilland from behind and kissed her affectionately on the cheek. She turned but didn't recognize him. The eyes, she said afterwards, were of a different man, a stranger she had never known.

Errol knew how ill he was. Yet with an optimism that was mainly a refusal to accept reality, he and Beverly were now talking about getting married. "Just a few details to fix up with Wymore, Woodsie," he told her, and instructed his lawyers to work out the clauses of a divorce settlement which they thought Pat would accept.

First, however, he gave Beverly a seventeenth birthday party. It was attended by Mickey Rooney and by as many of his old cronies as he could round up, as well as by a battery of cameramen and reporters.

"Isn't she too young for you?" one pressman asked bravely, looking at Beverly. Errol was courtesy personified. "I can only quote Al Jolson," he said, "I may be too old for her – but she's not too young for me." He protested that her passport gave her age as twenty-two. "I prefer to believe the Government." But nobody else did.

"I don't care what you fellows print about me," he added. "I'll be dead in five years." Ever the optimist.

The party at the Frascate Grill ended in a violent row between Nora and Beverly, who had made a few references to Errol's age that his former wife considered insulting. Errol complicated matters by using the foulest possible language – something which he had rarely done in the past.

The next day Errol felt even more sick. He was examined by Dr Jacques S. Gilbert, a heart specialist who took a cardiograph. He was not pleased with the findings. "You must modify your habits

or take the consequences," he warned. "Sure, doc," said Errol, "I'll
take the consequences. I'm not afraid."

In England, Professor Theodore Flynn saw *The Roots of Heaven*.
"You're looking fat," he wrote to his son. "You ought to watch
that." Errol did not let it bother him. He had other things on his
mind.

By this time, Beverly and he had stopped practising any form
of birth control. "We want a child very badly," Woodsie told a close
friend. Everything about their relationship was now in the open and
Beverly herself knew all about Errol's problems, most of all about
his financial worries.

There was talk of his being able to sell the *Zaca* to a couple living
in Vancouver and before long a deal was struck. If it sounded like
disposing of his assets as part of the business of putting his house
finally in order, he didn't say so. But the gesture of selling the *Zaca*
was like ringing down the Flynn ensign on everything that had gone
before.

He did, however, meet another television commitment, a comedy
sketch on the Red Skelton show, in which he played a hobo.

Errol almost looked like one when he arrived at Vancouver airport
with Beverly. He had a sports shirt under a blazer and wore a bowler
hat – not a usual combination. He wasn't going to make any more
films, he said. "The rest of my life will be devoted to women and
litigation." It was a statement of defiance, meaning that he had no
intention whatever of changing a pattern that had been so painstak-
ingly cut. One of the first things he and Beverly did together in the
city was to go to a nightclub. "I've always been one for burning
the midnight Errol," he joked.

While there, Beverly was officially described as his secretary-
cum-companion. He took her with him to the occasional business
meeting involved in tying up the sale of the *Zaca* and with her made
a tour of the nightclubs. That went on for a week until Errol felt
ill once more. It was 14 October 1959.

"I think I'd better go and see the doctor again." he called out
to Beverly and locked himself in his bedroom. There he jabbed himself with the hypodermic needle and took a couple of swigs at the
vodka bottle. It was early evening. Mr and Mrs George Galdough,

who were buying the *Zaca*, drove him and Beverly from their hotel
to the penthouse home of Dr George Gould. The doctor was entertaining friends at the time.

He broke off immediately and examined Errol, who neglected to
tell him about either the drinks or the jab he had self-administered,
and gave him an injection of his own. He tried to persuade him
to lie down, but Errol said that all he wanted to do was sit in the
company of interesting people and talk. For two hours, Errol
romanced about the glories of Hollywood and its people, holding
his minute audience spellbound as he mimicked Jack Warner and
John Barrymore. Occasionally he leant for support against the door
in the doctor's room. All the time, Beverly was looking his way,
hoping to catch some sign of improvement in his condition. She
couldn't.

Then, quite suddenly, Errol told the doctor: "I think I *will* lie
down now. I shall return." He walked towards the doctor's bedroom. In the corridor outside, he collapsed. Dr Gould rushed out
and helped him to his bed, ripped open his shirt and placed a stetho-
scope to his chest. The irregular dull beat told what he already
knew: Errol had had a massive heart attack. He tried mouth-to-
mouth resuscitation. An ambulance crew was called.

Errol was carried downstairs with an oxygen mask over his face.
During the 70-mph dash to the hospital, Beverly kept repeating to
the ambulance driver: "Are they keeping him comfortable? Do
these men know how to give him oxygen?"

At the hospital, she tried to follow the stretcher into the emer-
gency room, but the way was barred. A few minutes later, when
she saw the expression on the face of the doctor who came out to
talk to her, she fainted.

Errol was dead. Out – like Flynn.

21
Never Say Goodbye

I liked his fuck-you attitude.
Anthony Quinn

Errol Flynn was fifty when he died, leaving a distraught Beverly weeping uncontrollably even with the help of sedatives. But into those fifty years he had – as he so often said himself – crammed at least two lifetimes.

Nor when he died did the Flynn legend go with him. The two words Errol Flynn became synonymous with raucous high living and cinematic heroism beyond the possibilities of human endeavour. For the matrons who swooned from the stalls and gallery of the Northampton Rep. and for the millions who saw him only from a cheap cinema seat he had personified colour, excitement and romance.

Coroner Glen McDonald looked over the body soon after Errol's death. "It is," he said sorrowfully, "that of a tired, old man – old before his time." His verdict was that Flynn had died from coronary thrombosis complicated by a hardening of the arteries, degeneration of the liver and infection of the lower intestine. Even all that told only half the story, if that.

The man who had lived surrounded by a sea of controversy died that way, too, with women squabbling over him to the end. Nora and Beverly both said he wanted to be buried in Jamaica. Pat, the widow, said she considered it was his right to be buried where he would be recognized among his peers – in Hollywood. Yet, to date, there has been no marker over the grave to which he was taken in a slow freight train, escorted by Buster Wiles, once more looking after the comfort of his boss and friend.

There was a story that Raoul Walsh smuggled a dozen bottles of whisky into the coffin before the burial. Errol would have appreciated that. He would not have been happy to discover that so many of the Hollywood people he had known and with whom he had worked found excuses not to be present that day.

After the funeral, the women in his life quarrelled over the money that he left. More money than anyone had imagined. Beverly claimed there had been a new will written in Cuba, but that notion was ruled out by the courts. In the end, what remained of his estate and his property went to Patrice. "Woodsie" got nothing.

The taxman had most of the benefit, though. Flynn left something over $2 million. By his own estimate he had spent $5 million. His children were taken care of, and Sean was left an additional $5000 with which to enjoy himself "preferably on a world tour".

Sean's world tour included a film part as *Son of Captain Blood* and a period as a press photographer in Vietnam. He never returned from a mission in the jungle during the war there and was officially registered as missing, presumed dead.

Deirdre became a film stunt rider, but later gave up the work and settled down, unmarried, to a quiet life in Los Angeles. Rory was last heard of when she was involved with the courts on a fraud charge. Arnella has been out of the public eye since the time when, at the age of sixteen, she announced from her mother's home in Jamaica that she intended to go in for an acting career. Patrice Wymore has been running a boutique on the island.

Beverly Aadland's stormy life continued that way. Errol had made her promise: "Live for today and have a wonderful time doing it. No tears – break open a bottle and toast me in pink champagne." It was a long time before that bottle was opened. A short while after Errol's death, the Los Angeles police juvenile branch decided to investigate her moral responsibility in their affair, but took no action. Soon after that, a man was found shot dead in her bedroom; the verdict was suicide. Later, she married. Nora married again, too. Lili Damita has been living quietly in Iowa.

Errol's parents were not at his funeral. His father had just had a stroke and was not considered fit enough to travel. Later he started work on a biography of his son which he never completed. Both he and his wife died in England – she in a road accident.

The *Zaca* was sold and, as if in symbolic revolt at having a new master, broke down on its maiden voyage under his flag, never to sail again. It faded away, slowly disintegrating at a mooring on the French Riviera.

At Warner Brothers studios, one of the few remaining links with the Hollywood that Errol knew, practically no day goes by without someone mentioning the name of Errol Flynn and all that it stood for. It was, after all, his adversary Jack Warner who said at his funeral: "Errol had trials and tribulations in his life as almost everyone has. But he never knew dullness." Today those words are usually recalled as Errol would have wished them to be. With a twinkle in the eye and a glass in the hand.